PHOTOSHOP COMPOSITING
SECRETS

Unlocking the Key to Perfect Selections & Amazing
Photoshop Effects for Totally Realistic Composites

Matt Kloskowski

The *Photoshop Compositing Secrets* Book Team

CREATIVE DIRECTOR
Felix Nelson

ASSOCIATE ART DIRECTOR
Jessica Maldonado

TECHNICAL EDITORS
Kim Doty
Cindy Snyder

TRAFFIC DIRECTOR
Kim Gabriel

PRODUCTION MANAGER
Dave Damstra

PHOTOGRAPHY BY
Matt Kloskowski

SETUP SHOTS BY
Rafael Concepcion
Brad Moore

PUBLISHED BY
Peachpit Press

Copyright ©2012 by Kelby Corporate Management, Inc.

Composed in Univers, Interstate, Tertre Extra Bold, Mentone, and Openhouse by Kelby Media Group, Inc.

Trademarks

All terms mentioned in this book that are known to be trademarks or service marks have been appropriately capitalized. Peachpit Press cannot attest to the accuracy of this information. Use of a term in the book should not be regarded as affecting the validity of any trademark or service mark.

Photoshop is a registered trademark of Adobe Systems Incorporated.
Photoshop Lightroom is a registered trademark of Adobe Systems Incorporated.
Color Efex Pro Complete is a registered trademark of Nik Software, Inc.
Topaz Adjust is a registered trademark of Topaz Labs.

Warning and Disclaimer

This book is designed to provide information about compositing photography in Adobe Photoshop. Every effort has been made to make this book as complete and as accurate as possible, but no warranty of fitness is implied.

The information is provided on an as-is basis. The author and Peachpit Press shall have neither the liability nor responsibility to any person or entity with respect to any loss or damages arising from the information contained in this book or from the use of the discs or programs that may accompany it.

ISBN 10:   0-321-80823-1

ISBN 13: 978-0-321-80823-3

9 8 7 6 5 4 3

Printed and bound in the United States of America

www.peachpit.com
www.kelbytraining.com

To my grandparents, Catherine and Carl Zumbano.
As a child, you were there to spoil me. And as an adult,
I'm proud to say I'm able to share my children with you, so
they can see just how blessed I've been to have you in my life.
The strength, wisdom, and unconditional love you two have
given me is something I'll always treasure. I love you guys!

ACKNOWLEDGMENTS

Although my name appears on the cover of the book, creating what you're holding today is in no way a one-man job. It takes the support, hard work, and help from an entire team. One of my favorite parts of writing a book is that I get to thank them publicly, in front of the thousands and thousands of people who read it. So, here goes:

To my wife, Diana: No matter what the day brings, you always have a smile on your face when I come home. I could never thank you enough for juggling our lives, for being such a great mom to our kids, and for being the best wife a guy could hope for.

To my oldest son, Ryan: I love watching you grow up. Thanks for being my trusty photo assistant on several shoots for this book. I love that we're able to share in one of my passions and, whether or not it becomes one of your passions too, I'll always treasure those moments.

To my youngest son, Justin: I have no doubt that you'll be the class clown one day. No matter what I have on my mind, you always find a way to make me smile. And, it's just what I need to remind me what's most important throughout the day.

To my mom and dad: Thank you for giving me such a great start in life and always encouraging me to go for what I want.

To Ed, Kerry, Kristine, and Scott (my brothers and sisters): Thank you for supporting me and always giving me someone to look up to.

Thanks to Scott Kelby for not only becoming a great mentor to me, but for also becoming such a great friend. As I wrote this book, the advice and help you gave me was huge and I can't thank you enough. Thanks man!

Thanks to the folks that made this book look so awesome: Felix Nelson, Jessica Maldonado, and Dave Damstra.

Everyone should have a Corey Barker in their creative arsenal. Corey is the guy I turn to when I need to take things to the next level. Whenever I finished a composite for this book, I'd show it to Corey and he'd always have that one little tweak (or sometimes several tweaks) that helped take it up a notch. Plain and simple, Corey rocks and this book is much better because of his input.

Thanks to my other fellow Photoshop Guy here at NAPP headquarters, RC Concepcion. Your help in setting up photo shoots, lighting, and direction for several of the shoots in this book helped me in a big way.

I owe a huge thank you to Margie Rosenstein, Nicole Procunier, Calvin Hollywood, Eric Doggett, and Russ Robinson for allowing me to bounce ideas and images off them from time to time.

To my two favorite editors in the world, Cindy Snyder and Kim Doty: Thanks for making me look so good and keeping me on track.

To Dave Moser, the business powerhouse behind Kelby Media Group: Your militaristic, yet insightful, comments throughout the day help me way more than you know. Thanks for continuing to push me to be better each day.

I owe a special thanks to someone who has become a good friend of mine during the production of this book, Joel Grimes. Joel is one of the best compositors out there, and he was kind enough to share his techniques, thoughts, ideas, and overall creative approach with me.

Thanks to all my friends at Peachpit Press: Ted Waitt, Scott Cowlin, Gary-Paul Prince, and Sara Jane Todd. It's because you guys are so good at what you do that I'm able to continue doing what I love to do.

Thanks to all of my friends at Adobe for making a killer piece of software that I truly love to work with every day. I'd especially like to thank the team behind the Refine Edge dialog in Photoshop CS5: Sarah Kong, Alan Erickson, Jeff Chien, Gregg Wilensky, Scott Cohen, and Jue Wang. It sounds silly to thank someone for creating a dialog or feature, but I've gotta tell ya, without that feature in Photoshop, I don't think I would've even attempted to write this book. Selections have long been the bane of many digital artists' existence. But in Photoshop CS5, Adobe changed all that with Refine Edge. Selections that were once nearly impossible now happen in just a few minutes. No third-party plug-ins, no nuthin'. Thanks guys!

To you, the readers: Without you, well...there would be no book. Thanks for your constant support in emails, phone calls, and introductions when I'm out on the road teaching. You guys make it all worth it, and I feel honored that you've chosen me to help you learn more about Photoshop and photography.

Thank you.

Matt Kloskowski

OTHER BOOKS BY MATT KLOSKOWSKI

Layers: The Complete Guide to Photoshop's Most Powerful Feature

The Photoshop Elements Book for Digital Photographers

The Photoshop Elements 5 Restoration and Retouching Book

The Photoshop CS2 Speed Clinic: Automating Photoshop to Get Twice the Work Done in Half the Time

ABOUT THE AUTHOR

Matt Kloskowski

Matt Kloskowski, the Education and Curriculum Developer for the National Association of Photoshop Professionals (NAPP), is a Photoshop Guy whose books, videos, and classes have simplified the way thousands of people work on digital photos. Author of several best-selling books on Photoshop, as well as the *Lightroom Killer Tips* blog, Matt teaches Photoshop and digital photography techniques to tens of thousands of people around the world each year. He co-hosts the top-rated videocast *Photoshop User TV*, as well as *The Grid*, a live talk show about photography. He has built a massive library of videos that appear in DVDs and online training courses, and has written articles for *Photoshop User* magazine. You'll find Matt teaching for the Kelby Training Live seminar tour, as well as at the world's premier Photoshop event, the Photoshop World Conference & Expo. Matt lives in Tampa, Florida, and works at the National Association of Photoshop Professionals.

CONTENTS

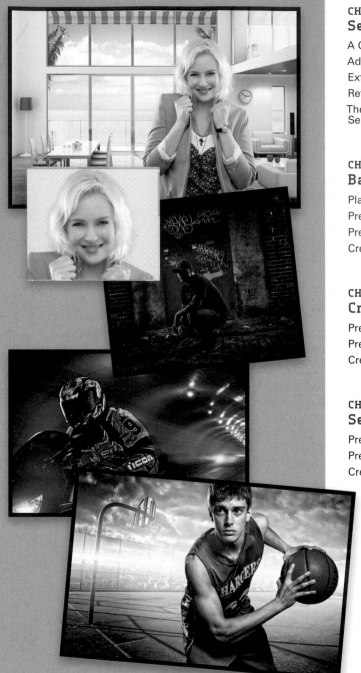

CONTENTS

CONTENTS

CONTENTS

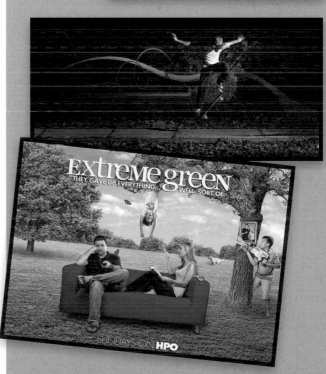

INTRODUCTION

Photoshop compositing has really blown up over the last few years. You see composites everywhere from magazine ads and covers, to movie posters, to athletic portraits, to, well, just about any kind of portrait. It really is everywhere. Clients and customers are very aware of Photoshop now and know what can be done, so they're requesting more from photographers and designers. As time goes on and the creative boundaries of photography and Photoshop continually push the envelope, even our own judgment and tastes have risen to new heights, because we know (and see) all of the possibilities. The good news is that, today, it's easier than ever to get into compositing.

For starters, the photography and lighting side of compositing has become much simpler to work with. Once you have the camera, lens, and memory card, experimenting is basically free. You can take as many photos as you need in an attempt to get the right one to work for your composite. Not only is the photography part easier, but the Photoshop part of the equation has changed big time. See, one of the key areas of compositing starts with a good selection. If you don't make a good selection, your composite is never going to look real. Before Photoshop CS5, selections used to be a royal pain in the a$$. But with the new Refine Edge technology in CS5, selections that were nearly impossible (or really time consuming) can happen in about 3–5 minutes. To me, that's a game changer in both the quality we get from our composites, and the time we have to invest in them.

The hardest part of the entire compositing process is, honestly, the creative side. No amount of technology will change that, though. But, to me, it's my favorite part and I hope it becomes yours as you read through this book. Let me first say that I love photography and I love capturing a beautiful photo right out of the camera. Whether it's a landscape or a portrait, there's something wonderful about making a great photo that looks awesome as soon as you open it on your computer. Hit Send, and you're done. That's a good feeling. However, I love Photoshop, too. I really do enjoy the creative process of making art on my computer. Compositing lets me combine my two passions and put them together to create photos that simply wouldn't be possible (or would be really difficult, at best) without both photography and Photoshop combined.

As you read through the book, you'll see I've covered the gamut when it comes to compositing. Compositing is many things to many different people, so I really tailored the projects so that everyone, no matter what type of photography and imaging you're into, would get something from the book. I've covered everything from ultra-grungy/edgy composites with dramatic lighting and Photoshop special effects, to real-world family/professional portrait composites that no one would ever know were composites, and everything in between. And you'll see the setup info, the background, the selection process, and the final compositing techniques that made it all happen.

Compositing has truly become a passion of mine over the years. I hope, as you read through this book, that it becomes yours, as well. Enjoy!

HOW TO FOLLOW ALONG WITH THIS BOOK

I know that people love to follow along with Photoshop books, so I wanted to take a quick moment here to tell you some things I've done to make it easier for you.

ACCESSING THE DOWNLOAD IMAGES
I've made all of the images I use in the book available for download on the book's download website. Here's the link: **www.kelbytraining.com/books/compositing.**

YOU DON'T HAVE TO READ THE BOOK IN ORDER
Most projects don't necessarily assume you've done another project in the book. So, feel free to jump in at one that looks appealing to you. I do refer back to other tutorials in certain projects, but you should be able to follow along wherever you jump in. However, I do think you should read "10 Things You Need to Know About Compositing" first, and follow it up with Chapter 1 (Selection Secrets) right after that. After that, just about anything is fair game. Also, I would work through at least four or five chapters before tackling the "Advanced Commercial Composite" in Chapter 16. That one assumes you know a lot of the selection, lighting, and shading tips and tricks we've used throughout the book, as well as how to do these things without a lot of explanation.

EACH CHAPTER (AKA: COMPOSITE) HAS SEVERAL TUTORIALS IN IT
Compositing isn't just about pasting a person onto a different background. There's lighting, shadows, selections, backgrounds, and special effects that all play a key role. Almost every project in the book includes a tutorial on: (1) the background photo, (2) the selection process, and (3) the overall composite. Each part is important. In fact, sometimes the background is just as important as the portrait, because our goal is to place people somewhere that they're not. If the background (or environment) didn't play a big role, then we'd never go through this trouble.

JUMP INTO A CHAPTER WHERE YOU WANT
I wanted to make this book as useful as possible to a wide audience, without making it too generic at the same time. So, I wrote each compositing project in a way that lets you jump in where you want. For example, if you're a photographer that does all of your own post-production Photoshop work, then maybe you'll want to read a whole chapter from the lighting setup, to the selection process, all the way through to the composite. But, let's say you're a designer or retoucher, and someone else usually hands you the photos to work on. No sweat. You may not care too much about the lighting setup part of the chapter. So, you can just jump into the selections and compositing tutorials. Or, maybe you're mostly interested in compositing. Skip the setup, skip the selections, and jump straight into the compositing tutorial.

Now, if you're really impatient and you just want to dive in and do the composite (maybe the background isn't of interest to you for a certain project), no sweat, you can skip the background tutorial. When you get to the compositing tutorial, I've included a PSD file of the finished background for you to start with. Let's say you don't want to spend the time selecting the person from their background, like I do in each chapter. Again, no sweat. I've got a PSD with the selection already done for you. So, you can literally jump to the composite tutorial in each chapter and start with the portrait and background photos already done. Or, if you're the kind that likes to do it all themselves, then you have all the originals, as well. Either way, it's your book and I've done everything I could think of to make it as useful and easy to follow along with as possible.

Okay, that's it for the up-front stuff. Now, it's time to dig in. Have fun!

10 THINGS YOU NEED TO KNOW ABOUT COMPOSITING

I wanted to kick off the book with 10 tips, secrets, and overall things you should know about compositing before we get started.

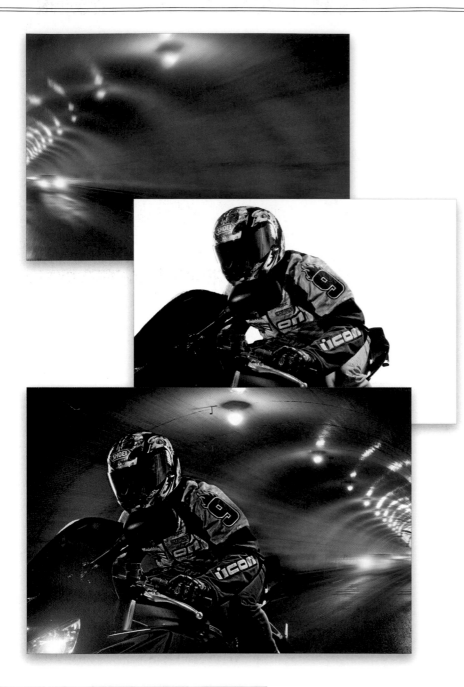

1. WHICH COMES FIRST, THE BACKGROUND OR THE SUBJECT?

I get asked this one all the time. Unfortunately, it's not a definite answer one way or the other. For me, I'd say that 75% of the time the subject usually comes first. Give me someone interesting to photograph, and I'll find a fitting background for them. Most of the time, I don't even know what that background is before I photograph the person. The other 25% of the time, I'll have a background specifically in mind before the photo shoot. I'll photograph the person in a way that I know will work for the background. Sometimes, I'll even try a quick composite in Photoshop while they're still in the studio.

2. STOCK PHOTOGRAPHY

If you're not a stock photographer, then you're probably thinking that stock photography doesn't play that important of a role in your work. In most cases, you're probably right (as a photographer, that is). However, when it comes to compositing, you can use stock in a much different way. Chances are you're going to want a certain element in the photo that you simply don't have. That's when stock photography becomes a supporting design element, an element to help add to the overall impact of your photo. Let's say you want a helicopter in your photo. Most people don't have the access to shoot a helicopter, so what do you do? Just go to a site like iStockphoto (www .istockphoto.com) and search for "helicopter." You probably won't find one isolated on a white background, but, hopefully, after reading this book and the selection secrets in Chapter 1, you won't care, because you'll know you can pull just about any image you want from its background.

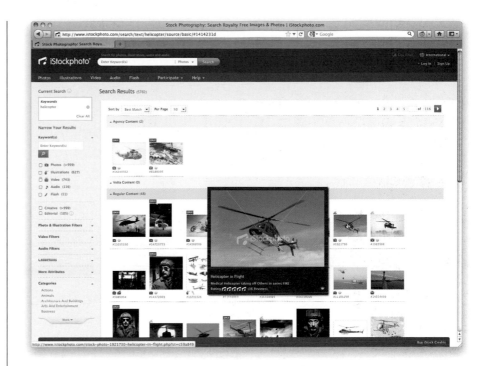

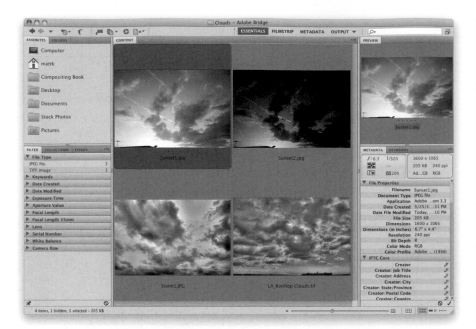

3. BUILD A BACKGROUND IMAGE LIBRARY

Building on the previous tip of using stock photography is the use of backgrounds. If you're compositing, the background is almost as important as anything else. And if you don't have to go to a stock photo website to get one, that makes it all that much better. I know you always hear, "Keep your camera with you at all times." But, before I started compositing, I never did. If I wasn't someplace spectacular, or in good light, I just didn't bother. But, since I've started creating more composites, I find that no matter where I am, it has potential. I literally take photos of everything, from clouds, to baseball fields, to streetlights, cars, doors, boats, old warehouses, alleyways, you name it. Anything you think you may one day use (and even if you think you'll never use it) becomes fair game for a photo. Why not, right? That click doesn't cost anything, so shoot it.

Once you start shooting backgrounds, make sure you organize them. I've created a Backgrounds folder, and in that folder are categorized subfolders. You don't have to have an official cataloging system—it doesn't have to be that sophisticated. As your collection grows, though, you may want to consider a program like Adobe Photoshop Lightroom (which I use for most of my photography), with all of its keywords and collections, but as you're starting out, keep it simple.

4. SELECTIONS IN PHOTOSHOP CS5 ROCK!

Everything you do in compositing is based around one key part of Photoshop—selections. Without a good, clean selection, your composites will never look professional. And as you'll see throughout this book, the selection technology in Photoshop CS5 absolutely rocks! Seriously, it has literally shaved hours off of compositing work and it has even made compositing attainable to people that simply didn't have the patience or time to try it before. It's leaps and bounds ahead of where it ever was before Photoshop CS5. So, the first secret is to make sure you have Photoshop CS5, if you want to make life easier. It all but eliminates the need for the old selection tricks using Channels, Calculations, and the Pen tool.

Now, if you're wondering if there are third-party plug-ins out there that make selections easier for you, there are. But, they cost more money. Photoshop CS5 has all you need and Chapter 1 will teach you all about it.

5. LIGHTING IS EVERYTHING

Lighting is the key to compositing, and not only makes selections easier, but also makes the composite look real. You can learn all of the selection tricks and Photoshop effects you want, but if the lighting on your subject vs. the lighting in the environment in which you place them is different, it'll never really look real. If you know the background up front, then you can plan ahead with your lighting. If not, using a setup similar to mine above gives you a lot of options later in Photoshop.

Most of the time, I use three lights: one main light up front to fill in the face and clothing, and then two lights on the sides that add a nice edge/accent light on the sides of the person. With two to three lights, you drastically increase your odds of getting a good selection from the background, as well as a head start to making the person fit into just about any other background. As for the backdrop, generally the lighter the better (make sure you check out Chapter 1 for more on the best color backdrop to use).

The Main Light: The main light source here is what fills in the face and front of the subject. The modifier you put on this light pretty much controls the mood of the light on your subject. I typically use one of two modifiers: The first is a beauty dish (as seen here) with diffusion material over it. It gives a slightly more contrasty look to your subject, because it produces harsher shadows on the face. The other is a small-to-medium-sized Rotalux Deep Octa softbox (as seen in the second setup photo on the next page), which I tend to use more when photographing families and kids. It tends to give a softer, flatter look vs. the contrasty look the beauty dish gives.

Edge Lights: This is the key to this lighting setup. The edge lights produce a fairly hard light right along the edge of the person. I've seen people go from using no lighting modifier at all on these (just the bare bulb) to using large softboxes. For me, the size of the modifier is important here, but not critical. The most critical part is that there is some sort of edge light on the person. Don't overthink this part—just make sure there's a light. Personally, I like to use a long strip bank softbox to get good coverage, from the subject's face all the way down the side of their body. But, a small-to-medium-sized softbox, if you don't have a strip light, can work really well, too. You'll also notice that I use grids on these edge lights to help control the light and focus it where I want. Remember, we just want a hard edge light along the side of them. We don't necessarily want that light to wrap around them and mix with the light coming from the front. With a grid, we can direct the light exactly where we want and get more controlled results.

Not every composite is going to start in the studio or be lit using a studio/off-camera lighting setup. As you flip through the book, you'll notice that we'll cover several natural-light composites. Natural-light portraits can work for lots of composites, but you're limited by that light. If you photograph someone in broad daylight at noon, you're probably not going to be able to place them in a dark alley, and make it look real. You'll be able to place them on another background that was shot at noon, but that's about it.

6. DON'T KILL YOURSELF ON A SELECTION IF THE DETAIL ISN'T IMPORTANT

Here's a good example: Jessica, here, was originally photographed on a gray background. After selecting her (and her hair), and placing her on a white background, the edges of her hair look horrible, right? If I plan on putting her on a bright background, then this is definitely a problem and something I'll need to fix (I show you how, by the way, in Chapter 1). But, if I plan on putting her on a darker background, take a look. Perfect! I didn't change one thing about the selection—only the color background that I placed her on. The point here is: don't waste time where it isn't needed or won't be noticed.

7. DARKEN THE FEET

This is one of the best-kept secrets in the compositing world. If you've got a full-body composite, and you place a person's feet on the ground, one of the telltale signs that it's fake is typically going to be around the feet. It's really hard to get shadows and lighting to look perfect when the person wasn't really standing there. We have tricks that we can do (and we will in the book), and one great way to hide what was done is to take people's attention away from it. Since we're drawn to looking at the brighter parts of a photo, darkening the feet helps keep people from focusing on them and the fact that something may not be quite right. Trust me, from this moment on, take a look at every ad or movie poster you see where you think something may be composited and look at the feet. Nine times out of 10, you'll see it's darker at the bottom.

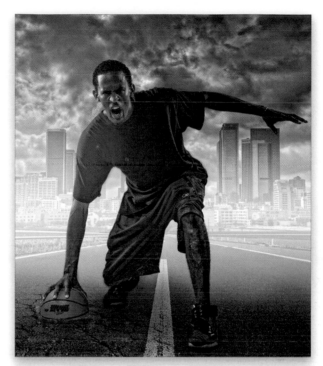

8. DON'T INCLUDE THE FEET

This is another great secret in the compositing world. If at all possible, create the image so that you don't have the feet included. You'd be surprised at how much feeling, movement, and mood you can create in an image, even if you don't see the person's entire body. Again, keep an eye out for movie posters and magazine ads, and you'll see that most of the images that seem like they must be a composite don't even have the people's feet in them.

9. COLOR GIVES EVERYTHING A COMMON THEME

One of the hardest parts of compositing is not necessarily putting various photos together. As you'll see, it's not really hard to select a person from one background and place them on another. What is more difficult is getting both the person and the background to share the same overall mood and color temperature. Color really does tie everything together, and it gives everything in the photo a common link. As we work through the book, we'll use a number of different tricks for this, like adjustment layers and blend modes, as well as a plug-in.

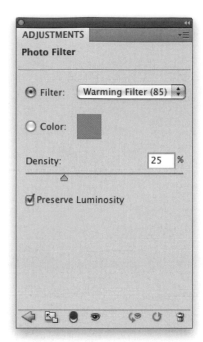

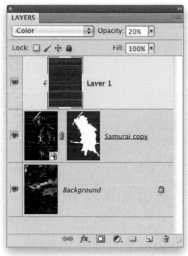

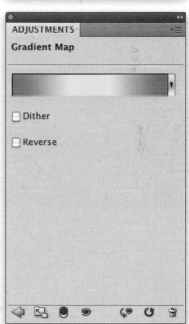

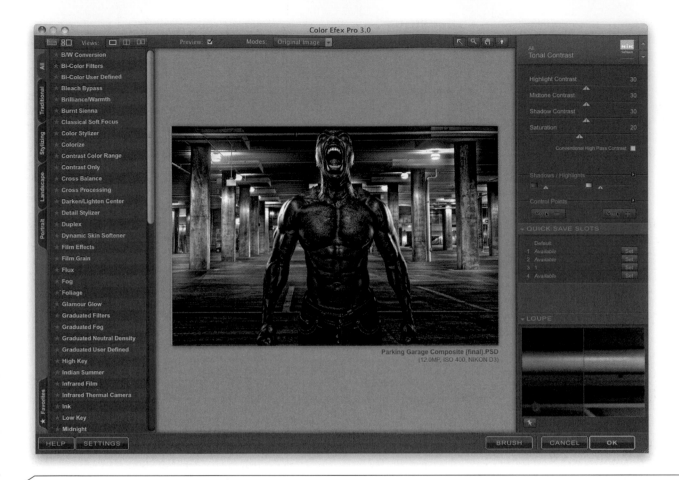

Parking Garage Composite (final).PSD
(12.0MP, ISO 400, NIKON D3)

10. THE COMPOSITOR'S SECRET WEAPON: PLUG-INS

Let me be the first to say that I know plug-ins aren't cheap. And I hate it when I read something that talks about all these third-party plug-ins you need in order to complete a tutorial. As if Photoshop isn't expensive enough already, along with all the photography gear you need to take the photos. So, here's what I've done: anyplace that I use a third-party plug-in, I first show you the free way to do something similar in Photoshop. You'll find that the free way has two issues, though: (1) it typically doesn't

look as good as the effect we get with the plug-in and (2) it takes much longer than it does with a plug-in. If you're into compositing, plug-ins will make your life easier, plain and simple. These are the plug-ins I use:

Nik Software's Color Efex Pro Complete
This plug-in gets used just about every single day in my work. Whether I'm compositing or not, I use Color Efex Pro. But for compositing, it's got so many filters that help finish your work. I swear by the

Tonal Contrast filter, which I use to finish off just about every one of my composites and backgrounds. The Bi-Color filter adds some really nice color to your photos. I use the Brilliance/Warmth filter on every landscape photo I take. Bleach Bypass is a great effect for portraits. The list goes on. I think these effects should be included in Photoshop, but they're not. Sure, you can go through a bunch of steps to create them in Photoshop, or you can just use the plug-in. At $199.95, it's not cheap, but it's the first one I'd buy.

Topaz Adjust by Topaz Labs

This one is another one of my must-have plug-ins. I use it to add an instant edgy/gritty look to my images. Plus, if I really want to add some mood and make a bright image look like it was taken at night, their Dark – Night preset (used in Chapter 10) is one of my favorites. And at $50, it's pretty reasonable.

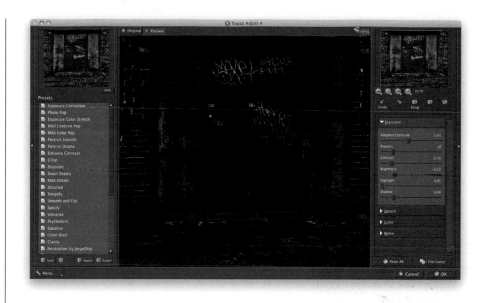

Knoll Light Factory for Photoshop by Red Giant Software

You'll notice I use a lot of lighting effects in the book. Lens flares and light streaks come in really handy to bring your composites to that next level of professionalism—things like enhancing the headlights on a car or light on a building, or adding a light source based on the way light is hitting your subject. You can do all of these things with layers, layer styles, and filters in Photoshop (and I did them in Photoshop in the book), but none of them give you the pro-fessional quality light effects that Knoll Light Factory does. That said, this one is probably the last one on my must-have list. It's not cheap, at $149, so you'd have to balance the good parts with how much you'd actually use it.

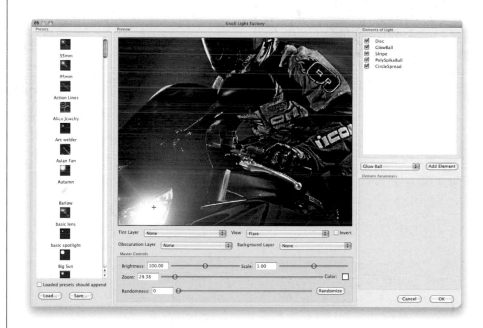

SELECTION SECRETS

When Photoshop CS5 came out in 2010, the natural question I heard from a bunch of people was "What's your favorite feature in CS5?" I've always been into HDR photography and I think everyone thought I'd say HDR Pro (the new and improved HDR feature in CS5). But it wasn't. I immediately found that the new features in the Refine Edge dialog were my favorite, because just about everything we do in Photoshop involves a selection at some point.

Today, I still stand by my favorite feature from over a year ago. Refine Edge, combined with the Quick Selection tool, is absolutely the best selection tool I've found in Photoshop, and most of the selections that we'll do in this book use this.

A COMPOSITOR'S BEST FRIENDS

When making selections, the Quick Selection tool and the newly enhanced Refine Edge dialog are going to become your best friends. I've demonstrated them in my classes since Photoshop CS5 came out and when people see the results, you can actually hear the oohs and aahs in the crowd. One of my favorite parts about them is that they're really easy to use. The Quick Selection tool is basically a brush, so if you can use a brush, you can use it. And, Refine Edge has only a few settings that we really need to worry about. Trust me, you'll have them mastered in no time and be well on your way to killer selections.

STEP ONE:

Go ahead and open a photo with a person you'd like to extract from the background. In this example, I'm using a photo of a person who is fairly well-defined all around, but there is a little more detail in his hair. Don't worry, though, I just want to get through some of the basics in this tutorial. We'll get to the flyaway hair stuff later in the chapter.

STEP TWO:

Grab the Quick Selection tool from the Toolbox (or just press **W**) and start painting over the subject in the photo. The Quick Selection tool works just like a brush. It's got Size and Hardness settings in the Brush Picker (up in the Options Bar), just like most brushes do. So, if you're selecting larger areas, then using a larger brush is faster. You can press the Right Bracket (**]**) key to quickly make the brush larger and paint in those areas.

STEP THREE:

The main idea behind the Quick Selection tool is that it's quick. At this point, just use a large brush and try to get as much of the subject selected as possible, even if you miss some smaller areas or over select some other parts. And you don't have to make the entire selection in one brush stroke. If you look at the left side of the Options Bar, you'll see three little icons: a brush with a dotted oval, a brush with a dotted oval and + (plus sign), and a brush with a dotted oval and – (minus sign). The Quick Selection tool is automatically always in Add mode (the middle icon; and you'll see a + in the middle of your brush). This means every time you click-and-paint with the brush, it adds to the selection.

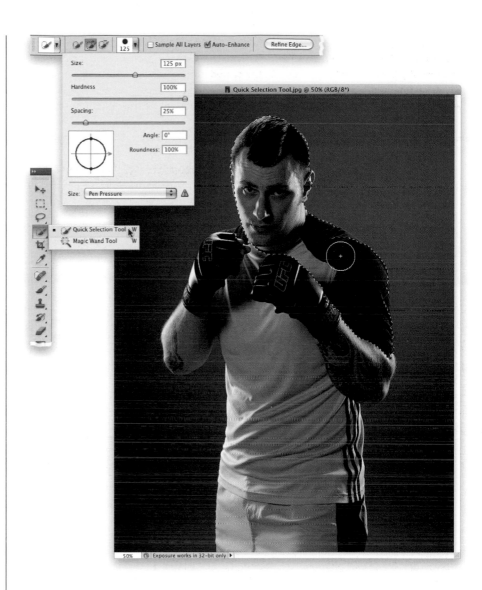

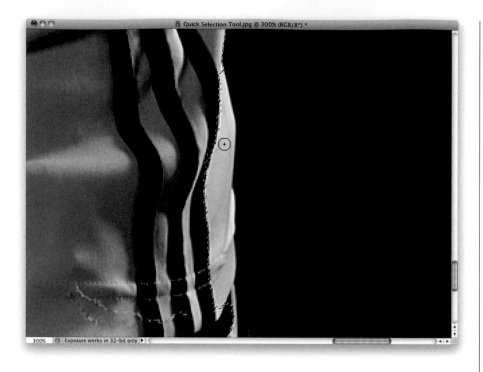

STEP FOUR:

I noticed a small area near the right edge of his shirt that wasn't selected. So, I zoomed in on this area (by pressing **Command-+ [PC: Crtl-+]** a couple times), made the brush smaller by pressing the Left Bracket (**[**) key, and painted in that area. Remember, the tool is automatically in Add mode, so it simply adds what I just painted on to the overall selection.

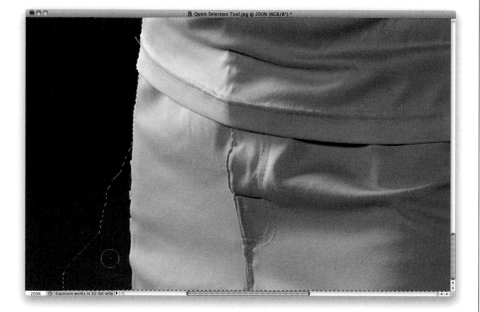

STEP FIVE:

The Quick Selection tool got a little overzealous in the bottom-left part of the photo (notice how I blamed the tool and not the user) and selected part of the background. No problem. Remember how I said the Quick Selection tool is always in Add mode? Well, you can temporarily put it into Subtract mode by pressing-and-holding the **Option (PC: Alt) key**. You'll see the – (minus sign) symbol in the middle of your brush, which means that anything you paint will be removed from the current selection. Now, just paint over any areas that shouldn't be selected.

STEP SIX:

It's a good idea to try and get most of the subject selected here. Even if you have to zoom in and spend a couple of minutes with a smaller brush, you'll be happy you did. Here, it also selected too much under his arm on the left, so I'll put the tool in Subtract mode again and paint to remove this from the selection. It doesn't have to be perfect, but you'll want to have a good selection around the subject before you move on.

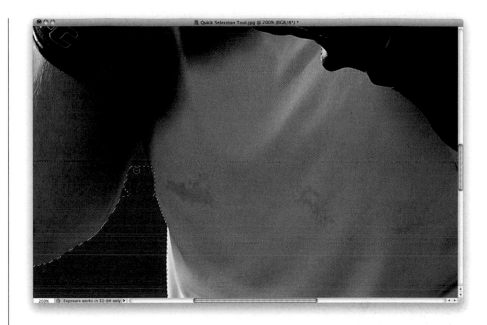

STEP SEVEN:

Okay, now that we have a pretty good selection around the subject, let's move on to the really good stuff—Refine Edge. At first glance, your selection may look really good, but it's definitely not great yet. Whenever you have a selection tool and a selection active in Photoshop, you'll see the Refine Edge button (circled here) become available in the Options Bar. Go ahead and click on it to open the Refine Edge dialog.

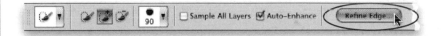

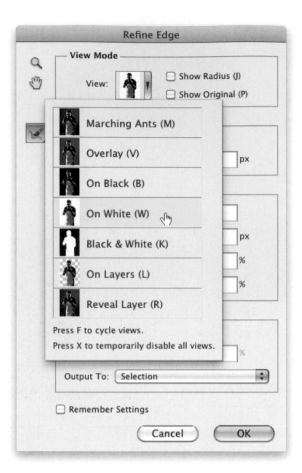

STEP EIGHT:

At the top of the dialog, there's a View setting. This lets you see how your selection looks on various backgrounds. I usually choose On Black or On White from the pop-up menu here. Most of the time, I pick the one that most resembles the brightness of the background I'm going to place the subject into. That way, I can get a good preview of how they're going to fit. In this example, white will give us a really good preview of the edge we're working with (since his clothes are darker than a pure white), so I'm going to choose **On White**.

TIP: EXPERIMENT WITH DIFFERENT BACKGROUNDS

It's always good to experiment with different background choices. If you usually choose black, then try switching to white once in a while. This way, you'll get a worst-case preview of what your selection looks like and any problem areas you may have to watch out for later.

STEP NINE:

You'll see that our selection is look-ing kinda jagged at this point. Well, the star of this dialog is the Edge Detection section (new in CS5), and it's going to help out a lot. Its job is to automatically figure out what areas you want to keep around the edges of your selection and what areas you want to get rid of. So, the first thing I do is increase the Radius setting. This gives Photoshop some information about how far out from the existing edges of the selection you want to look for things that may need to be selected. If you don't have wispy hair or any stray details that are really far out of the original selection (like in this example), then you can get by with a low setting of around 10–15 pixels or so.

STEP 10:

Try turning on the Show Radius checkbox at the top of the dialog. This gives you a preview of the Radius setting, so you can fine-tune just how far you need to drag the Radius slider. If you still don't see the edges of what you eventu-ally want selected, then you need to keep increasing the Radius set-ting until you do. If not, Photoshop won't look that far outside your original selection for any more details to select.

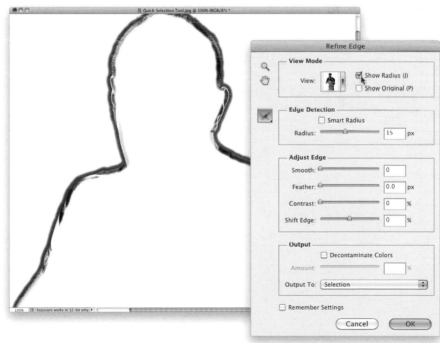

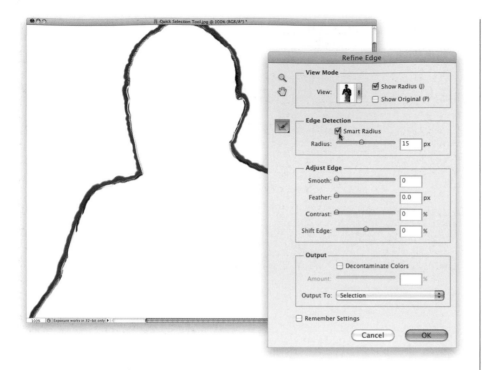

STEP 11:

Right now, I have the Radius set to 15 pixels. This means that Photoshop will look within 15 pixels on either side of the selection for details. But, you'll see there's a Smart Radius checkbox above the Radius slider. Turning this checkbox on tells Photoshop to be a little smarter about what it chooses to select. If it sees a hard edge, it'll automatically bring the radius in closer, so it doesn't accidentally select something it shouldn't. If it detects details near the edge (like hair), then it'll hold the radius farther out, near the original Radius setting you chose.

STEP 12:

The rest of the dialog isn't actually new to CS5—it's been around for a while. The Smooth setting will smooth off any jagged edges, and most of the time, like now, I leave it set to 0 because I want all of the edges, like the hair on his arms and head. If the edges start to look too jagged, I'll increase it to 5, maybe 10 at the most. The Feather setting makes the edges blurry or soft. Typically, you don't want an extremely crisp edge no matter what the subject is. So, feathering has always been a selection trick we used to make things look more realistic, but it doesn't have much of a place anymore. The Radius (and Smart Radius) settings work much better. But, I usually set Feather to a really small setting, like 0.3 pixels, anyway, just to soften the edge a tiny bit.

STEP 13:

Contrast firms up any soft edges. It's typically not something we'll use for extracting people, though, because the Radius setting gives us such a good result. The Shift Edge setting tells Photoshop to shift the entire selection inward or outward depending on which way you move the slider. Again, we've done our work already, so you generally don't need to move the selection edge at this point. Decontaminate Colors is only used when you have your subject on a colored background. We'll talk more about what color to photograph people on later in this chapter, so for now just leave it turned off.

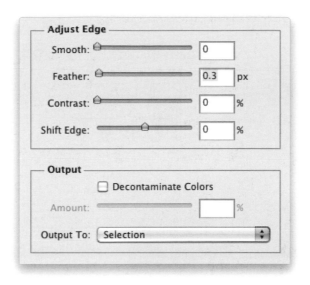

STEP 14:

When you're done with your selection and ready to move on, head down to the Output To pop-up menu at the bottom of the dialog. Instead of just outputting the results of this dialog to a selection, we can put it on a new layer with a layer mask, so we can always go back and change it if we need to. In fact, we'll adjust the selection in the next tutorial. For now, though, just choose **Layer Mask** from the pop-up menu and then click OK.

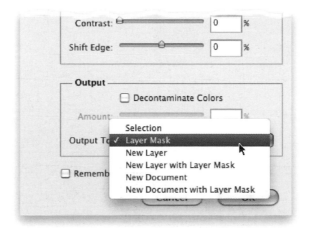

STEP 15:

Sweet! (FYI: I say "Sweet!" a lot.) You've successfully selected a person from a background. Now when you look in your Layers panel, you'll see the original layer has a layer mask on it. Sometimes your selection will look perfect. If it does, then great, but sometimes it still needs a little more work. If that's the case, then check out the next tutorial.

I know it seems like it took a lot of steps to do this, if you look back through the tutorial. But, really, it was just because I was explaining things as we went along. Most of the time, after I make a selection with the Quick Selection tool, I generally use the same settings in Refine Edge over and over. Trust me, you'll develop a knack for it and, after the first few times you do it, you'll see it only takes a few minutes.

ADJUSTING THE SELECTION

In the last tutorial, we used the Refine Edge dialog to get Photoshop to do the bulk of the work when selecting someone from their background. Sometimes we get lucky and our selection looks awesome when it's done. But other times, it needs a little adjusting. Since we created a mask along with our selection, it's really easy to adjust. That's the cool thing about layer masks for compositing—they let us go back and adjust the selection as much as we want with the Brush tool, so we can get really detailed if we need to.

STEP ONE:
We finished the last tutorial with our subject selected on his original layer with a layer mask, so all we see is a transparent background. (If you haven't done the last tutorial yet, feel free to download the file and open it here to start from where I left off.)

STEP TWO:

Before we go any further in adjusting the selection, let's add a new background behind the subject, so we can see how things are looking. Command-click (PC: Ctrl-click) on the Create a New Layer icon at the bottom of the Layers panel to add a new blank layer below the existing layer. Then, with this new background layer active, choose Edit>**Fill**, and choose **White** from the Use pop-up menu, so our subject stands out pretty well from the new background.

STEP THREE:

Now, get the Zoom tool (**Z**), zoom in, and start looking around the edges of the photo. If you're lucky, everything looks awesome and there's no more work to be done. Most of the time, though, you won't be that lucky. In my example here, I noticed that some of his shirt is missing at the top of his shoulder on the right.

STEP FOUR:

To adjust the selection, we'll use the layer mask that Refine Edge added to our layer. The way that the layer mask works is that wherever there is white on the layer mask, the image on the layer is visible. So, if you look at the layer mask, you'll see that the white figure is the exact shape of our subject (what was selected in the last tutorial). Basically, wherever the layer mask is white, that part of the photo is selected. In fact, just to prove my point, press-and-hold the Command (PC: Ctrl) key and click on the layer mask. Photoshop will put a selection around whatever is white on that layer mask on your image. Go ahead and Deselect (Select>**Deselect**), since we don't really need the selection just yet.

STEP FIVE:

In my case, I need to add to the selection. Remember, the selected areas are white on the layer mask, so I'm going to paint with white on the mask. First, make sure the layer mask is still active (you'll see a black highlight border around it), then press **D** to set your Foreground color to white. Select the Brush tool **(B)** from the Toolbox and use the **Left and Right Bracket keys** on your keyboard to set the brush size to around 20 pixels. Zoom in on the shoulder (or other area) that was cut off and start painting until you see the rest of it appear.

STEP SIX:

If you happen to paint too much and accidentally bring back some of the background, then press the **X key** to swap your Foreground and Background colors. Now you'll be painting with black, which is the same as taking away from the selected area. Paint back over the photo and you'll see those areas you don't want to show (like that small area of the gray background in Step Five) disappear.

STEP SEVEN:

Ready for a really cool trick? Zoom in and look at the left side of the photo where he's holding his hand up near his face. See how there's a dirty fringe-like edge that follows the contour of his glove? This happens sometimes if your original background was too dark (like mine was here). Sure, you could paint on the mask in black very carefully to remove it, but there's an easier way.

STEP EIGHT:

With the layer mask still active
and the Brush tool still selected,
up in the Options Bar, set the blend
Mode to **Overlay**. Then, choose
a brush size that is about the size
of the fringe you see, set your Foreground color to black (because black
will hide whatever we paint on), and
start painting on that fringe.

STEP NINE:

Don't worry if your brush starts
to spill over onto the subject.
Normally, if we weren't using the
Overlay blend mode for the brush,
we'd start hiding part of his hand
if we painted in black. But because
of Overlay mode, Photoshop hides
the fringe, but still keeps everything
else the brush touches. Now, if you
kept brushing over and over on the
same area, you'd eventually ruin
the edge. But one quick swipe with
the brush will remove the fringe
and keep the rest of what you selected intact. Best of all, you didn't
have to be very precise about it.
Give it a try around the rest of him,
if you see any other areas where
the background shows through.

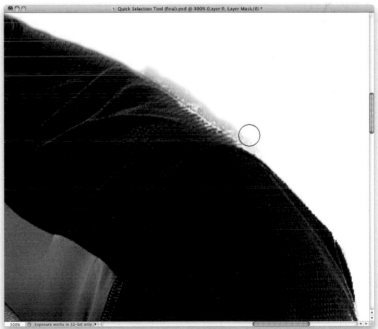

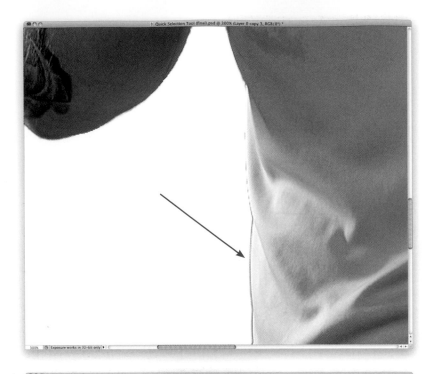

STEP 10:

One last tip for pulling off a good selection: Zoom in on the left edge of his shirt, just above his shorts. Notice that really dark edge or fringe? It's thin, but it's definitely there. It doesn't happen all the time, but I always zoom in to check for it.

STEP 11:

To fix this, we have to put our selection up on its own layer, because it won't work on a layer with a layer mask. So, Command-click on the layer mask to load our selection around the subject.

STEP 12:

Click once on the layer thumbnail itself to target it, and then press **Command-J (PC: Ctrl-J)** to duplicate the selected area onto its own layer. Next, click on the little Eye icon to the left of the original layer to hide it, along with the layer mask (this hides it, but keeps it just in case you need to go back to it later). Now you'll see the subject selected from his background on a separate layer, but without a layer mask.

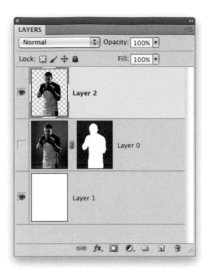

STEP 13:

Go to Layer>Matting>**Defringe**, enter a Width setting of 1 pixel, and click OK. Most of the time, you'll immediately see the fringe disappear. If it doesn't, go to Edit>**Undo** and reapply Defringe with a 2-pixel setting instead. Like I said before, it doesn't happen for all photos, but if you do see a small fringe around the edges, the Defringe feature works great.

TIP: COMPARE A BEFORE/AFTER

After applying Defringe, zoom in on the area that had the fringe and press **Command-Z (PC: Ctrl-Z)** to Undo and then Command-Z again to Redo to see the difference. Sometimes you'll think "Eh, not that great" and other times you'll think "Holy crap!!! That's awesome!"

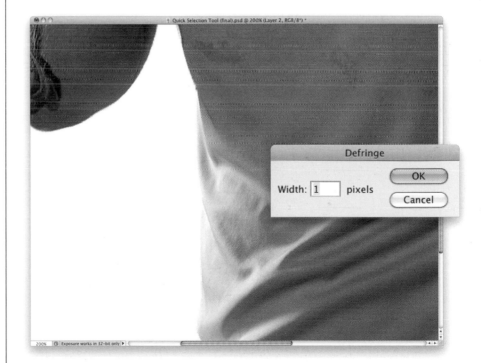

EXTRACTING HAIR

There's one question that I get all the time whenever I'm out teaching Photoshop: "How do you select a person from one background and move them to another background with all of their hair intact?" Well, you're in luck. If you followed along with the previous tutorials, you've already learned how to get yourself most of the way there. There's just one small tool we need to help out with the hair.

STEP ONE:

Go ahead and open a photo that has some wispy hair in it. While the subject here has got some clean, defined edges around her clothing, she definitely has some flyaway hair.

STEP TWO:

Use the Quick Selection tool **(W)** to put an overall selection around her. Just like we did earlier, spend a minute or two to get the selection as close as possible around all of the well-defined edges. But don't worry about the hair—just get the overall selection close, like you see here. Don't even try to select the hair edges at this point.

STEP THREE:

When you're ready, click the Refine Edge button in the Options Bar to get the Refine Edge dialog. For starters, press the **F key** to cycle through the View settings until you get to black (since the black background shows off the hair selection really well).

TIP: VIEW SHORTCUTS

Under the View pop-up menu, you'll see each option has a letter next to it, which is a quick shortcut key to jump directly to that background view. It's probably a good idea to memorize your favorites like B for black, W for white, and K for black and white.

STEP FOUR:

Now, drag the Radius slider to around 10, and you should immediately see a *big* improvement. Seriously folks, if you've ever doubted how powerful this Edge Detection stuff is, then take a look at what it's doing here. Zoom in on the subject's head, press the **P key** to see the original, and then press P again to see the current selection. All we've done so far is move one slider and we're already starting to pick up more hair!

STEP FIVE:

Okay, we still have some work to do. Notice how you can definitely see the gray peeking through around the edges of her hair, especially near her shoulders. This is where we call in the ringer. The big dog. The head honcho (okay, I'll stop). The big kahuna here (sorry, last one) is the Refine Radius tool. It's the little brush icon (circled here) just below the Zoom and Hand tools near the top left of the dialog.

STEP SIX:

Just like other brushes in Photoshop, it has a size setting that can be controlled with the **Left and Right Bracket keys**. Go ahead and resize the brush, so it'll cover the entire radius of any flyaway hair. Then simply start painting around the edges of the hair. As you paint, you'll reveal part of the original background, so you can see just how far out you have to paint to get all of the hair selected. When you release your mouse button, sit back in awe as Photoshop selects the hair, but leaves out the background (sometimes it takes Photoshop a few seconds to catch up, so be patient when using this tool). I know I sound like a total Refine Edge fan boy, but you have to admit, this tool rocks!

STEP SEVEN:

Now, continue to brush around the edges of the hair to bring all of the wispy hair edges back. You can paint in one long brush stroke around the entire head, or use smaller strokes in more concentrated areas. Honestly, I've tried both and I haven't noticed better (or worse) results from either way.

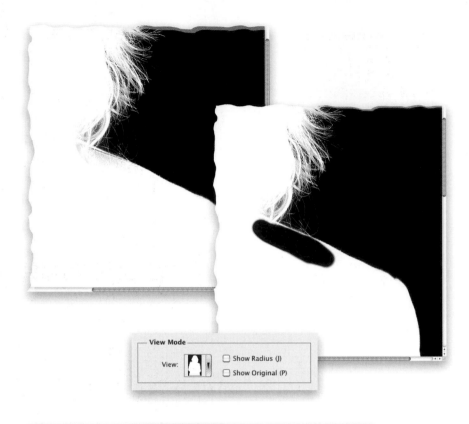

STEP EIGHT:

Every once in a while, you'll use the Refine Radius tool and paint over an area that you didn't want to paint over. You may notice it immediately, but sometimes it's hard to spot. Either way, it's always good to press the **K key** to set the View mode of Refine Edge to the On Black & White view, where you can see missed areas more clearly. Here, you can immediately see that we're missing part of her jacket on the right where her shoulder meets her hair. So, press-and-hold the **Option (PC: Alt) key** and paint over that area to bring it back.

STEP NINE:

The selection is looking good now. So, just choose **Layer Mask** from the Output To pop-up menu at the bottom of the dialog, and click OK. Now, we have our subject selected from the background, with a layer mask.

STEP 10:

Open a background image to place the subject on. In this case, I'm using something that has a lot of bright natural light in it, since our subject has light on both sides of her hair and I think a bright background fits her best. Once the background is open, switch back to the photo of the subject, select the Move tool from the Toolbox (just press **V**), and then drag the photo of the subject onto the new background and position her on the right. If your subject is larger than the new background, press **Command-T (Ctrl-T)** to bring up Free Transform, press-and-hold the Shift key, and then click-and-drag a corner handle inward to resize (press **Command-0** [Zero; **PC: Ctrl-0**] if you can't see the corner handles). Press **Return (PC: Enter)** to lock in your transformation. *Note:* If you had to resize your subject to fit in the new background, you may see an outline of your layer mask. Just use a black brush to paint this away on the layer mask.

STEP 11:

Things are looking pretty good. We've selected our subject and we have lots of hair detail selected along with her. But if you zoom in and really look closely at the edges, you'll see we have a problem: there's some gray left over from the original background. In the next tutorial, we'll look at how to fix this.

REFINING HAIR

We're seeing a problem with the image in the previous tutorial because we placed our subject on a bright background. If you recall, in the Refine Edge dialog, we were previewing the selection on a black background, so we didn't see the original background coming through at all. That just goes to show that the background plays a big role in compositing. If we were keeping her on a dark background, we'd be fine and I wouldn't bother with the edges. But, since that's not the case, let's take a look at several ways to refine the hair edges even more using the composite we created in the last tutorial.

METHOD #1:
INNER GLOW LAYER STYLE

STEP ONE:
The first method is one of my favorites and has become my go-to technique for refining hair edges. Click on the Add a Layer Style icon at the bottom of the Layers panel and choose **Inner Glow**.

STEP TWO:

When the Layer Style dialog opens, click on the color swatch near the top of the dialog to open the Color Picker. With the Eyedropper, click on an area in the hair that is closest to the overall hair color around it (don't click on any dark roots or shadows) and then click OK to close the Color Picker. This sets the color of the glow.

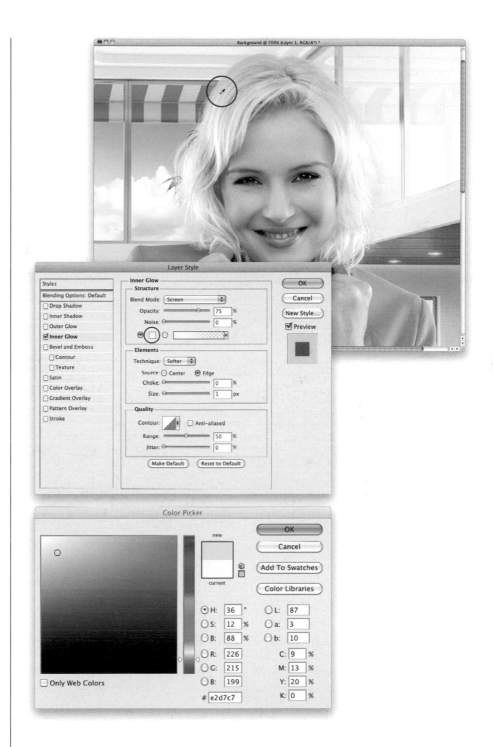

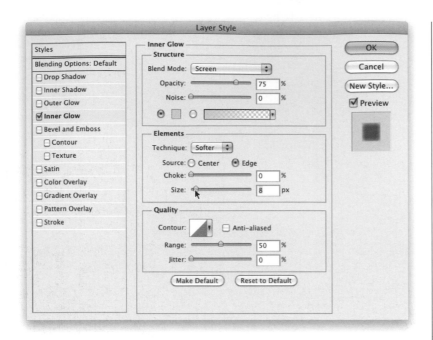

STEP THREE:
Depending on how far the gray background encroaches on the hair, adjust the Size setting to make sure you take all of it away. Then, if needed, adjust the Opacity setting at the top to make the fix brighter or darker, depending on how bright the background is. When you're done, click OK.

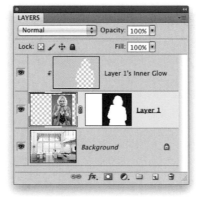

STEP FOUR:
This works great, but it does leave us with one tiny problem. The Inner Glow effect is applied to the entire photo, so even the edges of her jacket get the glow. Now, in this photo, I actually kinda like it. I think it works, since she's got so much natural light coming from behind her to begin with. But if it doesn't work for your particular photo, then we can always remove it from the parts we don't want it to affect. Go to Layer>Layer Style>**Create Layer**. This puts the effect onto its own layer, so it's no longer a layer style.

STEP FIVE:

Click on this new layer to make it active, then click on the Add Layer Mask icon at the bottom of the Layers panel. Select the Brush tool **(B)** and set your Foreground color to black. Then, just paint away the inner glow from any areas you don't want it to affect. Again, this technique is my favorite and it's the one I turn to the most when selecting hair.

STEP SIX:

I just wanted to let you know this works for dark hair, too. You just have to change a few settings. Here's another photo with crazy hair. In fact, I'm not sure it gets any crazier than this. I used the same exact steps as before to select her and her hair from the background. The subject is selected on her original layer with a layer mask and then I added a white layer below. Since it's white, everything looks great.

PHOTOSHOP COMPOSITING SECRETS

STEP SEVEN:

But look at what happens when I place her on a dark background. You'll see remnants of the brighter background around the edges of her hair. Just a quick aside: In all honesty, I'd never place her on a black background to begin with. I just don't think it looks right. She's so brightly lit that she fits in perfectly with a bright background. To me, she looks fake and "pasted in" on the black background, regardless of what's happening with the edges of her hair. That said, let's try out the Inner Glow trick just to show you it works here, too.

STEP EIGHT:

Add the Inner Glow layer style just like before. But, this time, first change the Blend Mode from Screen to **Multiply** (at the top of the dialog), then click on the color swatch to open the Color Picker. Use the Eyedropper to sample a color from her hair and adjust the Size and Opacity settings.

So, for brightly colored hair, use the Screen blend mode (the default) and for dark hair, use Multiply.

METHOD #2:
LAYER MATTING OPTIONS

STEP ONE:

Another method for removing that fringe is to use the Matting options found under the Layer menu. You can't use them on a layer with a layer mask, though, so you'll want to make sure you've got your selection as good as possible before you do this. So, let's go back to our blonde subject and Command-click (PC: Ctrl-click) on the layer mask to load it as a selection. Then, click on the layer thumbnail (not the mask) to target it and press **Command-J (PC: Ctrl-J)** to copy the selected area onto its own layer. Click on the Eye icon to the left of the original layer with the layer mask to hide them, so only the top copy layer is showing.

STEP TWO:

Go to Layer>Matting>**Remove Black Matte**. This removes those gray edges and sometimes it's amazing how well it does. It does, though, have two bad side effects, which both affect this photo: (1) it tends to make the darker edges of the hair really bright, like it did here, and (2) sometimes it fries the edges of the hair—meaning they become really crispy. I know it sounds funny to say they're fried or crisp, but it just tends to make the edges jagged and overly contrasty in certain places. Now, if the edges appear brighter (rather than darker, as they did in this example), then try using Layer>Matting>**Remove White Matte**.

METHOD #3:
DODGE AND BURN

STEP ONE:

I usually use the Dodge and Burn trick as a follow-up to one of the previous techniques. It's really simple for fixing just a few small stray hairs and not the entire head. In our example, our subject has blonde hair. So, when the hair is light, select the Dodge tool from the Toolbox (or press **O**). Then, in the Options Bar, set the Range to **Midtones**, the Exposure to 10%, and turn on the Protect Tones checkbox.

STEP TWO:

Now, just paint on the layer along the edges of the hair that are too dark. Each brush stroke will lighten them, since you're only using 10% exposure (it's like opacity). The same thing applies to darker hair with white fringes around it. The only difference is that you'll use the Burn tool instead. It's nested beneath the Dodge tool in the Toolbox (or just press **Shift-O** until you have it). Use the same settings, though.

THE BEST BACKGROUND COLOR FOR SELECTING & EXTRACTING

There has been a lot of debate about what the best color is to photograph a person on so they're easy to extract in Photoshop. Let's put this one to rest and take a look at all of them (white, gray, black, and green). You'll find that, as long as there's a good amount of contrast between your subject and the background, just about anything will work. In fact, later in the book, you'll see we don't have real studio backdrops behind some of the people we're working with. But, if you're in a controlled environment (like a studio), when it comes to shooting specifically for compositing and extraction, there's one color that just makes the most sense.

GRAY:

Let's start with my favorite choice, gray. Actually, light gray. Here's a photo of a woman on a white seamless backdrop that has no light aiming at it. The lighting setup is similar to one I wrote about in "10 Things You Need to Know About Compositing"— one light in front and one light on the side to get that nice edge/accent light on her body, face, and hair. Because there's no light pointing at the background, it falls to a light gray. For me, and the selection tools I work with, light gray seems to work best. Once in a while, if the subject happens to be wearing gray, it can miss a few edges, but it's always a quick, easy fix. For hair and detailed edges (the hardest part about selecting), gray seems to do the best job.

WHITE:

Here's a photo of the same woman taken on the same white seamless backdrop, but here it has been lit. In the studio, to keep the background white, you need to point a light at it. If you take a photo of it with no light aimed toward it, the background turns a light (or dark) shade of gray, depending on what other lights are pointed toward it, and how far away the entire setup is from it. White actually works really well for extracting. In fact, I've found it's one of the best colors for Refine Edge to work with. Here are the problems, though:

❶ When we point a light directly at the white background, some of that light inevitably reflects back to the subject and causes a bright light to wash over the edges of their body and clothing. If you're placing them onto a brightly colored background, it's not a huge problem. But, if you're putting them on a darker background, it won't look right. It's hard to describe, but when you see it, there's just something that looks off, because there's so much bright light around them.

❷ The other problem with the all white background is that we're using one or two edge lights (check out "10 Things You Need to Know About Compositing" for more on lighting). These lights make the edges of the subject's clothing and skin almost white. Not all-white mind you, but close enough to confuse Refine Edge and make selecting the hair and body a pain.

BLACK:

Here's another photo of the same subject and the same lighting setup we saw with the gray backdrop, but this time we're using a black backdrop. With no light pointing directly at the background (our main light will cast some light on it), the black stays mostly black. The problem with black is that dark clothes (which are pretty common) don't give Photoshop enough contrast to select with. Even worse, someone with dark hair really presents a *big* problem. You have to make sure you light all of the hair to give enough separation for the selection tools to work. Otherwise, dark hair pretty much blends with the black background and is nearly impossible to select.

GREEN (OR BLUE):

Finally, here's a different subject, with the same lighting setup, on a green backdrop. Green (or blue) has always been popular in the video world. A process called "keying" allows most video-related programs to automatically extract people from the background and place them on other backgrounds. Movies (especially those with lots of special effects) use this all the time. But, here's why I don't like it for compositing:

❶ The main reason I don't like it is the green spill that can occur. Light picks up the color of any surface it hits, right? So if you're lighting your subject in a studio,

there's a good chance that the lights you're using can reflect off the background and spill green light onto the edges of your subject. There are ways around this, though. Standing a good distance in front of the background always helps to reduce the spillover, but that also means you need a studio with enough depth and space to accommodate.

❷ You need more lights. You have to light the background evenly, which usually requires at least one, if not two, lights. Then, you need to light your subject. So, lighting can quickly go from three lights to five.

❸ It's just more difficult. Chances are there's a white backdrop nearby in a photo studio, but unless you're set up only for compositing, green probably isn't as close at hand as white.

I'm not saying that green backgrounds are always bad. If you've got the setup and are comfortable lighting it, it can work really well. It just takes a little more setup and know-how to do it. For me, a white background (and letting it turn to a light gray) is the way to go.

I thought we'd jump right in with a basic composite. Here, we have a background and we have a person who was shot in a studio. The subject is a friend of mine, Justin. He practices mixed martial arts (MMA) and I took some studio portraits of him in his MMA gear. But, I also grabbed some photos of him in casual dress, as well. When I shot the photo we're working with here, I had an idea—put him in a dark alley with a very grungy feel to it.

PLANNING AHEAD

This is one tutorial where planning ahead really helped out. From the portrait shoot all the way to the background, I knew this was going to be a composite. I also knew it was going to be a full-body composite, which makes things a little more difficult. When that's the case, there are a few things you can do to help make sure everything fits together nicely.

STEP ONE:

During the photo shoot of Justin (seen here), I knew that I would be compositing him onto a different background. So, the first thing I did was note the focal length on the lens I was using. I mostly shoot my portraits and backgrounds with the Nikkor 24–70mm f/2.8 lens, and the focal length of this portrait was 70mm. The next thing I did was note the camera height. I had the camera on a tripod about 2.5 feet off the ground. It's really important that you shoot your background at the same height, or your subject's feet won't line up with the ground.

STEP TWO:

Finally, I noted how far away I was from the subject. In this example, I was about 8 feet away from Justin. Again, if you want your full-body composites to line up nicely, you'll need to make sure you know the camera-to-subject distance, so you can use the same distance when shooting your background.

STEP THREE:

Now comes the background. Once I found a background I liked, I set the focal length of my 24–70mm lens to 70mm. I didn't have my tripod, but I knew that I was 2.5 feet from the ground for the portrait, so I got on my knees (similar to how I was crouched in Step One) and got the camera position to nearly the same height. Then, I moved back until I was about 8 feet from where I envisioned placing the subject. Not 8 feet from the background, though. This is camera-to-subject distance, so I picked a mark on the ground (it was a crack in the street, circled here) where I envisioned placing Justin. Then I backed up 8 feet from there and took the photo.

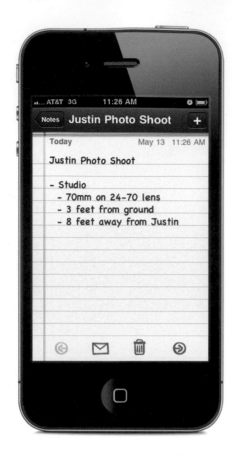

STEP FOUR:

So, how do you remember all of this info? Write it all down on a piece of paper, or put it in your phone. I have an iPhone, and I use the built-in Notes app to write this stuff down. It all seems like a lot to remember, but trust me, if you're doing a full-body composite, you'll be thankful you did. You'll see in this chapter that everything fits together really easily, because I took the time up front to keep the settings for the two separate shoots as close together as possible.

PREPPING THE BACKGROUND

The background photo was taken specifically with a composite in mind—it was specifically for the shoot of Justin (the MMA fighter) I had done the day before. The sun was nearly down behind me, and was casting a warm light onto this doorway, and I remembered all of the details of Justin's photo: how far he was from the camera, the camera angle, and the focal length that I used. So, I set myself up at the same perspective here and grabbed a couple of frames of this doorway.

STEP ONE:

Open the background image for this example. First, let's add a really grungy feel to it. It's not an HDR photo, but we can fake it with a Photoshop adjustment, so go to Image>Adjustments>**HDR Toning**.

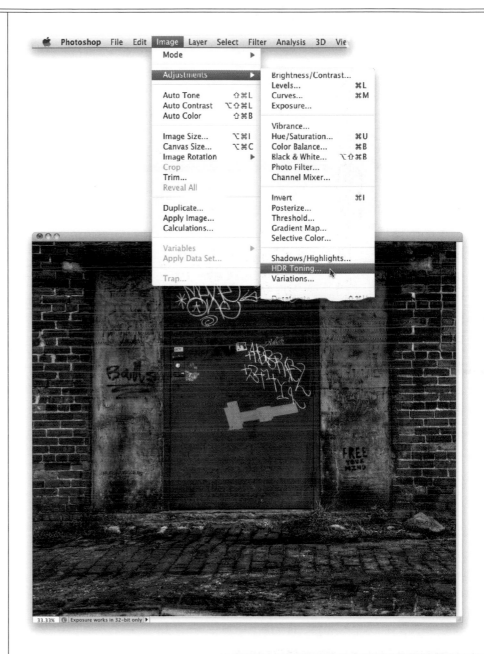

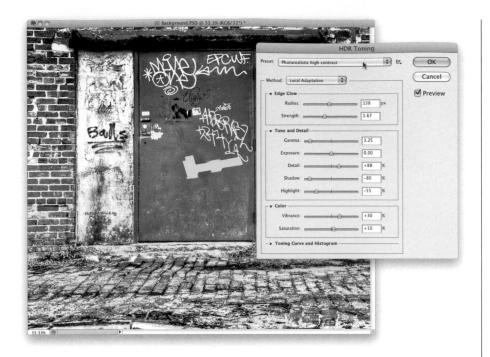

STEP TWO:

The adjustment comes with some presets at the top of its dialog. Choose **Photorealistic High Contrast** from the Preset pop-up menu to give us a starting place. Yep, I know it does crazy things to the photo, but we'll tone it down a bit next.

STEP THREE:

Bring the Exposure setting down to –3.00, which will darken the entire image. Then, increase the Highlight Detail amount to +110%. This should give us a really detailed and grungy look for our image. Click OK when you're done.

STEP FOUR:

Now is a good time to clean up any distractions. I like most of the graffiti here, but there is one word on the wall on the left side of the door that I think I'll remove. I'm not assuming the word means anything derogatory, mind you. Let's assume it simply means that inside this door is an indoor sports facility where people play with various footballs, basketballs, baseballs, etc. Either way, it's easy to remove. Press **J** to select the Spot Healing Brush (or press **Shift-J** until you get to it if you last used one of the other tools in the group), make sure the Content-Aware radio button in the Options Bar is turned on, and then paint over the graffiti on the left wall next to the door.

STEP FIVE:

It should disappear pretty quickly. If you see a repeating pattern left behind, try painting one more time on the wall and that should do it.

STEP SIX:

To really finish this background off, we'll add an edge darkening effect to it. Press **Command-J (PC: Ctrl-J)** to duplicate the Background layer and then change the blend mode to **Multiply** (as shown here), which will darken the entire image. Use the Rectangular Marquee tool **(M)** to make a rectangular selection around the area where we'll place our subject.

STEP SEVEN:

Go to the Select menu and choose Modify>**Feather**. Enter 200 pixels and click OK to soften the edges of the selection. You'll see the edge of the selection gets rounder, but that's about it. It doesn't visibly get soft yet.

STEP EIGHT:

Head up to the Select menu one more time and go to Select>**Inverse** (or press **Command-Shift-I [PC: Ctrl-Shift-I]**). This flips the selection because we really want the darkening effect applied on the edges, not the middle, right? Then, click on the Add Layer Mask icon at the bottom of the Layers panel and you'll see the Multiply blend mode layer gets hidden in the middle (where our subject will be), but stays around the edges. We're pretty much done with our background image, so go to File>**Save** and save it as a PSD file, and we'll move on to the next step of the composite.

PREPPING THE PORTRAIT

Like I mentioned, I took this portrait with the intention of placing Justin on a new a background. I took the portrait in the studio, and a few days later, while walking around an old bar district in Tampa, I shot the background that we just worked on. But it's the tone and feeling of the photo we'll work with here that sets the stage for the entire image.

STEP ONE:
Open the photo of Justin. Since it's a RAW file, it'll open directly in Adobe Camera Raw. You'll notice the background is a dark gray and, in Chapter 1, I talked about the best background to select people from. Well, dark gray isn't it. I prefer a light gray instead, especially if the subject is wearing darker clothes, like Justin is. That said, we don't always have a choice. Sometimes we have to work with what we've got, so we'll cheat a little in the next step.

STEP TWO:
Increase the Exposure setting to +2.50. This overexposes the entire photo, but it brings the background to a lighter gray, which will work well for our selection. Don't worry, we'll come back and adjust it when we're done with the selection.

STEP THREE:

Press-and-hold the Shift key and you'll see the Open Image button turn into the Open Object button at the bottom right of the Camera Raw window (circled here). Click that button to open the photo in Photoshop as a Smart Object. By working with the photo this way, we have the ability to go back and forth between Photoshop and Camera Raw if we ever want to adjust the photo later. It gives us a lot of flexibility, especially when we're working on composites, because sometimes we need to change things as the entire composite begins to come together.

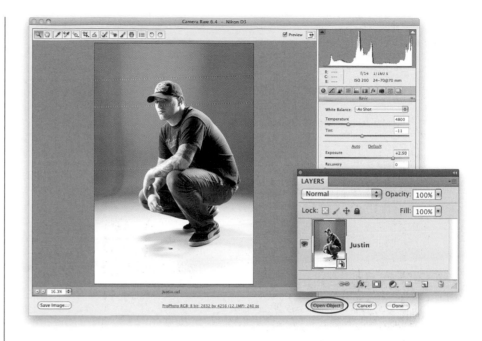

STEP FOUR:

Now that we're in Photoshop, press **W** to select the Quick Selection tool from the Toolbox, and then use the tool to paint a selection around Justin. Photoshop will select the overall figure pretty fast. Keep in mind, though, it's worth spending an extra couple of minutes here to zoom in and use a small brush to make sure you get all of the tiny edges that the larger brush will miss the first time around. Just paint again to add to the selection, or press-and-hold the **Option (PC: Alt) key** to remove part of the selection.

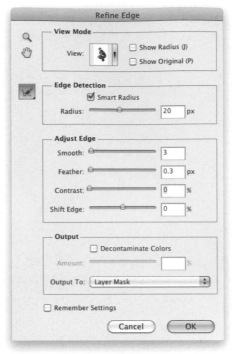

STEP FIVE:

Once you get your selection looking good, click the Refine Edge button up in the Options Bar. Press the **F key** to toggle the View setting until the background turns white. This'll be a good color to really see the edges of our selection. Turn on the Smart Radius checkbox and set the Radius to 20 px. Set the Smooth setting to 3, the Feather to 0.3 px, and the Output To pop-up menu to **Layer Mask**, and click OK.

STEP SIX:

Now, you'll see that Justin has been masked out and put on a transparent background. Press **Command-+ (PC: Ctrl-+)** to zoom in on his shoulder on the left side of the photo. If you look around the edges of your selection, you may see some rough fringes or missed edges, like I have here. This happens a lot when the person in your photo is wearing something that matches the background too much.

STEP SEVEN:

Back in Chapter 1, we saw a quick way to fix this without having to tediously perfect the mask edge to make it perfect. First, press **B** to get the Brush tool and choose a smaller, soft-edged brush. Then, in the Options Bar, change the blend Mode of the brush to **Overlay**.

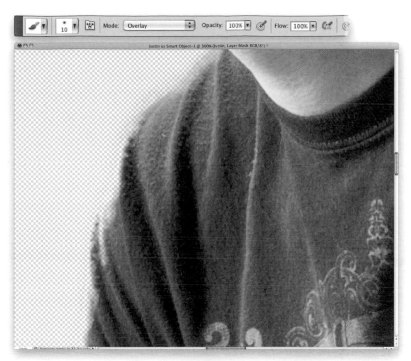

STEP EIGHT:

If it's not targeted already, click on the layer mask to target it. In this case, part of the shirt is missing, so press **D** to set your Foreground color to white, and then paint along the edge where the shirt is missing (no need to be precise here, it's okay if the brush extends beyond the edge). Photoshop starts revealing the missing edges of the shirt, but won't bring the background back in. That's because the Overlay blend mode is simply fixing the edge of the mask. Even though your brush may be larger and it looks like you'd bring the background back into view, it doesn't.

PHOTOSHOP COMPOSITING SECRETS

STEP NINE:
Continue the same process around the edges of the selection, until you clean everything up. Also, don't forget, if you see too much of the background in any areas, the opposite also works. In this case, the area near his shoes had some background showing through. Press **X** to change your Foreground color to black and paint on the mask. Since you're still in the Overlay blend mode for the brush, it'll bring the edge in closer to whatever you're selecting.

STEP 10:
Once the selection is done, we need to fix the overall exposure. Remember, this layer is a Smart Object, so this means we can go right back into Camera Raw and readjust the Exposure setting. So, double-click on the Smart Object layer's thumbnail to open the Camera Raw window. Set the Exposure slider back down to around 0 and click OK to return to Photoshop. Now, go to File>**Save** and save the photo as a PSD file. We're done with Justin, now let's put him into the new background.

CREATING THE COMPOSITE

Let's bring everything together now. Remember, our background photo was taken at a specific focal length, knowing exactly where we'd place the subject, so there wouldn't be any perspective or distortion problems. By shooting this way, you'll be amazed at how easily your subject fits into the background image. Our main goal here is to make it look realistic, and the shadows are going to play a big part in it.

STEP ONE:

Open the background image (if it's not open already). Since we only need one layer for the background, go to Layer>**Flatten Image** to flatten it into one layer.

STEP TWO:

Open the photo of Justin where he's been selected from the studio background (if you don't still have it open) and use the Move tool **(V)** to drag him into the background image. Now, you should have two layers: the Background layer and the Smart Object layer with Justin on it.

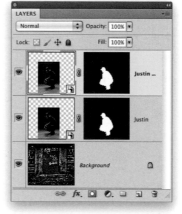

STEP THREE:

As you can see, Justin is too big for the background, so click on his layer to target it and go to Edit>**Free Transform** (or press **Command-T [PC: Ctrl-T]**). Press-and-hold the Shift key and click-and-drag one of the corner handles inward to resize him and make the photo smaller (press **Command-0** [zero;**PC: Ctrl-0**] if you can't see the corner handles). Press **Return (PC: Enter)** to lock in the transformation when you're done.

STEP FOUR:

We're missing one key thing to help pull this composite off—shadows. This isn't true for all composites, though. If you've cropped the feet and don't see the ground, then shadows aren't as much of an issue. But any time you try to put someone standing in one scene into another scene, you need shadows to pull it off. The cool thing about the technique you're about to see is that we'll use the existing shadows, so we don't have to create new ones. To start, press **Command-J (PC: Ctrl-J)** to make a copy of the Justin layer.

STEP FIVE:

Click on the layer mask on the original Justin layer and go to Edit>**Fill**. Set the Use pop-up menu to **White** and click OK to fill the layer mask with white (which reveals the original studio background again).

STEP SIX:

While we don't want to keep everything from the studio background, we do want to keep the shadows and make them blend with the new background. So, change the layer blend mode to **Hard Light** and you'll see a lot of the original background disappear (not all of it, but a lot). You'll also notice the original shadows look like they blend in with the ground below his feet now.

STEP SEVEN:

To get rid of the rest of the studio background, select the Brush tool **(B)**, use a medium-sized, soft-edged brush, and make sure the Mode pop-up menu in the Options Bar is set to **Normal**. Since the layer mask is white right now, we want to paint with black, so press **D**, then **X** to set your Foreground color to black, and start painting away the remnants of the original studio background. Paint everywhere except the area around his feet where the original shadows now cast on the ground. Don't worry if you paint over him, because we have another copy of him on the top layer.

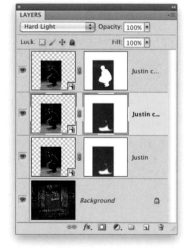

STEP EIGHT:

If you want to intensify the shadows (I think it would help here), then just press Command-J to duplicate the shadow layer and the shadows become even darker. If it's too dark, just reduce the Opacity of the layer until the shadows look real. Cool huh? Instant shadows!

STEP NINE:

While we're on the topic of shadows, I think we need to add one of our own right below his foot. These shadows are essential when someone is standing on the ground, because our feet usually cast a very dark and thin shadow on the ground right below them. So, zoom in on the front foot, then click on the Create a New Layer icon to create a new blank layer, and click-and-drag it below all of the other shadow layers, as seen here.

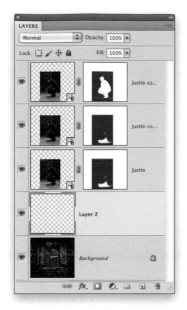

STEP 10:

With the Brush tool still active, choose a small, soft-edged brush from the Brush Picker, set your Foreground color to black, and paint a very slight shadow right under the shoe on the right. Keep it close to the shoe, though, as you don't want this one to spread out. Remember, it's just his shoe casting the shadow on the ground and because the shoe is so close to the ground, it's not going to be a large shadow.

STEP 11:

Another telltale sign that Justin has been placed into the new background is the color. He's got a cool/blueish color to him, while the background is very warm. Well, remember how the layer that Justin is on is a Smart Object layer? That means we can change the color temperature with just a few clicks. So, double-click on the topmost layer of Justin to reopen the image in Camera Raw. It's going to vary for each photo, but for this one I moved the Temperature slider toward the right to 5750 to warm things up a bit. Click OK when you're done to update the photo back in Photoshop.

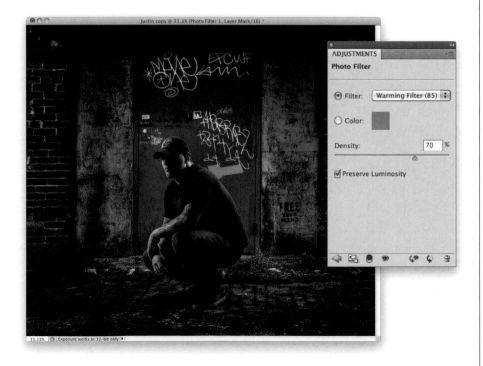

STEP 12:

While we're on the color temperature topic, I think his clothes still look too cool/blue for the environment he's in. Remember, this is one of the main things we need to get right when compositing. But, I don't want to warm the photo any further in Camera Raw, because it's going to warm his skin, and I think we're good there. So, this time, click on the Create New Adjustment Layer icon at the bottom of the Layers panel and choose **Photo Filter**. This adjustment is the compositor's best friend. In the Adjustments panel, it defaults to **Warming Filter (85)**, which works well for this photo. Just drag the Density slider to 70% to make it warmer.

STEP 13:

Adding the Photo Filter adjustment warmed everything in the photo, but we only want to warm his clothes (mainly the back of his shirt, which would be picking up that warm light we see in the image). So, to make this happen, first go to Layer>**Create Clipping Mask** (or press **Command-Option-G [PC: Ctrl-Alt-G]**). This forces the Photo Filter layer to only affect the layer right below it (the selection of Justin).

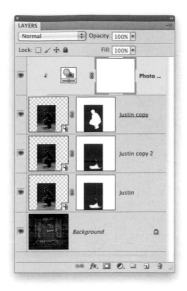

STEP 14:

But, it's still warming his skin. No sweat. The Photo Filter adjustment layer came with layer mask, so set your Foreground color to black and use the Brush tool to paint on his skin to remove the warming filter. Now, it only affects his clothing. In fact, I'd probably go a step further and paint on his jeans, too, since they're already warm enough. We mostly want to warm the black shirt, so it looks like it's absorbing all of that warm color we have in the photo.

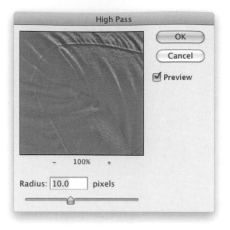

STEP 15:

On this particular image, the background is already pretty gritty and edgy. So, let's add some of that grit to the portrait, too. Click on the topmost layer with Justin on it to target it. Then, go to Filter>Other>**High Pass**, set the Radius to 10 pixels, and click OK.

STEP 16:

Of course, the layer looks horrible because it's all gray now, but remember that this is a Smart Object layer. Since we've applied a filter to it, we get all kinds of advantages—one of them being blend modes. If you look at the layer in the Layers panel, you'll see a tiny little icon, at the very bottom right, next to the words High Pass (circled here). Double-click that icon to open the Blending Options for the High Pass filter.

STEP 17:

Here, change the Mode setting to **Hard Light** to hide the gray, but keep all of that gritty detail. You can also reduce the Opacity in this dialog if it's ever too gritty, but I think it looks good on this photo at 100%. Click OK when you're done.

STEP 18:

Okay, I like the gritty look everywhere but on his face. You'll notice, though, that the High Pass filter has a layer mask (it's circled in red here). This means we can paint the High Pass filter away from any parts of the photo where we don't want it. So, click once on the mask to target it. With your Foreground color set to black, paint with a small, soft-edged brush over his face to hide the High Pass filter effect there, but keep it on the rest of his body.

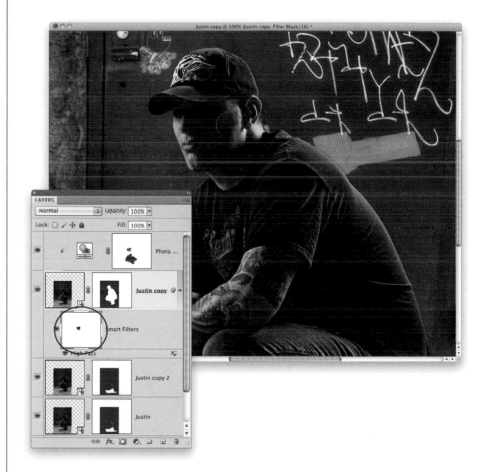

STEP 19:

For the last step, let's go ahead and sharpen the overall image. Click on the topmost layer and then press **Command-Option-Shift-E (PC: Ctrl-Alt-Shift-E)** to merge everything below it into one new layer at the top of the layer stack. Go to Filter> Sharpen>**Unsharp Mask**, use an Amount setting of 134, a Radius setting of 1, and a Threshold setting of 4, and then click OK.

Hopefully, you can see how this composite is pretty much all just finishing touches. We spent most of the time on shadows and color. But, when it came to perspective and angles, fitting Justin into this new background was simple because some extra time was taken up front to make sure the camera settings, distance, and height matched.

FINAL IMAGE

CREATING MOTION

I first came up with this composite idea when I saw some photos of an actual motorcycle photo shoot. The photographer was tethered into the back of a pickup truck driving down a road, with an assistant holding a light (also tethered into the truck). Now, the photos were great, but it got me thinking, "What about shooting the motorcyclist in the studio, where I could control the exact lighting that I wanted, and then placing him onto the background I wanted?" To me, a project like this really shows the power of compositing, because the alternative can be costly, requires a lot of setup, and is pretty much just a pain in the neck to pull off.

PREPPING THE BACKGROUND IMAGE

My idea for this shoot was a motorcycle speeding through a tunnel, but I live in Tampa, FL, and there are not many tunnels around here. Luckily, I was in Los Angeles recently attending a workshop by a friend of mine, Joel Grimes (an awesome photographer and compositor), and we stumbled across the 2nd Street Tunnel. So, I grabbed my tripod, went into the middle of the tunnel, and snapped off a few frames (with Joel looking out for cars).

STEP ONE:
Open the photo of the tunnel. The first thing we need to do is change the perspective a little. To me, the sidewalk on the left doesn't add anything of interest to the background and I envision only seeing the road the motorcycle will be on (plus, we need to remove the tripod leg on the far left). So, let's make a copy of the image layer to work on by pressing **Command-J (PC: Ctrl-J)**.

STEP TWO:
Instead of cloning away the sidewalk, let's just stretch the photo a little. Since the background will eventually have some motion blur to it anyway (because the motorcycle is speeding), we can get away with quite a bit here. Go to Edit>**Free Transform**, click on the bottom-right corner of your image window and drag it out, then click on the middle-left handle and drag it to the left until you bring the vanishing point of the tunnel to the far-left edge (as shown here).

STEP THREE:

Then, instead of just dragging the bottom-right corner handle downward (which will simply enlarge the entire image), press-and-hold **Command-Shift (PC: Ctrl-Shift)** and drag it downward to change the perspective a little, so it really looks like whatever is in the tunnel is coming at us. When you've got the transformation in place, press **Return (PC: Enter)** to lock it in.

STEP FOUR:

If we push and pull the background any more, we're going to distort it too much, but we still want to get rid of the sidewalk, right? So, grab the Rectangular Marquee tool **(M)** and make a rectangular selection on the bottom third of the photo (as shown here). Then, press Command-J to copy that selected area up onto its own layer.

STEP FIVE:
Next, get the Move tool **(V)** and move the duplicated portion of the road over to the left side of the image. I know it doesn't look quite right yet, but we do have some erasing to do, which we'll do with a layer mask in the next step.

STEP SIX:
Click on the Add Layer Mask icon at the bottom of the Layers panel (shown circled here) to add a white layer mask to the top layer. To erase away parts of this duplicate road layer, we'll need to paint with black on the white mask. So, with your Foreground color set to black, get the Brush tool **(B)** and, in the Options Bar, choose a medium-sized, soft-edged brush from the Brush Picker. Now, paint over the right side of the duplicate road to make it disappear and show the road that's below. Continue painting over toward the left and over the car to make it reappear. What we want to do here is bring back the original road that is under the duplicate copy, but we want to keep enough of the dupli-cate, so it appears that the road extends all the way to the left edge of our image.

STEP SEVEN:

When you're done bringing back the road, if you see duplicate lines on it, try this: Click on the Create a New Layer icon at the bottom of the Layers panel to create a new blank layer, then select the Spot Healing Brush from the Toolbox (or just press **J**). In the Options Bar, make sure the Content-Aware option is selected and the Sample All Layers checkbox is turned on, then paint over any extra lines and cracks with a small brush. They'll disappear in no time flat.

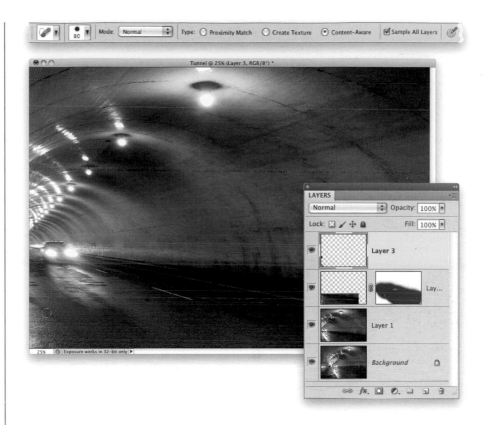

STEP EIGHT:

The next thing we'll do is add some blur. Since the motorcycle is going through the tunnel, we'll want to convey that movement. So, first, let's create a merged layer of everything we've done so far by pressing **Command-Option-Shift-E (PC: Ctrl-Alt-Shift-E)**. This creates a new flattened layer of all our work, but still keeps all of our layers below it in case we need them again.

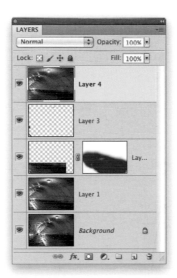

PHOTOSHOP COMPOSITING SECRETS

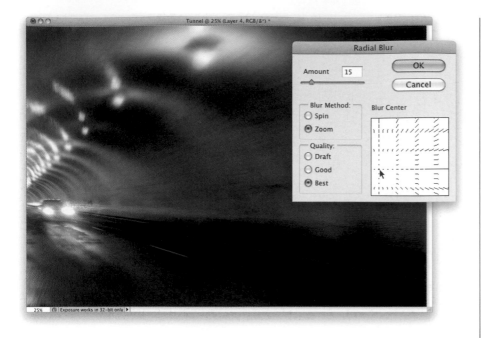

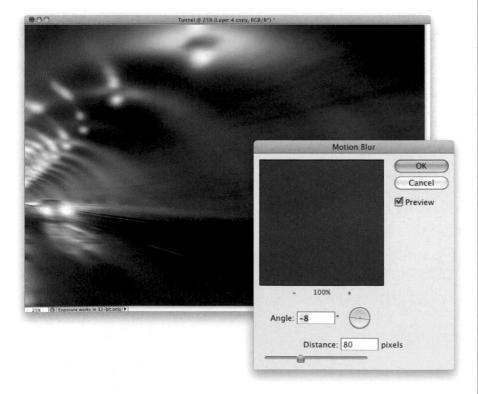

STEP NINE:

Go to Filter>Blur>**Radial Blur**. Radial Blur simulates movement from a panned camera, rather than just blurring everything in the photo. Set the Amount to something pretty low, like 15 (we don't want to blur it too much). Under the Blur Method, choose Zoom, and under Quality, choose Best. Also, the default Blur Center will come from the middle, which won't work for this photo, since the vanishing point of the tunnel is in the lower left. But you can change it by clicking on the Blur Center preview point and moving it to the lower left of the preview (as shown here). Click OK when you're done and you'll see a slight blur added to everything in the tunnel (lights, car, and road).

STEP 10:

Let's add a slight motion blur to the car next. Duplicate the layer, then go to Filter>Blur>**Motion Blur**. Set the Angle to about –8° (slightly downward to match the direction of the car) and the Distance to 80 pixels. Click OK to apply the blur.

TIP: RENAME YOUR LAYERS

It's not a bad idea at this point to double-click on each layer's name in the Layers panel and rename them to something more descriptive, so they're easier to keep track of.

STEP 11:

Press-and-hold the **Option (PC: Alt) key** and click on the Add Layer Mask icon to add a black layer mask to the motion blur layer, which completely hides the layer. It's still there, we just can't see it. Then get the Brush tool, and with your Foreground color set to white, paint the motion blur layer back in only on the car in the lower left.

STEP 12:

Lastly (and this is purely artistic), I imagined the entire image having a blue tint to it, so we'll do this by adding a Hue/Saturation adjustment layer. Click on the Create New Adjustment Layer icon at the bottom of the Layers panel and choose **Hue/ Saturation** from the pop-up menu. Then, turn on the Colorize checkbox at the bottom of the Adjustments panel and it'll apply a tint to the entire photo. Drag the Hue slider to 217 to add a blue tint and then drag the Saturation slider to 32. We now have the background photo prepped and ready for the motorcycle.

At this point, it's probably a good idea to go to File>**Save** and choose **Photoshop** from the Format pop-up menu to save this as a PSD file, so you're covered just in case.

PREPPING THE MOTORCYCLE IMAGE

In the last tutorial, you saw how to get the background image ready for the composite. Now, it's time to get the motorcycle photo ready. We'll first take a look at how the motorcyclist was photographed and any changes I made to the photo, before adding it to the tunnel background. An interesting side note on this image is that I originally thought I'd go with a head-on straight shot of the motorcyclist. In fact, I created the entire composite that way. Then I started working with a photo from a lower angle on the side and as soon as I dropped it onto the background, I knew this was the angle I wanted. It conveyed the idea of speed to me more than the straight shot did. Funny how things work out, huh? Goes to show you it's worth shooting a few more angles or poses than you think you need. Okay, let's get started.

STEP ONE:

Here's a photo of the overall setup for the motorcyclist shoot. The pose isn't exactly the same one we're using for this project, but this will give you a good idea of where the lights are positioned. Pretty standard for this edgy type of photo—a strip light on each side (with grids) and one main light in front (along with my buddy RC's elbow at the top right).

STEP TWO:

Open the photo of the motorcyclist in Camera Raw. Now, I took shots of several different poses—some straight on, some from a lower angle on the side, and some from directly on the side of him (I just had him turn the bike, so his side was facing me). In the end, this one was the one that really caught my eye for a composite. There's one problem, though: because I changed the shooting angle, the white seamless background isn't behind him near his helmet on the left. I normally would move the subject, so the backdrop did fall behind them, but that would have meant moving the bike (which wasn't light) and the lighting setup. Since I was pressed for time, and I knew the edges along the helmet were pretty hard edges, I didn't worry too much about the selection I'd end up making later.

STEP THREE:

As for the photo, I think there's a lot of detail in the shadows that we can bring out. So, increase the Fill Light slider to about 60 and you'll see those shadows open up quite a bit.

STEP FOUR:

There's not much more we can do in Camera Raw at this point, so let's move over to Photoshop, however, we're not locked into these settings. We have a trick for making Photoshop and Camera Raw work together, in case we want to come back and tweak anything (like the overall exposure or white balance of the photo), and trust me, we probably will, once we see the image on the background. Just press-and-hold the Shift key and the Open Image button will turn into the Open Object button (shown circled here). Click it to open this photo in Photoshop as a Smart Object.

STEP FIVE:

Now, let's start making the selection. First, use the Quick Selection tool **(W)** to put a selection around the entire motorcyclist. Keep in mind that part of his jacket is gray, as well as the background, so take a few minutes to zoom in and get the selection as good as possible here.

Note: Don't forget, you can always open the practice files that I've provided and they'll already have a layer with a layer mask of the selected image for you. You can find out where to download them in the book's introduction.

STEP SIX:

Once your selection looks good, click the Refine Edge button up in the Options Bar. We're putting the motorcyclist on a fairly dark background, so in the Refine Edge dialog, choose **On White** from the View pop-up menu—this way, we'll really see any selection edges that are off. Turn on the Smart Radius checkbox, increase the Radius setting to about 17 pixels, the Smooth setting to 3 (since there aren't any rough or detailed edges), and the Feather setting to 0.2. Then, in the Output section, from the Output To pop-up menu, choose **Layer Mask**. If you look closely at the edges around his shoulder, you might see a dirt-like fringe around certain places. This happens a lot when the background color is so close to the edges of what we're selecting. But we have a trick (that we covered in Chapter 1 and will get to in a minute) to get rid of it using the layer mask, so just click OK here when you're done.

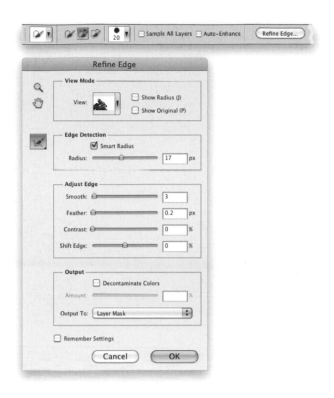

STEP SEVEN:

Now, in the Layers panel, Command-click (PC: Ctrl-click) on the Create a New Layer icon at the bottom of the panel to add a new blank layer under the existing one. Go to Edit>**Fill**, choose **White** from the Use pop-up menu, and click OK to fill the new layer with white. This simulates the same white background we just used with the Refine Edge dialog.

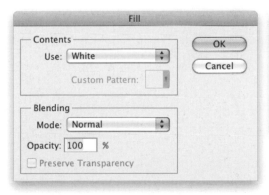

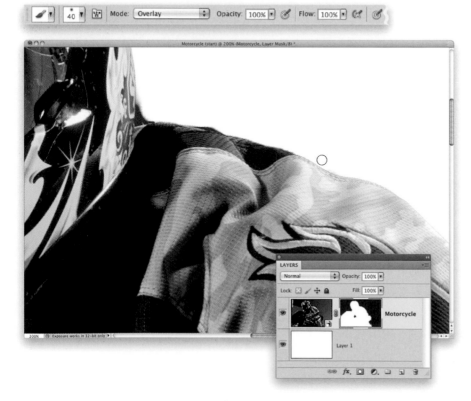

STEP EIGHT:

Press **Z** to get the Zoom tool and zoom in to the photo until you can see those dirt-like fringes around his shoulder (and anywhere else). Because the original background color was so dark and matched the edges of the motorcyclist so closely, we have this fringe that Refine Edge just couldn't select out that well.

STEP NINE:

To get rid of it, in the Layers panel, click on the layer mask thumbnail to make it active. Press **B** to get the Brush tool and, in the Options Bar, choose a small, soft-edged brush and change the Mode to **Overlay**. With your Foreground color set to black, start painting along those edges. You'll see the fringe disappear, but because you're using the Overlay blend mode, Photoshop won't let it affect the actual edge of the motorcyclist. Then, change your brush blend mode back to **Normal** and use the layer mask to paint out (using a black brush) or paint in (using a white brush) any edges (basically, any cleanup work) that didn't get selected perfectly back in Refine Edge.

TIP: PAINT IN WHITE IN OVERLAY MODE

The same works in reverse, too. If your selection ever cuts out part of the person along the edges, change your Foreground color to white and, while still using the brush in Overlay mode, paint along the edges on the layer mask. It'll bring the edges back without bringing back the original background.

STEP 10:

Okay, now that the motorcyclist is selected from the background, go to File>**Save** and save it as a PSD, so all of your changes are saved. Next, we'll put it all together.

CREATING THE COMPOSITE

Now, it's time to put this one together and everything actually comes together really well with this one. There's not much that we have to do to fit the motorcyclist into the background other than place him there. Our main hurdle here, though, is to convey speed. Since neither the background image nor the motorcycle were really moving, we have to make it look like it isn't just a photo of a guy sitting on a bike.

STEP ONE:

First, open the background image. Here, I've opened the background image where we left off in this chapter's first tutorial. At this point, I don't need all of the layers with this image anymore. I know I'm not going to change anything, and keeping them all just makes our Layers panel more complex. So, go to Layer>**Flatten Image** and now there's just a Background layer.

TIP: DUPLICATE BEFORE FLATTENING

If you're morally, or otherwise, opposed to flattening your layers, then try going to Image>**Duplicate** to make a copy of the image, then flatten the copy to make it easier to work with. If you ever need to go back, you still have your original with all of its layers.

STEP TWO:

If you remember from the previous tutorial, the motorcyclist is aiming toward the left side of the image. But our background looks as though he would be heading to the right, so we have a problem here. We can't flip the guy on the motorcycle, because the writing on his helmet and jacket would be backwards. So, we'll flip the background image instead. Go to Image>Image Rotation>**Flip Canvas Horizontal**. Now the tunnel is angled in the same direction the motorcycle will be traveling.

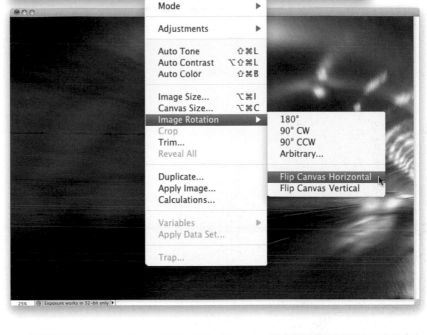

STEP THREE:

Next, open the motorcycle image and position the images so you can see them both onscreen (or at least their tabs, if you're using Photoshop's tabbed interface). Using the Move tool (**V**), click on the motorcycle layer, then drag it over onto the background image, and position it up against the far left of the background.

STEP FOUR:

The first thing I noticed is that the motorcyclist has a warmer tone to him than the background does, and since the motorcyclist layer is a Smart Object, we can edit the white balance back in Camera Raw. Just double-click on the image thumbnail and it will open in Camera Raw. Move the Temperature slider toward the left to 4400. I also ended up decreasing the Fill Light and increasing the Blacks a little.

STEP FIVE:

While we're here, there's one more thing we can adjust: Notice how bright his jeans are? They're one of the brightest things in the photo and really the last thing we want to draw attention to, right? But there are some headlights in the background photo that would probably be casting some light on them. So, let's even this out with some selective brushing. Select the Adjustment Brush tool **(K)** from the toolbar up top (the fifth icon from the right), then set the Exposure slider to −2.00 and the Brightness slider to −25.

STEP SIX:

Using a pretty small brush, paint over his jeans to darken them. It doesn't have to be perfect here, so don't spend too much time on it. Just darken the general area, so it doesn't look so distracting, but leave the back of the jeans alone, so it looks like the light from the car's headlights is shining on them from behind. Click OK when you're done to return to Photoshop.

STEP SEVEN:

Next, let's add some motion behind the motorcycle—we have a couple of cool tricks to help do this. First, we'll add some motion blur to the motorcyclist. But, remember, his layer is a Smart Object. We won't have the control we need to apply a blur directly to this layer, so we need to put him onto a regular layer. Click on the layer with the motorcycle to make it the active layer, and then Command-click (PC: Ctrl-click) on the layer's layer mask to load the selection around him.

STEP EIGHT:
Press **Command-J (PC: Ctrl-J)** to copy that selected area (the entire motorcyclist) onto its own layer. The image looks exactly the same, but now in the Layers panel, you'll see the Smart Object layer and mask, and a regular layer containing only the motorcyclist on top of it.

STEP NINE:
With the new layer active, go to Filter>Blur>**Motion Blur**. Set the Angle setting to –11, set the Distance to 250 pixels, and click OK.

STEP 10:

Obviously, the blur wouldn't normally be all over his body, so click on the Add Layer Mask icon at the bottom of the Layers panel to add a white layer mask to this layer. Then, with your Foreground color set to black, get the Brush tool **(B)**, and paint over the mask to hide the blur from everything except the right edge of the motorcyclist, so it looks like the panning camera left some motion blur (even though we know the camera wasn't panning). To soften the blur a little, at the top of the Layers panel, lower the layer's Opacity (here, I lowered it to 73%).

STEP 11:

Here's another lighting trick to give the appearance of motion: Click on the Background layer to target it, then click on the Create New Adjustment Layer icon at the bottom of the Layers panel and choose **Gradient**. In the Gradient Fill dialog, change the Style to **Angle** and then click on the gradient to open the Gradient Editor. From the Gradient Type pop-up menu, choose **Noise**, set the Roughness to 61%, and then from the Color Model pop-up menu, choose **HSB**. Drag the white knob under the S (Saturation) slider halfway to the left and then drag both knobs under the H (Hue) slider toward the middle, under the blue area, so the gradient becomes blue (the color of the tunnel). Lastly, click the Randomize button until you see something similar to what I have here in my gradient.

STEP 12:

Click OK to close the Gradient Editor and go back to the Gradient Fill dialog. Move your cursor over onto the image and with the Move tool, reposition the center of the light source over to the bottom right, where the vanishing point of the tunnel is (as shown here). Click OK to close the Gradient Fill dialog. Now, if you change the adjustment layer's blend mode to **Soft Light**, you'll drop out all of the black that was in the gradient and you'll only be left with something that looks more like a ray of light. I lowered the layer Opacity a bit, as well, to soften the effect.

STEP 13:

Right now, the effect is applied to the entire image, but you'll notice the Gradient Fill adjustment layer was automatically created with a layer mask. With your Foreground color set to black, select the Brush tool and choose a fairly large, soft-edged brush. Start painting away the effect everywhere but behind the motorcyclist, so it looks like he left this motion streak–like effect behind him.

STEP 14:

Next, we'll add some reflections to his helmet's visor by copying the background and warping it to fit the visor. Click on the topmost layer in the Layers panel to target it and choose Select>**All.** Then click on the Eye icons to the left of the two motorcycle layers to hide them, so only the background is visible. Choose Edit>**Copy Merged** to copy everything (except the motorcycle), and then choose Edit>**Paste** to paste it on its own new layer.

STEP 15:

Click where the Eye icons used to be to the left of the two motorcycle layers to turn them back on. Then, go to Edit>**Free Transform** (or press **Command-T [PC: Ctrl-T]**), press-and-hold the Shift key, click on a corner handle, and resize the new background layer, so it's roughly the size of the helmet, maybe a little larger (as shown here).

STEP 16:

Next, go to Edit>Transform> **Warp** and in the Options Bar, from the Warp pop-up menu, choose **Inflate**, and then increase the Bend amount to 100%. Press **Return (PC: Enter)** when you're done to lock in the changes.

STEP 17:

Add a layer mask to the warped layer and, with a black brush, just paint away the warped background everywhere, except the right side of the visor. You may need to switch to the Move tool and move it around a little to get it to fit into place. When you're done, reduce the Opacity of the layer to around 40%–50%. You just want a little reflection in there, but not much. Repeat Steps 14–17 and add a reflection to the wind guard on the front of the bike. But, this time, don't transform it as small and reduce the opacity of the layer to 20%, so it's even less visible than the other reflection. (*Note:* Be sure to move the new background layer that you create in Step 14 to the top of the layer stack after you create it.)

TIP: CLEAN UP THE VISOR

If you want to get really detailed here, you can add a new blank layer and use the Clone Stamp tool **(S)** to clone the light stand out of the existing visor reflection. But I'm not going to bother doing that here.

STEP 18:

Okay, we're almost done. Now for some finishing touches: Let's create a new layer to do some dodging and burning. Click on the topmost layer in the Layers panel to target it, then press **Command-Option-Shift-E (PC: Ctrl-Alt-Shift-E)** to merge everything together into one new layer on top. Select the Burn tool from the Toolbox (or press **Shift-O** until you have it), and in the Options Bar, set the Range to **Midtones** and the Exposure to 20%. Now, paint in any places where you want to make the image darker. I painted over the front of his helmet and the front of his jacket because I thought the light was too bright compared to the rest of the image. Do the same thing with the Dodge tool (press **Shift-O** until you have it) if you want to brighten any parts of the image, like the edge of the jacket, to accentuate the back lighting on him, along with the lighting behind him.

STEP 19:

It's time for a little grit and sharpening effect. Again, merge everything together on a new layer at the top of the layer stack. Then, go to Filter>Other>**High Pass**, set the Radius to 15 pixels, and click OK.

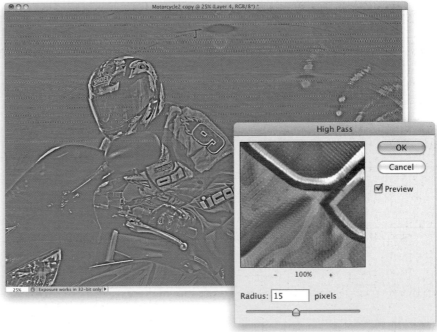

STEP 20:
Now you have a grayish layer on top of all the others. Change the layer blend mode to **Hard Light** and it'll hide the gray, but keep that gritty detail effect the High Pass filter applied. It has the appearance of not only sharpening the photo, but it also adds some depth and dimension to it, as well. It does brighten some parts of the photo, too, though. So, try adding a layer mask to the layer and painting the brightness away from the areas where it doesn't look good (like the front of his jacket and the lights along the top of the tunnel).

STEP 21:
Next, we'll add an effect to the headlight. I know I'm beginning to sound like a broken record but, once again, merge everything into one new layer, then go to Filter> Render>**Lens Flare**. Set the Brightness to around 100% and choose 105mm Prime for the Lens Type. Then, click in the preview window and move the flare to the bottom-left corner of the photo, over the headlight, and click OK to apply it. Because we just created the flare on its own layer, you could add a layer mask to the flare layer and use the Brush tool set to black to paint away any excess flare in the image. You can also reduce the Opacity of the layer to lessen the brightness, if needed.

STEP 22:

One last thing to do: A vignette will really help darken the edges and draw our attention to the motorcyclist. So, create a new merged layer one last time and then change the layer blend mode of the new layer to **Multiply** to darken the entire image. Add a layer mask to the layer, grab the Brush tool, and use a large, soft-edged brush (with your Foreground color set to black) to paint away the darkened layer from the motorcyclist and the motorcycle. Reduce the Opacity to tone it down a bit, if needed.

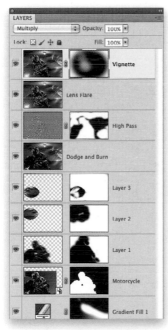

FINAL IMAGE

Another great use of compositing is for high school senior portraits. It's become a really hot trend to take seniors out to a cool, fun, or dramatic location for their graduation photo shoot. But, with compositing, you don't have to take them anywhere. It really has a ton of uses for this style of photo: maybe the weather didn't cooperate on the day of a location shoot, maybe you don't have the location that works for your subject, etc.

PREPPING THE BACKGROUND

The background for this one is an outdoor basketball court. It's got a nice blue sky behind it, along with a city skyline. It's cool, but doesn't do much if we're looking for something edgy here. Once we add some dramatic clouds and a few effects, it'll look totally different, though.

©ISTOCKPHOTO/JOSE GIL

STEP ONE:

The subject we'll be placing in this background is wearing a basketball uniform, so while we're going to go with a basketball-themed background here, we'll take it in a very dramatic direction. First, open the main image for the background. It's pretty simple at this point: a basketball court with a city skyline in the background.

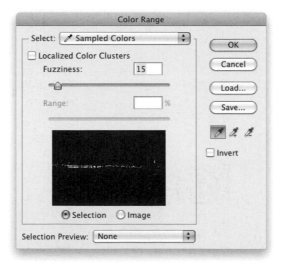

STEP TWO:

Since we're going in a dramatic direction for this one, let's add some really dramatic clouds in place of the blue sky. We'll need to make a selection first, though. Now, I know I've been touting the Quick Selection tool with Refine Edge as the best selection tools around, but for this one, we're going to use another selection tool called Color Range. Since the sky is all blue, it'll be the fastest way to select it. So, go to Select> **Color Range** to open the dialog.

STEP THREE:

The way Color Range works is that, with the Select pop-up menu set to **Sampled Colors**, you click on the color in your image you want to select. In this case, it's the blue sky, so just click with the eyedropper on the blue sky. If you have the Selection option turned on (below the preview window), you're going to see a black-and-white preview of your selection. Everything that's white is now selected, and everything that's black isn't. You'll see just a small area of the sky shows up in white at this point.

STEP FOUR:

There's obviously more than one shade of blue in the sky, so we'll need to add to our selection. To add to it, press-and-hold the Shift key and click in other areas of the blue sky. Each time you Shift-click, you'll add more blue to the selected area. Don't forget to Shift-click inside those areas in the fence right above the skyline.

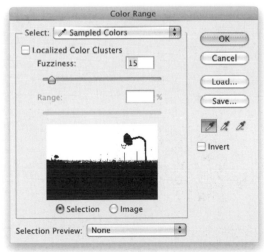

STEP FIVE:

You'll also notice a Fuzziness slider near the top of the Color Range dialog. Fuzziness pretty much loosens the edges of your selection. At 0, the selection remains very tight and only the colors you clicked on will be selected. As you increase the Fuzziness amount, the edges loosen a little and become softer, so more areas around what you clicked on become part of the selection. I found 15 works pretty well for this photo. When you're done, click OK to lock in the selection and close the Color Range dialog. If the selection looks like it bleeds over into other parts of the image, don't worry about it for now. You'll see, later, that we'll hide a lot of those imperfections and you'll never even see them.

STEP SIX:

Now, let's add some clouds. Go ahead and open the photo of the clouds for this example. I took this photo on a rooftop on a really cloudy day. Overcast days work well for this, too, but shadowed, puffy clouds work best, since they give a lot more detail.

STEP SEVEN:

Let's add to the drama by adding an HDR effect to the clouds. Even though it's not a bracketed photo with several different exposures, we can fake it with Photoshop. Go to Image>Adjustments>**HDR Toning**. The main thing here is to bring the Radius and Strength sliders way up. Take Radius to 230 px and Strength to 3.25. I brought the Exposure down to –0.50, Detail to +60%, and both Shadow and Highlight to –80%.

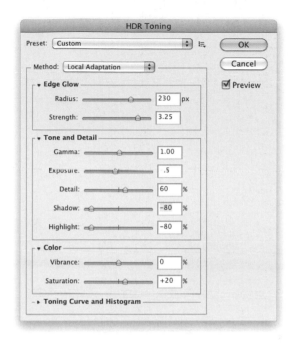

STEP EIGHT:

Click on Toning Curve and Histogram at the very bottom of the dialog to open the Curve for the photo. Click on the Curve to add two points, drag the bottom one down, and then drag the top one up, like you see here. This will add some nice contrast to the clouds. When you're done, click OK.

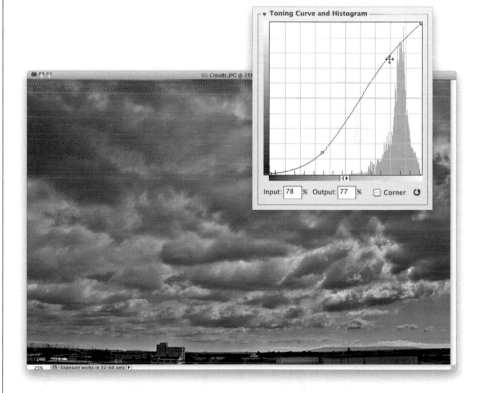

STEP NINE:

Okay, now our clouds are nice and dramatic. Let's add them to the basketball court image. Go to Select>**All** (or press **Command-A [PC: Ctrl-A]**) to select the entire cloud image. Then go to Edit>**Copy** (or press **Command-C [PC: Ctrl-C]**) to copy it. Switch over to the basketball court photo (where we should still have a live selection from Step Five) and go to Edit>Paste Special> **Paste Into**. This pastes the clouds into the selection that we created earlier. The best part about doing it this way is that Photoshop automatically creates a mask for us, so we can adjust where the clouds appear if we need to.

STEP 10:

Press **Command-T (PC: Ctrl-T)** to go into Free Transform mode. Notice how you can't see all of the handles around the Free Transform box? Here's a little tip: Press **Command-0** (zero; **PC: Ctrl-0**) and Photoshop will zoom your image out, so that all of the handles fit in view. Then, press-and-hold the Shift key and drag the bottom-right corner handle inward until the transform box is closer to the size of the basketball court image. Press **Return (PC: Enter)** when you're done to lock in the transformation.

STEP 11:

Grab the Move tool from the Tool-box (or just press the **V key**) and move the clouds up so the horizon line from the clouds image falls just behind the buildings in the city skyline.

STEP 12:

There's one last thing we'll do to the background. See, compositing has a lot to do with the background, but at the same time, you don't want the background to overpower the photo. In this example, there's a lot going on with the background, so we'll use a little trick to help tone it down a bit. Press **G** to select the Gradient tool from the Toolbox. Click on the gradient thumbnail in the Options Bar to open the Gradient Picker, and choose the second gradient from the top left (circled here), which is Foreground to Transparent. Immediately to the right of the gradient thumbnail are the gradient type icons. Click on the Reflected one (the second from the right) and then set your Foreground color to white by pressing **D**, then **X**.

STEP 13:

Click on the Create a New Layer icon at the bottom of the Layers panel to create a new blank layer. Then, position your cursor in the middle of the image and drag downward to the bottom to add the gradient on this layer. It creates a white gradient in the middle, and the gradient appears to fall off as it gets further away from the middle. What we've done here is give the appearance of adding a lot of light to the background. It's this light wash that lets us pull off the composite more easily and keep focus on the subject that we'll eventually be adding. When you're done, go to File>**Save** (or press **Command-S [PC: Ctrl-S]**) and save this as a PSD file.

PREPPING THE BASKETBALL PLAYER

This one breaks all the rules on how I've been telling you to set up your backgrounds to make the selection process easier. While teaching at a small workshop in Tulsa, OK, I decided to do a live compositing tutorial for the class—the shoot, the extraction, and the Photoshop work all in one class. Well, because of the classroom setup, we didn't have any seamless backgrounds to use. In fact, we didn't have any background at all. And all we had were two lights (not the three I would normally use). So, the setup wasn't ideal, but because the background was light enough and because there was at least one edge light, we're still able to pull off a great selection.

STEP ONE:

Open the basketball player photo. It's a RAW photo, so it'll open in the Camera Raw window. Our model, a young guy named Tyler, did great here. But, as you can see, the setup wasn't ideal. The yellow wallpaper from the small hotel conference room isn't the background I was hoping for (you gotta love the power cords in the background, too). I only had one edge light, and you can see it in the photo here. The only other light, which you don't see, is a beauty dish with a diffuser just to the right of the camera, above and in front of the subject, to add some fill to his face and uniform.

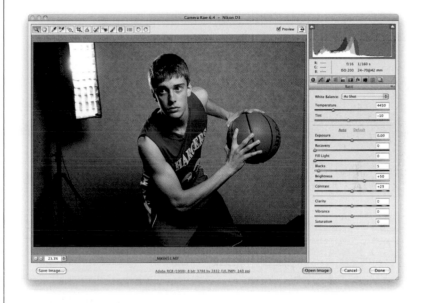

STEP TWO:

To make the selection process easier, increase the Exposure setting to +1.00. The brighter the background, the easier job Photoshop will have at selecting Tyler from it. Press-and-hold the Shift key and the Open Image button, at the bottom right of the window, will turn into Open Object (circled here). Click it to open the image in Photoshop as a Smart Object, which means we'll be able to easily come back to Camera Raw if we need to later.

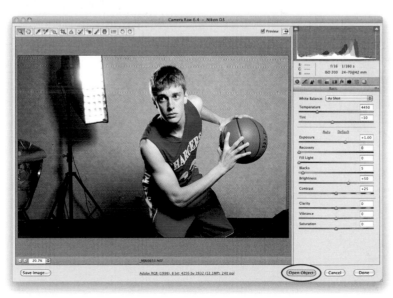

STEP THREE:

Believe it or not, the selection for this one is really simple. First, press **W** to get the Quick Selection tool. Then, paint your selection on Tyler until you have the entire body and basketball selected. As I always say, spend a couple of minutes here to make sure you get all of the edges as close as possible. To remove an area from the selection, just press-and-hold the **Option (PC: Alt) key** and click on it.

STEP FOUR:

Press the Refine Edge button in the Options Bar to open the Refine Edge dialog, and then press the **F key** until you have the white background. Since our final background is fairly light, white works best for previewing our selection. For this one, I dragged the Radius slider to 15 px and turned on the Smart Radius checkbox.

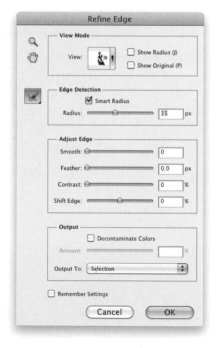

STEP FIVE:

Press the F key one more time to switch to the black and white View mode. I'll do this every once in a while to see if I'm missing any edges in the selection. In this case, zoom in to the area at the top right, where his shoulder meets his ear. You'll see a jagged fringe near it. If we leave it alone, it'll eventually pull in some of the yellow wallpaper.

STEP SIX:

To fix it, click and hold on the Refine Radius tool to the left of the Edge Detection section, and choose the Erase Refinements tool. Use the **Left Bracket key ([)** to make the brush pretty small, so it fits into that area, and then paint along the edge until the fringe goes away (as shown here). When you're done, set the Output To pop-up menu to **Layer Mask**, and press OK to close the Refine Edge dialog.

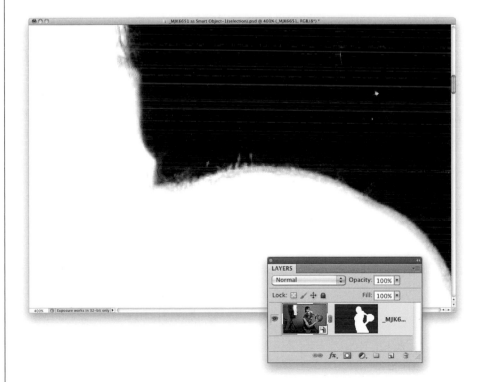

STEP SEVEN:

Now, we'll clean up some fringes around the selection on the layer mask using the Overlay mode Brush tool trick I first covered back in Chapter 1. Click on the layer mask to target it, press **B** to select the Brush tool, and then set the Mode pop-up menu in the Options Bar to **Overlay**. Zoom in really close to the edges and start painting with either black or white. Paint with white on areas like you see here, where part of Tyler's uniform is actually missing from the selection. Painting in Overlay mode with white will bring it back, but it won't bring back the original background.

STEP EIGHT:

Paint with black in areas like you see here, on the left side of his jersey. Remnants from the yellow background are still there, and painting with black will remove them, but not his already-selected jersey.

STEP NINE:

Now, double-click on the Smart Object thumbnail to go back into Camera Raw and set the Exposure setting back to 0 (zero), since we don't need it to help with the selection anymore. Click OK to go back to Photoshop.

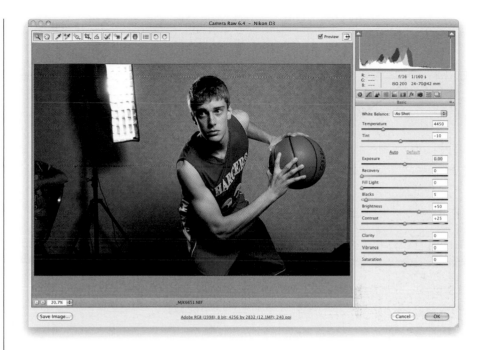

STEP 10:

Part of prepping the portrait also involves any retouching that needs to be done. There are a few blemishes that we can get rid of quickly and it's easier to get it done now than worry about it later when we're trying to composite the two images together. So, click on the Create a New Layer icon at the bottom of the Layers panel to add a new blank layer. It's always good to try to rename your layers as you go, too (double-click on the layer's name to do this). I can't say I'm always good at remembering to do it, but I do try when I know I'm compositing, because the layers can get out of hand really fast.

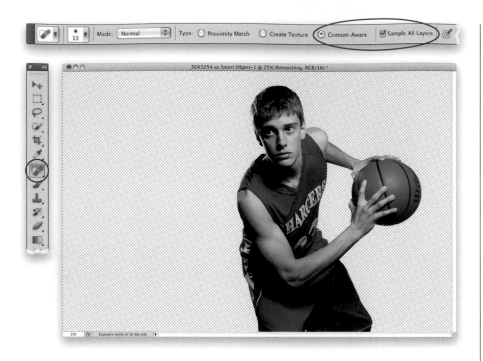

STEP 11:

Select the Spot Healing Brush tool from the Toolbox by pressing the **J key**. Make sure that the Content-Aware radio button and Sample All Layers checkbox are both turned on in the Options Bar.

STEP 12:

Zoom in on the face to get a closer look. The Spot Healing Brush is pretty simple to use, especially when you turn on the Content-Aware option, like we just did. There's no sampling involved, just position your cursor over a blemish. Use the **Left** or **Right Bracket key** to resize the brush to something just a bit larger than the blemish. Then, click to paint over the blemish, and it'll disappear. Use the same process to remove any tiny spots on his arms and face. Okay, we're done with the prep work for the portrait, so save it as a PSD file and move on to the composite.

CREATING THE COMPOSITE

Now that we've got the portrait selected and the background created, the composite comes together pretty quickly. We'll have to make some adjustments to carry over the atmosphere we added to the background in the final image. Plus, we'll need to do some overall dodging and burning, so he's not too bright for the background that we've placed him in.

STEP ONE:

Start out by opening the background image we created in the first part of the chapter. Don't forget, if you skipped that part, I've got the completed background in the download images ready for you to start with. Since we don't need all of the layers anymore, go to Layer>**Flatten Image** to flatten everything.

STEP TWO:

Now, open the photo of the basketball player that we worked on in the last tutorial. Again, the completed image is ready for you if you need something to start with. Use the Move tool (**V**) to drag the basketball player onto the background photo.

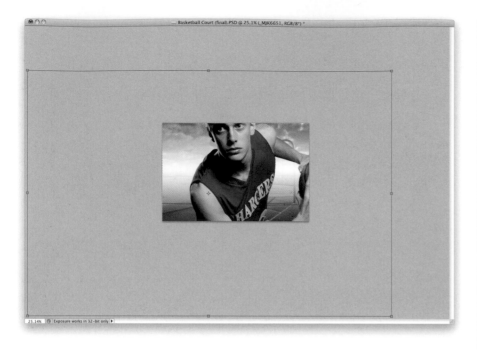

STEP THREE:

He's a little too big for the background, right? So, press **Command-T (PC: Ctrl-T)** to go into Free Transform mode. You probably can't see the transform handles around him, so press **Command-0** (zero; **PC: Ctrl-0**) to zoom out to where you can.

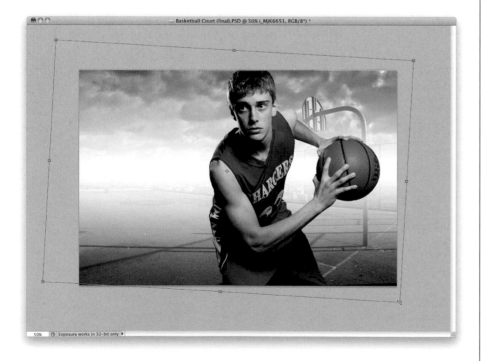

STEP FOUR:

Press-and-hold the Shift key and drag one of the corner handles inward to make the basketball player smaller. You can also move your cursor outside the bounding box, and click-and-drag to rotate the image a little, as I did here. I deliberately left this image so the top of his head is cropped a little at the top of the image, but that's more of a creative choice. I just felt it conveyed more depth with him in the photo this way. Feel free to make it a little smaller if you want to fit the subject's entire head in the frame. Press **Return (PC: Enter)** to lock in the transformation when you're done.

STEP FIVE:

The next thing I noticed is that I'd rather have the basketball hoop be on the side of the image that Tyler is looking at (the left side). Not that I think he's looking at the hoop, I just think it serves as a better focal point to have it on that side of him. Since I can't flip Tyler (the writing on his shirt would be backwards), we'll have to flip the background. So, click once on the Background layer and press **Command-J (PC: Ctrl-J)** to duplicate it.

STEP SIX:

Go to Edit>Transform>**Flip Horizontal** to flip the background the other way. Now, the basketball hoop is on the left side of the image, but Tyler stayed the same.

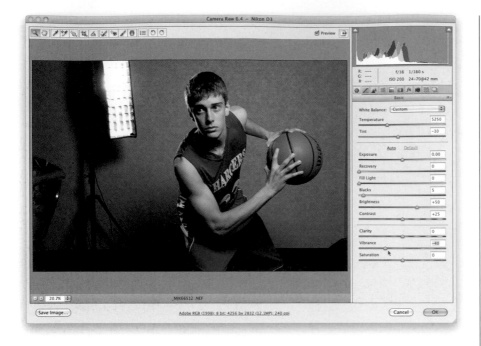

STEP SEVEN:

Okay, things are looking better, but we need to help the portrait fit into the background better. Part of what's wrong here is that his skin tone has too much color compared to the muted background we're using. This is why I love working with Smart Objects when doing my composites. Since we originally opened the basketball player photo as a Smart Object, it's easy enough to adjust. Double-click on the Smart Object thumbnail to reopen the photo in Camera Raw. Drag the Vibrance slider to –40 and it'll take some of the red out, and then increase the Temperature slider to 5250 to warm the photo up a little, too. Click OK when you're done to go back to Photoshop.

STEP EIGHT:

It's looking better, but we still need to add some contrast/edginess and a little more of that desaturated look. We'll need a duplicate of the basketball player layer for this trick, but you can't just duplicate the layer the way we're used to doing it, because it's a Smart Object. Instead, Right-click on the Smart Object layer and, from the pop-up menu, choose **New Smart Object via Copy**. That makes a duplicate that we can work with and not affect the original layer.

STEP NINE:

Double-click on the image thumbnail on the top copy layer to go into
Camera Raw again. In order for this
edgy trick to work, we need to have
a black-and-white photo. So, click on
the HSL/Grayscale icon (the fourth
one from the left beneath the histogram) and turn on the Convert to
Grayscale checkbox at the top of
the panel. Go back to the Basic panel
and increase the Fill Light setting to
+30 to brighten the shadows a little,
too. Click OK when you're done.

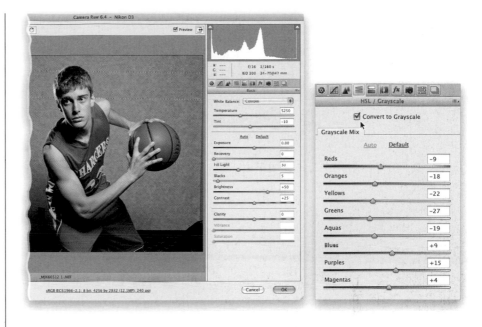

STEP 10:

Change the blend mode of the top
copy (the one we just converted to
black and white) to **Soft Light** and
reduce the Opacity to around 80%.
This adds a little more contrast, but
also gives the photo more of that
edgy and slightly desaturated look.
You can always try the Overlay or
Hard Light blend modes, too. Sometimes they work well, but they have
a little more punch to them than
Soft Light.

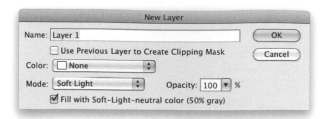

STEP 11:

Next, we'll do some dodging and burning on Tyler's skin. This is another finishing technique that helps add some depth and dimension to a person's skin. Go to Layer>New>**Layer**. In the New Layer dialog (seen here), change the blend Mode pop-up menu to **Soft Light**, then turn on the Fill with Soft-Light-Neutral Color (50% Gray) checkbox, and click OK. This adds a new layer filled with 50% gray, but because it's set to Soft Light, it appears transparent, which makes it perfect for dodging and burning, because it gives us an easier way to see our dodging and burning areas (by just changing the blend mode back to Normal).

STEP 12:

Now, grab the Brush tool **(B)**, and choose a medium-sized, soft-edged brush from the Brush Picker in the Options Bar. Also, lower the brush Opacity setting to 15%. This lets us build the amount of dodging and burning we do with each stroke.

STEP 13:

Here's how dodging and burning will work on this new layer: We're going to paint in black over the dark shadow areas and anything we want to darken to make them darker. Then, we'll paint with white over the brighter highlight areas to make them brighter. Start by pressing **D** to set your Foreground color to black, then paint with black along the outside edges of his arms where the natural shadows are falling to darken them a little. I don't think we have to darken all the shadows, though, just the ones on his arms and maybe even his shoulder to make it a little darker.

STEP 14:

Press **X** to switch your Foreground color to white to brighten the highlight areas. I painted along the inside of the forearms, his shoulders and upper arms, and his face. Don't forget, since you're working with a low-opacity brush, the more you brush, the more you'll build up the brightening or darkening effect. This one is hard to see, but if you turn the layer visibility on and off, you'll definitely see the results. You might even try pressing **Command-J (PC: Ctrl-J)** to duplicate the dodge/burn layer to see what it looks like if you intensify it more.

STEP 15:

Part of finishing this image off will be to add some more light to the photo. Since we have this large, bright wash of light behind the subject, we're going to work with that and even add to it. Click on the Create a New Layer icon at the bottom of the Layers panel to create a new blank layer, then double-click on the layer name and rename the layer "Light." Then, with the Brush tool still selected, make sure your Foreground color is still white and your brush Opacity is still set to 15%.

STEP 16:

Using a fairly large, soft-edged brush, paint a few brush strokes over the shoulder near the basketball hoop on the left. Since there's a light source back there (you can see from the clouds), we'd expect more light to be pouring in from that direction. I also painted some brush strokes, using a slightly smaller brush, in between his arms and the basketball and above his other arm on the right.

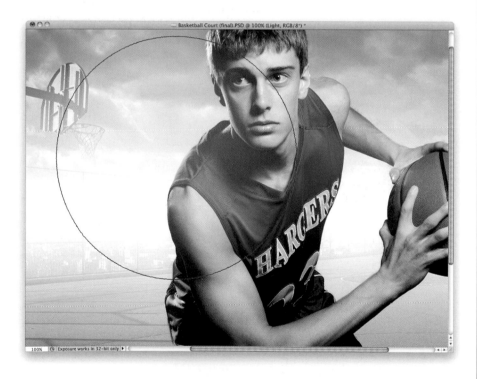

STEP 17:

We're almost done. Merge all of the layers into a new one by pressing **Command-Option-Shift-E (PC: Ctrl-Alt-Shift-E)**, and rename it "Edge Darkening." Change the blend mode of the layer to **Multiply**. Now, everything will be darkened. Click on the Add Layer Mask icon at the bottom of the Layers panel to add a layer mask. Then, with the Brush tool still active (don't forget to change the Opacity back to 100%), set your Foreground color to black, and use a large, soft-edged brush to paint away the Multiply effect from the middle of the photo, so just the edges and bottom are darker (as seen here).

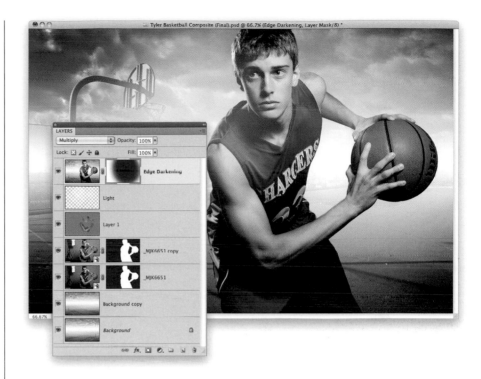

STEP 18:

One more thing: I'd like to add some overall extra-edginess to the photo. I'm going to show you two ways to do this: one is free and comes with Photoshop, and one isn't (but it's the method I actually use, because I can't get the same results in Photoshop). First, we'll look at the free way. Press Command-Option-Shift-E, again, to combine all of the layers into a newly merged layer on top, and rename it "Edgy Effect."

STEP 19:

Then, go to Filter>Other>**High Pass** and use a Radius setting of 9 px. Click OK when you're done, and the image will now look gray.

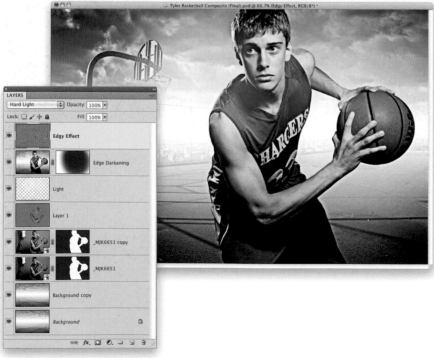

STEP 20:

Change the blend mode of the layer to **Hard Light** to hide the gray. Now you're left with a sharpened and gritty effect on the photo. It's a perfect (free) way to finish off images like this.

STEP 21:

Now for the not-free way. It's a plug-in called Topaz Adjust from Topaz Labs (www.topazlabs.com). I cover this plug-in, and the entire plug-in topic, in the "10 Things You Need to Know About Compositing" section at the beginning of the book. I wanted to show you the way I'd *really* finish off this photo to get the best effect, and Topaz Adjust is one of my best-kept secrets. Once you install it, you can delete the High Pass layer we just created, merge your layers to a new layer again, and name it "Edgy Effect," again. Then, go to Filter>Topaz Labs>**Topaz Adjust**. *Note:* Topaz Adjust is available as a free trial in case you want to try it out.

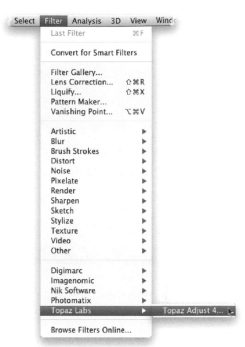

STEP 22:

The filter I like for most of my portrait composites is called Portrait Drama. It has the effect of doing what we did with the High Pass filter, and then some. It sharpens the entire photo, but it also adds this contrasty/edgy look and some color that, well, I just can't seem to add any other way in Photoshop without adding a bunch of layers, filters, and blend modes (and I'm still not usually that happy with it). So, click on Portrait Drama in the Presets panel on the left and leave the settings at their defaults. Click OK when you're done. Now, you know the way I *really* finish off most of my composites.

STEP 23:

Sometimes, the effect is too heavy (which I think it is here). The skin will tend to get overly gritty, and any dramatic clouds get really contrasty. If that happens, then add a layer mask and paint it away from those areas. Here, I painted with a 30% opacity black brush on the layer mask to remove some grit from his face, arms, and the clouds.

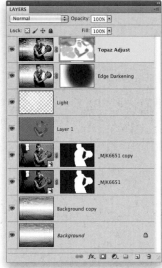

FINAL IMAGE

Let's say you're a portrait photographer who lands a job to shoot a professional office staff of some sort. You immediately go into planning mode, and quickly realize that it ain't gonna be easy. I mean, from 9:00 to 5:00 they're all working, right? Who wants to come in to work early for a photo shoot? And I'm sure some have to drop their kids off at school. After work is just as hard. There are soccer practices, dinner plans, and all kinds of other things that a professional office staff would probably be doing on their own time. That's where compositing can come in really handy. In this chapter, we'll be using a doctor's office as an example. Trying to get the doctor and any supporting staff together at the same time isn't easy. But if you set things up and make it easy for them to stop in when they have 10-15 minutes, you'll have a lot better chance of making the shoot happen.

THE SETUP

For this composite, I photographed the doctor and nurses on a white background. They came in at various times, so none of them were actually there in the studio together. With a little planning ahead, though, it was easy to re-create the same exact lighting setup and same settings, so they all looked as if they were photographed together.

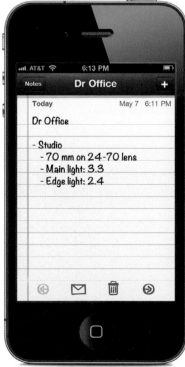

STEP ONE:

I set up the studio and used blue painter's tape (that you can buy in just about any hardware or home do-it-yourself store) to mark the floor where the lights were, as well as where the subject should stand. I also put some tape where I was standing while taking the photo. That way, I knew that the perspective was good and everyone would appear at his or her correct height when I put the composite together.

STEP TWO:

I also made a quick note (on my phone) of the focal length, and the power settings on the lights. Again, just to make sure that the lighting would look exactly the same on each person, regardless of when I photographed them.

STEP THREE:

I shot the subjects in two different ways for this. First, I used two lights: one main light coming from the front left, and one edge light coming from the back right. You can see this setup in the shot here. Then I turned off the edge light, so there was just the one main light coming from the front left.

STEP FOUR:

Here's the result of one of the photos with both lights on. That edge light gives the appearance that there's a bright light coming in from one side. It adds a lot of depth, dimension, and background separation to the portrait.

STEP FIVE:

Without the edge light, there's more shadow on the half of the face that's positioned away from the front main light. Photographing both ways just gives me more options when compositing. If I place them in a background with a light source on one side, then maybe I'll use the first photo. If not, maybe I'll use the other one. Options are great when compositing, especially if they're easy to do while shooting.

STEP SIX:

Lastly, I shot several poses of each subject. Again, this just gives us some options later. You can see from the Grid view in Lightroom here, that I had them turn to each side, arms folded in some, and facing straight ahead in others.

PREPPING THE PORTRAITS

Since everything was shot under the same lighting conditions, our main job here is to get a good selection. And since they were all photographed on a bright background (and my original vision for this one was to place them on a bright background), we'll have a lot of flexibility with our selections. We'll also mix in a little retouching to help finish things off.

STEP ONE:

Go ahead and open the first photo—we'll start off with one of the nurses. Press **W** to get the Quick Selection tool from the Toolbox and then start painting a selection on her. This one is pretty easy to get all of the details. Don't forget to press-and-hold the **Option (PC: Alt) key** and paint away the background selection between her arms and torso, though (you learned all about selections in Chapter 1).

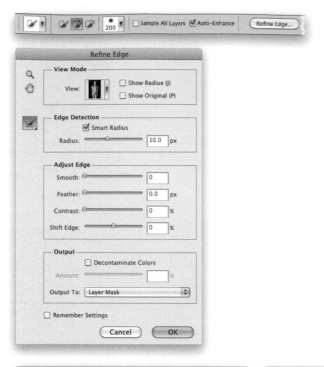

STEP TWO:

Click on the Refine Edge button up in the Options Bar to open the Refine Edge dialog. Again, this one is really easy, especially since she had her hair pulled back, so there was not a lot of flyaway hair. Turn on the Smart Radius checkbox, set the Radius to 10, and use the Refine Radius tool to brush around the edges of her hair near her neck. Choose **Layer Mask** from the Output To pop-up menu at the bottom of the dialog and click OK.

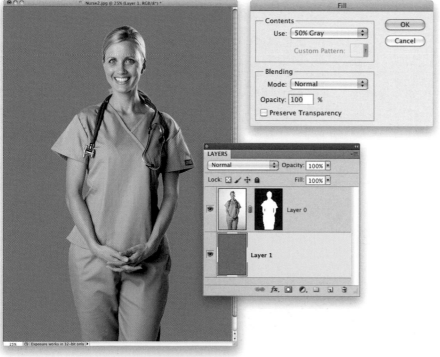

STEP THREE:

Now, you've got the nurse selected from the background with a layer mask. If you wanted to put her onto a white background with the other office staff, then you could probably skip this step. But for this tutorial, she's going to end up on a slightly darker background. Not black, but a light gray. To simulate that and to help refine the selection to make sure she fits, click on the Create a New Layer icon at the bottom of the Layers panel. Drag the new layer to the bottom of the layer stack and then go to Edit>**Fill**. For the Use setting, choose **50% Gray** and click OK. Now you've got a slightly darker (but not black) background to preview and refine your selection on.

STEP FOUR:

Next, zoom in to any areas that still show the original white background—I noticed a small area near her arm on the left that still shows white. Click once on the layer mask to target it, select the Brush tool **(B)** from the Toolbox, and with your Foreground color set to black, paint with a small brush to get rid of it. Do the same for any other white areas that still show through. Like I said earlier, though, don't bother with this if you're putting the subject on a white background. You won't ever see these little problems, so it's not worth the extra time.

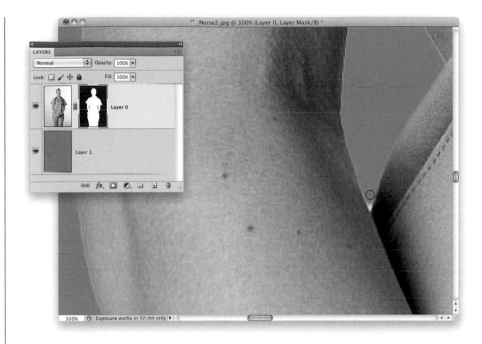

STEP FIVE:

Remember that fringe problem we learned about in Chapter 1? Well, zoom in on her shoulder on the left side of the photo. See that little tiny white line that still remains? It's not a major problem, but it's just going to look weird when we place her onto another background, so we have to get rid of it.

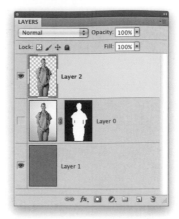

STEP SIX:

In order to do this, we need to put the nurse onto a regular layer without a layer mask. So, Command-click (PC: Ctrl-click) on the layer mask to load it as a selection, click once on the image thumbnail to target it, then press **Command-J (PC: Ctrl-J)** to copy the selected area onto its own layer. Once you have that new layer, click on the Eye icon to the left of the original image layer to hide it, since we don't need it (it's there if you ever need it to change the mask edge, but we don't need it to be visible anymore).

STEP SEVEN:

With the new layer of the nurse active, go to Layer>Matting>**Defringe**, enter 1 pixel for the Width, and click OK. The fringe will immediately disappear and you didn't have to do any detailed masking work to get rid of it. You gotta love that little Defringe feature!

STEP EIGHT:

Time for some quick retouching to remove any blemishes. Press **J** to select the Spot Healing Brush and make sure that Content-Aware is chosen in the Options Bar. Then, simply click on any small blemishes to remove them.

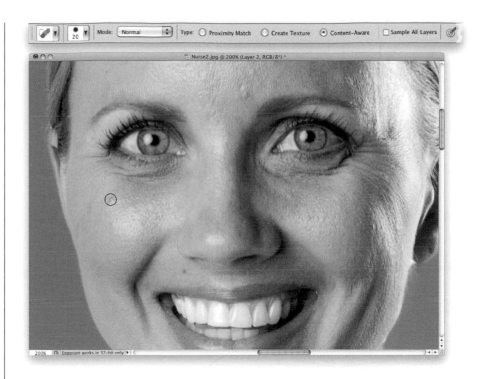

STEP NINE:

Lastly, let's fix her scrubs. Notice how the sleeves on her shirt flare out quite a bit? It's a little distracting and now's the best time to fix it. So, go to Filter>**Liquify** to open the Liquify dialog and select the top tool in the Toolbox, the Forward Warp tool **(W)**. Use the Left **([)** and Right Bracket **(])** keys on your keyboard to resize the brush, so it's about the same size as one of the flared-out sleeves (as seen here).

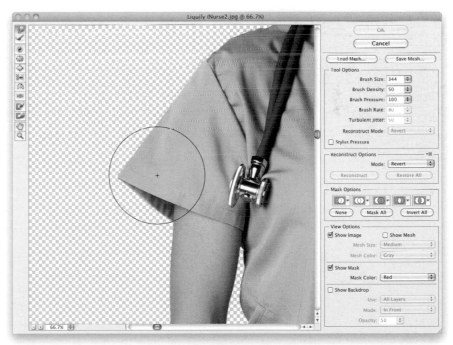

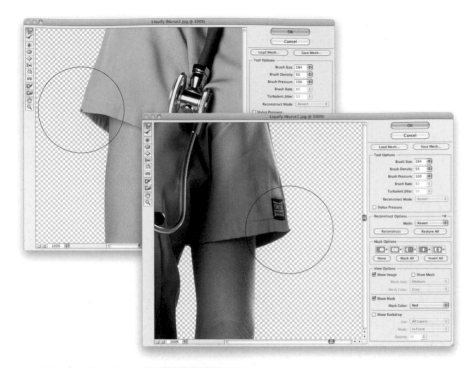

STEP 10:

Now, position the middle of the brush on the area you want to move, and just click-and-drag it in the direction you want to tuck it in. You'll find tiny clicks and small moves work best when you're dragging. Then, do the same for the other sleeve. I even zoomed in on the bottom of her shirt on the left and pushed that in slightly, because it was flaring out there, too. Click OK when you're done.

STEP 11:

All right, the first portrait is done, so go to File>**Save** and save it as a PSD file. You'll do the same thing to the rest of the portraits that you did to this one: open the photo, make your selection, Defringe if needed, and finish each one up with minor retouching, like we did here in Steps 8–10.

CREATING THE COMPOSITE

I originally thought I'd place all the subjects on a nice, clean, white background. But, once I started creating the composite and had them on a white background, I had another idea. I found an excellent photo of the interior of a building. It looked like a really fancy hospital with lots of bright sunlight coming in and it fit perfectly with the photos. That said, if you or your client still prefer white, you'll see it's just as easy.

STEP ONE:

Open the background photo you'd like to use. In this example, you'll see it's got a nice, clean look, which fits well with the medical theme that we have. It's also got a lot of window light coming from one side, which works really well with the nice edge light we used in the studio.

STEP TWO:

Open the three photos with the subjects already selected from their backgrounds. They should each be on their own layer if you followed what we did in the previous tutorial. Using the Move tool **(V)**, drag each of them onto the background image, so they're all in the same document. We're going to want the doctor to appear in the front, so if he wasn't the last one dragged in, in the Layers panel, drag the layer with the doctor to the top of the layer stack. You can also move any other layers that you want to at this point. Here, I've also moved the blonde nurse to appear second in the layer stack.

PHOTOSHOP COMPOSITING SECRETS

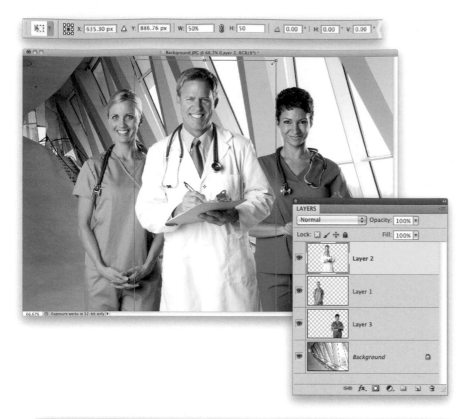

STEP THREE:

Now, they're probably going to be too big for the background image. So, starting with the top layer in the Layers panel, go to Edit>**Free Transform**. Click on a corner handle, press-and-hold the Shift key, and drag inward to resize the image (if you can't see the corner handles, press **Command-0** [zero; **PC: Ctrl-0**]). Keep an eye on the W (width) and H (height) settings in the Options Bar and remember the percentage setting from this first subject (in this case it was 50%), because you'll need to resize the other people by the same amount, so the perspective and overall size of one subject compared with another isn't off. Press **Return (PC: Enter)** to lock in your transformation, and then do the same thing for the other two images.

STEP FOUR:

Once you have them in place, we'll need to add some shadows. We've got two things that'll cause shadows in this example: First, look at the shadows on the bottom right of their noses. We can tell that there's a light source coming from the front left (remember the main light in the setup shots?). This will cause anyone in front to cast a shadow on anything that is behind and to the right of where they're standing. Next, anyone standing in front of someone else will simply cast an overall shadow on the person behind them, because they're blocking the light from hitting them.

STEP FIVE:

Layer styles have a lot of uses and shadows are a perfect example. But, we're not going to use the usual Drop Shadow layer style for this one. Instead, click on the Add a Layer Style icon at the bottom of the Layers panel and choose **Outer Glow** to open the Outer Glow options in the Layer Style dialog. Since a glow is usually bright, we need to change a few settings. First, change the Blend Mode at the top from Screen to **Multiply**, then click on the color swatch and change it from yellow to black.

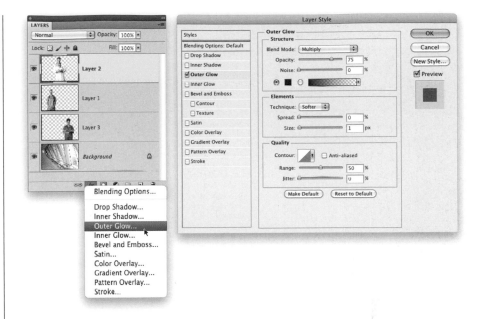

STEP SIX:

Right now, the outer glow is just a small, dark fringe around the doctor. So, try increasing the Size setting to spread it out more and widen its reach. I set mine to 200 pixels. I know it starts to spread out from behind the doctor's head, too, but we'll take care of that in a minute. When you're done, click OK to close the dialog.

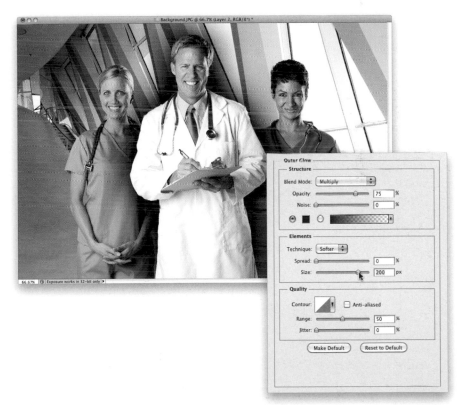

STEP SEVEN:

Obviously, we have some problems. The shadow cast on the nurses is fine, but it has also cast behind the doctor's head into thin air. To help fix this, we'll need to put the shadow on its own layer, instead of leaving it as a layer style. So, go to Layer> Layer Style>**Create Layer** to put the shadow on a separate layer below the doctor.

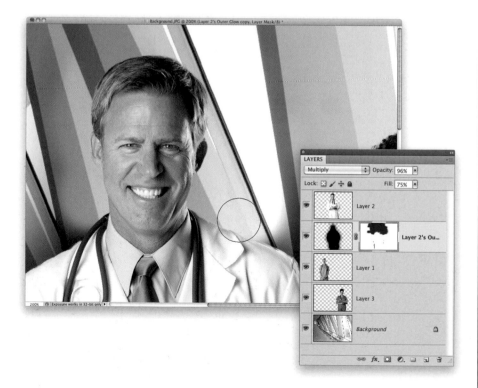

STEP EIGHT:

Click on the new shadow layer to make it active, and with the Move tool selected, press the **Right Arrow key** on your keyboard a few times to nudge the shadow over to the right, so it's more directional. Remember, the main light source was coming from the front left, so more of the shadow should be falling to the back right. You can also lower the layer's Opacity a little, as I did here, if it seems a little too dark. Then, click on the Add Layer Mask icon at the bottom of the Layers panel to add a layer mask to it. Get the Brush tool (**B**), and with your Foreground color set to black, paint away the excess shadow.

STEP NINE:

Don't forget to zoom in and use a smaller brush to paint away the shadow from the background that's in between the nurses' arms and the doctor. The light source is too far away to have a shadow that dark cast there. You can also click on the middle nurse layer and, using a black brush set to a low Opacity in the Options Bar (like 10%), brush away a little of the shadow on her arm on the right.

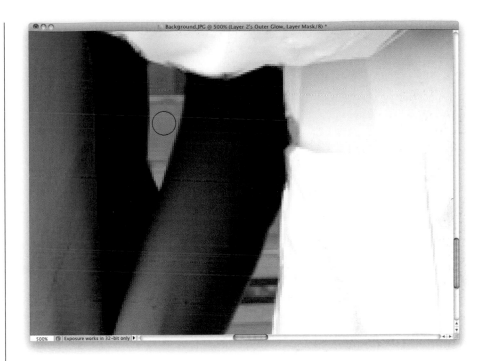

STEP 10:

After sitting back and looking at the photo for a minute, I thought the background was too dark. Everything had a really bright, natural light feel to it, and I thought the background needed to be brighter to pull this off. So, click once on the Background layer to target it, then click on the Create New Adjustment Layer icon at the bottom of the Layers panel, and choose **Exposure**. Set the Exposure to +0.30 and the Offset to +0.05 to brighten the entire background. You can always use the layer mask on the adjustment layer to paint in black over any areas that became too bright (like I've done here, on the right side of the background image).

PHOTOSHOP COMPOSITING SECRETS

STEP 11:

If you (or your client) want a white background, it's easy enough to add. Just create a new blank layer on top of the Background layer (or above the Exposure adjustment layer), then choose Edit>**Fill**. From the Use pop-up menu, select **White**, and click OK to fill that new layer with white. You'll see the people fit right in on top of a white background, too.

STEP 12:

I realize that not everyone will want their staff placed on a nice, bright, modern background like we used. Just to show you this can work, even if you have to use their office or place of work (which may not be quite as nice), here's another example with a hospital-like photo behind them.

©ISTOCKPHOTO/VAL LAWLESS

ALTERNATE IDEA:

Another really popular idea that you'll see used with professional offices and businesses is the blurred group shot. Basically, one person is in focus up front, and the others are blurred in the background. It works great for practices that have several doctors (or lawyers) involved, because you can showcase a different person when needed. And the really cool part about this one is that you can create it with the photos we've already taken. So this one photo shoot can be used in multiple ways. I've recorded a video for you that goes over how to create it. You'll find it on the book's companion website, mentioned in the book's introduction, along with the images used here.

FINAL IMAGE

First off, I have to give credit for this idea to Drake Busath over at http://busath.com. I read an article of his in *Professional Photographer* magazine last year where he photographed a large family in smaller groups, and then put them all together in Photoshop later. As I was writing the outline for this book, I realized this concept would be a perfect example of real-world compositing, especially if you're photographing a large family or group. First, the entire family doesn't even have to be there at the same time. So, if part of the family can only be there on one day, but another part of the family can't, no sweat. Just shoot them whenever they can get there. The other thing I found when shooting these photos was that the family was incredibly relaxed. The best part about this photo is that everyone doesn't have to be "on" at the same time. Once everything was set up, each smaller group is able to step in and have their photo taken. The rest of the family can sit back and relax, get ready, put makeup on, play with the kids to keep them in good moods, etc. Plus, you can even use the other groups that aren't "on" to help capture the attention of and get smiles from the kids that are being photographed. Seriously, it was a great experience for the family and I'd recommend this setup in a heartbeat for any large family or group portraits.

THE SETUP

The setup for this photo is similar to the setup for the doctor composite we created in the previous chapter. The only big difference is that this was taken on-location at one of the family members' houses. See, it was the little boy's baptism weekend and all of the family was coming to town on Saturday night for the Sunday baptism. The schedule was so tight that they were not able to comfortably make it by the studio, but did offer to let me come by the house to take the photo before they left for the church. Luckily, this setup is easy to move. So with a little help (from my buddy RC), we made it happen.

STEP ONE:

The key to this composite is that every group is standing in the same place. That way, I knew that the perspective was good and everyone would appear at their correct height when I put the composite together. I placed a piece of clear Scotch tape on the floor near their feet, so they all stood in the same place. It's really hard to see here, but trust me, it's there.

STEP TWO:

As you can see from this setup photo, I placed the camera on a tripod. Once I established the tripod height and set the focal length (I used 50mm for this one), I never touched it again, except to press the shutter button. Again, everything is now locked down, so the position of the people relative to the camera, the height of each person relative to each other, and the overall perspective will be perfect.

STEP THREE:

Another thing I learned from studying Drake's work is that children need to be placed higher in the image, whether a parent holds them, or you have them standing on a small chair or box (we did both in this example). This allows us to crop the final image right above or below the knees and keep from showing the feet on the ground.

STEP FOUR:

I shot the family in two different ways, just like I did the doctors and nurses. First, I used two lights: one main light (with a medium-sized Wescott Octabank Softbox) coming from the front left, and one edge light (a strip bank with a grid) coming from the back right. You can see the setup shot here.

STEP FIVE:

Then I turned off the edge light (circled here), so it was just the one main light coming from the front left.

STEP SIX:

Here's the result of one of the photos with both lights on. That edge light gives the appearance that there's a bright light coming in from one side. It adds a lot of depth, dimension, and background separation to the portrait.

STEP SEVEN:
Without the edge light, there's more shadow on the half of the face that's positioned away from the main light in front. I've mentioned this before, but shooting the photo both ways just gives me more options when compositing. Sometimes you'll find it works better for the people in the photo to use the photo with more shadows and depth, and sometimes you'll like the ones with the hard edge light instead. Remember, options are great when compositing, so if you can easily add some options while shooting, then go for it.

PREPPING THE PORTRAITS

Since everything was shot in the same lighting conditions, our main job here is to get a good selection. And since they were all photographed on a bright background (and my vision for this one was to place them on a white background), we'll have a lot of flexibility with our selections. We'll also mix in a little retouching of the layer mask to help finish things off.

STEP ONE:

Go ahead and open one of the family portraits. They're all pretty much the same, so I'll use the one I thought was the hardest to select here. Press **W** to get the Quick Selection tool from the Toolbox. Click to start painting a selection on the family. Remember that we're going to crop this right around the knee area, so don't worry too much about the feet.

STEP TWO:

Zoom in to the shoulder on the left. Her dress has some white in it, so it may take a little longer to select. Just make your brush smaller and spend a minute to get the selection as close as possible. Trust me, it's much easier to deal with now. Remember, if the selection accidentally spills out onto the background too much, just press-and-hold the **Option (PC: Alt) key** to put the Quick Selection brush into Subtract mode and remove it.

STEP THREE:

Click the Refine Edge button in the Options Bar to go into the Refine Edge dialog. I chose the white option to view the selection on, since my final image will have a white background. Photos like this are probably one of the easiest to select, since we don't have to worry about all of the hair detail all of the time (sometimes it's still a problem, as you'll see in a minute). Most of the time, even if we carry over some of the white background near the hair, we'll never see it, because we're putting them on the same color background. Set the Radius to 6, the Output To setting to **Layer Mask**, and click OK to close the dialog.

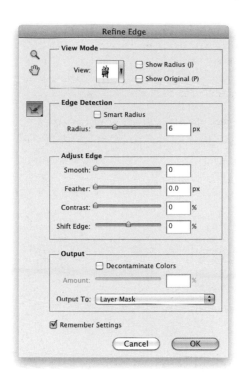

STEP FOUR:

The family is now selected on their original layer with a layer mask in the Layers panel. Let's see if we need to refine the mask at all. Go ahead and Command-click (PC: Ctrl-click) on the Create a New Layer icon at the bottom of the Layers panel to add a new layer below the family layer. Then go to Edit>**Fill** and set the Use setting to **Black**. I'm using black here because the woman on the left is eventually going to be in front of a man with a dark blue jacket. This'll give me a similar background, so I can decide if the edge around her needs any more refining. Click OK, and now you'll see every tiny bit of detail that doesn't fit in.

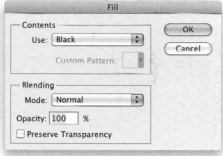

STEP FIVE:

Before you start working on the layer mask to remove any white areas, think about the final image for a minute. In this example, I know they're going to be put on the far right of the entire group. And since we're moving them to another white background, all we need to worry about is how the left edge of the woman and her hair look, since that's the only area that'll intersect with anyone else in the photo. The guy on the right is going to go from one white background to another white background, with nothing else behind him, so there's no need to worry about any fringing there.

STEP SIX:

Zoom in to the neck area of the woman. You may see some white still showing through her hair. If you do, click once on the layer mask to target it. Select the Brush tool **(B)** from the Toolbox, set your Foreground color to black, and paint with a very small, soft-edged brush to get rid of it. Do the same for any other white areas that still show through (except for the hair). Like I mentioned earlier, though, don't worry about this part if the person is not going to intersect with another person in the final image.

STEP SEVEN:

Now, we're back to that overall fringing problem that we'll usually get from the original background. Zoom in on her hair on the left side of the photo. There's still some fringing around the edges. As soon as we place her over another person in the photo, especially someone with a dark jacket on, that fringe will stick out like a sore thumb.

STEP EIGHT:

We covered this problem back in Chapter 1. So far, we've had a lot of luck by putting the selected area on its own layer and going to Layer>Matting>**Defringe**. Usually, we enter 1 pixel and it looks great. Not in this photo, though. Instead, we're going to use the Inner Glow trick from Chapter 1. First, let's put them onto a regular layer without a layer mask, so Command-click (PC: Ctrl-click) on the layer mask to load it as a selection. Click once on the layer thumbnail to target it. Then press **Command-J (PC: Ctrl-J)** to copy the selected area onto its own layer. Once you have that new layer, click on the little Eye icon to the left of the layer below to hide it, since we don't need it. Now, you have them on a blank layer with nothing else.

STEP NINE:

Click on the Add a Layer Style icon at the bottom of the Layers panel and choose **Inner Glow**. When the Layer Style dialog opens, change the Blend Mode to **Multiply**, then click on the color swatch toward the top of the dialog to open the Color Picker. Click on an area in the hair that is closest to the overall hair color around it (don't click on any highlights or shiny areas). This sets the color of the glow to something dark, and you'll start to see the bright edges go away. Adjust the Size setting to make sure you take all of it away. I used 15 pixels in this example. Then adjust the Opacity setting at the top to around 70% to soften the effect. When you're done, click OK to close the dialog.

STEP 10:

This works great, but it does leave us with a problem: the Inner Glow effect is applied around the entire layer. Even the man on the right has a dark edge around him now (you may need to turn off the black background layer to really see it). So, go to Layer>Layer Style>**Create Layer**. This puts the effect onto its own layer, so it's no longer a layer style.

STEP 11:

Click the layer style's layer to make it active, and then click on the Add Layer Mask icon at the bottom of the Layers panel. Select the Brush tool, and set your Foreground color to black. Then, paint away the inner glow from any areas you don't want it to affect.

STEP 12:

Turn the black background layer back on. If you still see a white fringe, now is a good time to try the Defringe feature. Click once on the layer with the family to target it. Go to Layer>Matting>**Defringe**, enter 1 pixel for the Width setting and click OK. The selection edge should be looking really good now, especially around her hair. And since she's going to be standing in front of someone with a dark jacket, we need it to look really convincing. Go to File>**Save** and save it as a PSD file. Then, using the same selection techniques we used here, select the families from the other two photos. In fact, I thought they were a little easier, since the hair seemed to select better from both of them.

CREATING THE COMPOSITE

The more compositing you do, the more you'll find that sometimes you spend more time on the composite and sometimes you spend more time on the setup. I think this composite is a perfect example of one where you spend more time on the setup. Since everything was photographed at the same distance and same focal length on the camera, putting this composite together is probably the easiest part of the project. The main thing we'll need to do in Photoshop is make sure we place the shadows correctly whenever we put one person in front of another.

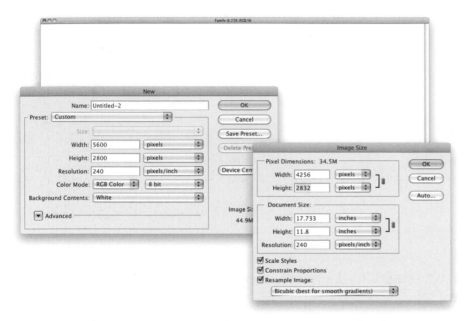

STEP ONE:

There is no background photo in this one. Instead, we're going to use a white background. So, go to File>**New** and create a new image that's 5600x2800 pixels at 240 ppi, and make sure the Background Contents pop-up menu is set to **White**. Where'd I get those numbers from? Well, if you open one of the portraits in Photoshop and go to Image>**Image Size**, you'll see the height is about 2800 pixels. So, we know the overall height of the final image won't exceed that. Then, I just doubled it for the width, since I knew 5600 pixels would be plenty wide enough. We can always crop later.

STEP TWO:

Now, open the three photos with the people already selected from the background. Each family should be on its own layer if you followed the previous tutorial (if you have a layer style as a layer, like we did in the previous tutorial, turn off the other layers below the selected family, and press **Command-Option-Shift-E [PC: Ctrl-Alt-Shift-E]** to merge them into a new layer at the top of the layer stack). Use the Move tool **(V)** to drag them onto your new background image, so they're all in the same document. Make sure you place the couple's layer below the other families' layers, since they'll go in the middle, behind everyone else.

STEP THREE:

We know the perspective is right on because of the way we photographed everyone, and everyone is at their correct height. But when you get them together like this and start moving people around, you sometimes lose one person's height relative to another. One thing I found that helps is to make a note of similar height people, so you have a good place to start. So, use the Move tool to put all three photos in place. I made a note that the two brothers on opposite ends are the same height, so that's a great starting place. The man in the middle is slightly shorter, so just make sure to place him slightly below the other two.

STEP FOUR:

Once everyone is in place, the rest of our job is all about shadows. That's really the last thing we need to make this composite convincing. We know the main light source is coming from the front left. This will cause anyone in front to cast a shadow on anything that's behind and to the right of where they're standing. And just the nature of one person standing in front of another person will cast a slight shadow on the person behind them, too.

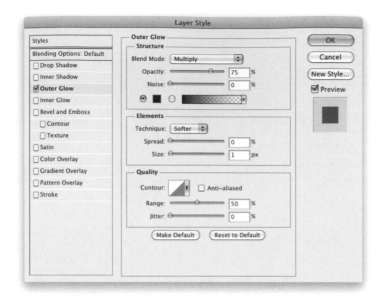

STEP FIVE:

We'll use the same layer style we used in the doctor composite for the shadows—the Outer Glow layer style. Click once on the layer of the family on the left to target it. Then click on the Add a Layer Style icon at the bottom of the Layers panel and choose **Outer Glow** to open the Outer Glow options in the Layer Style dialog. Since a glow is usually bright and a shadow is dark, we need to change a few things. First, change the Blend Mode pop-up menu at the top from Screen to **Multiply**. Then, click on the color swatch and change the color from yellow to black.

STEP SIX:

Right now, the Outer Glow is just a small, dark fringe. Increase the Size setting to spread it out more and widen its reach. I set mine to 205 pixels, here. It'll also start spreading out from behind everyone's heads, too, but we'll erase that next. Click OK when you're done.

STEP SEVEN:

Next, we'll erase the shadow from the areas where it doesn't fit. To help fix this, though, we'll need to put the shadow onto its own layer, instead of leaving it as a layer style. Go to Layer>Layer Style>**Create Layer** to force the Outer Glow layer style onto a separate layer below the family.

STEP EIGHT:

To paint away the excess shadow, click on the Outer Glow (shadow) layer we just made, then click on the Add Layer Mask icon at the bottom of the Layers panel to add a layer mask to that shadow layer. Get the Brush tool **(B)**, set your Foreground color to black, and on the layer mask, paint away the shadow from wherever it shouldn't fall. Don't forget about way down at the bottom of the photo, too, near their legs. The background should still be white, and the shadow shouldn't affect it at all.

STEP NINE:

Do the same thing for the other family on the right side. This one isn't as crucial, for this photo in particular, because the man in the middle is wearing a dark jacket and we won't see the shadow that much. But you'll still want to make sure there's some sort of shadow there.

STEP 10:

As a finishing touch, you can paint your own shadows, too. I'd paint an even darker shadow behind the woman in the family on the left side. But keep it close to her arm and torso. She's really blocking all light from hitting the woman in blue behind her, but only where her arm is in front. The light would still hit the rest of her blue dress, so it shouldn't be as dark. To add your own shadows, click on the shadow layer for the family on the left, and then click on the Create a New Layer icon at the bottom of the Layers panel to create a blank layer behind the family, but in front of their shadow and the couple in the middle. Then, use a low (10%) opacity black brush to brush in more shadows. And since it's on its own layer, you can always control the layer's Opacity if you need to make it more subtle.

STEP 11:

Back in Step One, we created a larger document than we really needed. So, go ahead and select the Crop tool **(C)** from the Toolbox, drag the cropping border around the photo, and crop right near the knees. Also, leave about half a head's height of headroom at the top.

STEP 12:

As a finishing touch, I think we could use just a little more color saturation here. Click on the top layer in the Layers panel, then click on the Create New Adjustment Layer icon at the bottom of the panel and choose **Vibrance**. In the Adjustments panel, drag the Vibrance slider to around +50 to +60. It does a good job of adding more color to the photo, without making their skin look too red. You can see the final image on the next page. That's it! Go to File>**Save** and save it as a PSD file, in case you ever need to adjust anything.

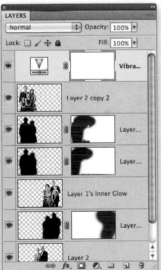

FINAL IMAGE

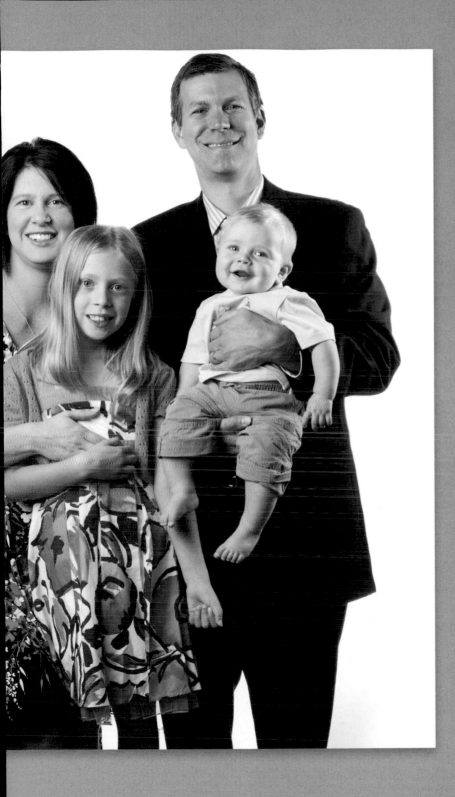

STUDIO SPORTS PORTRAIT

7

This is probably one of the hottest compositing trends today. A lot of photographers are now choosing to photograph athletes in a studio and then composite them into a background that's more fitting to their sport, or simply more dramatic. Whether it's for an advertisement (Nike and Under Armour do it all the time), or whether the athlete just wants a great photo of themselves, shooting this way offers a ton of opportunities. Plus, it makes things a lot easier if you don't have access to some of the cool locations that you'd ideally like to shoot in.

PREPPING THE BACKGROUND

As always, our background is almost as important as the portrait itself. After all, we're doing all this work so that we can put them into a really cool place, so it's worth spending some time to set this up. We'll have to combine a few elements to make this background. First, we'll need a road that has the correct perspective to it. Since we'll be including our subject's feet, this part is really important. Then, we'll need a city skyline for the background. Throw in some dramatic clouds (I love clouds, if you haven't realized) and you're good to go.

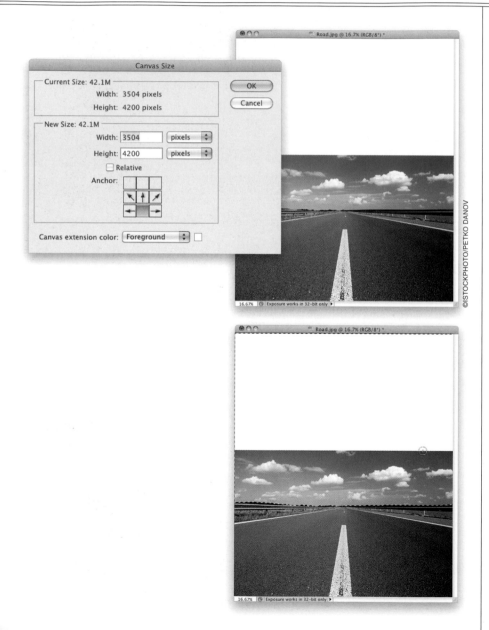

©ISTOCKPHOTO/PETKO DANOV

STEP ONE:

Open the photo of the road. The first thing we'll need to do is extend the canvas, since we'll be adding some buildings and sky to it. You'll see later that this is sort of a ballpark size for now. It gives us some room to work with, but you can always crop it later if you'd like, depending on the end result. Go to Image>**Canvas Size**, and in the dialog, make sure the Relative checkbox is turned off, then change the Width and Height unit pop-up menus to **Pixels**. Let's keep the Width the same, but increase the Height to 4200. Also, go to the Anchor grid, at the bottom of the dialog, and click the bottom-middle square to keep the road anchored at the bottom of the image and only extend the canvas toward the top. Click OK when you're done.

STEP TWO:

Press **W** to get the Quick Selection tool. Then, brush over the sky and solid area at the top of the image to select it. Don't worry about refining it with the Refine Edge dialog, because it's in the background and we'll never really see any detailed area back there.

STEP THREE:

Open the clouds photo. Go to Edit>**Select All** to select the entire photo, and then to Edit>**Copy** to copy it. Switch back over to the background image (where we already have an active selection from the last step), and go to Edit>Paste Special>**Paste Into** to paste the clouds into the selection. This automatically creates a layer mask, so the clouds only appear in the top of the photo.

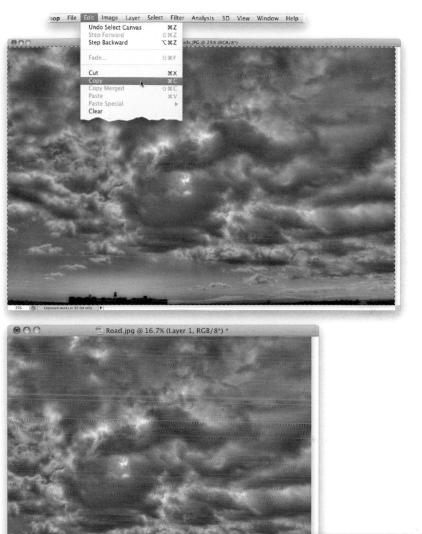

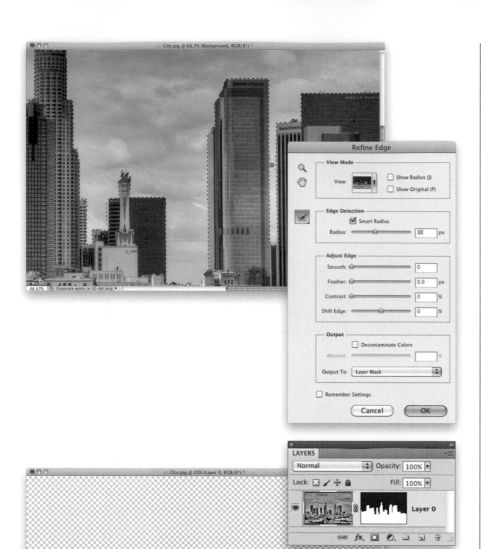

STEP FOUR:

Open the photo of the city skyline. Use the Quick Selection tool to select the buildings. Make sure you zoom in and use a smaller brush to get all the tiny edges that the Quick Selection tool probably won't pick up on the first pass. Remember, you can **Option-click (PC: Alt-click)** to remove anything it selected that you didn't want selected. Then, click the Refine Edge button up in the Options Bar. Since there are lots of tiny little details around the edges of the buildings that we'll want to select, turn on the Smart Radius checkbox, so that Photoshop will look outside of the selected edge for them. Then, set the Radius to 10 pixels, set the Output To setting to **Layer Mask**, and click OK.

STEP FIVE:

To copy the city photo, we have to use a different command because it has a layer mask with it. So, go to Select>**All** to select everything, then Edit>**Copy Merged** to copy the photo. This copies exactly what you see onscreen with the transparent sky. Go back to the background image and Command-click (PC: Ctrl-click) on the layer mask of the clouds layer to put a selection around the sky once again. Then go to Edit>Paste Special>**Paste Into** to paste the city skyline into our background image. Use the Move tool **(V)** to move it into place. Because the Paste Into command automatically created a layer mask, you don't have to worry about moving it over the road. It'll automatically stay hidden from the bottom of the photo.

TIP: RESELECTING THE SAME AREA

If you want to reselect the same area you previously had selected, go to Select>**Reselect** and Photoshop will automatically bring up your last selection.

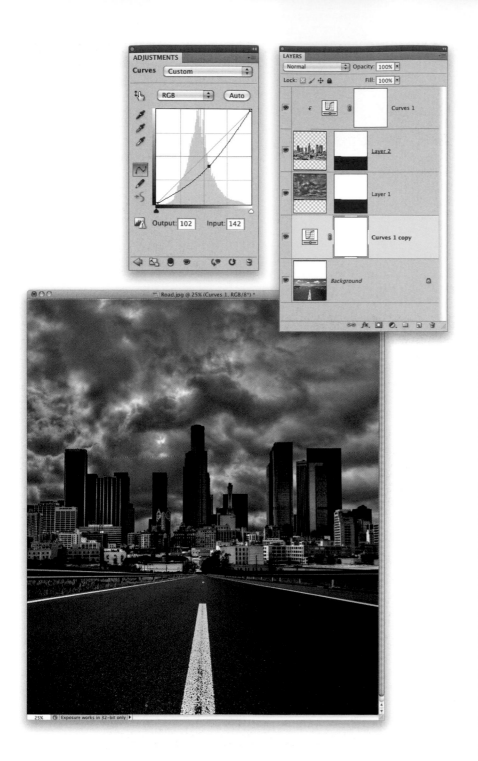

STEP SIX:

Next, we'll add some contrast and darken the city a little. Click on the Create New Adjustment Layer icon at the bottom of the Layers panel and choose **Curves**. Click in the middle of the curve and drag it downward. Then, click on the Create a Clipping Mask icon at the bottom of the Adjustments panel (it's the third icon from the left, and looks like an Oreo cookie with the top being pulled off). While you're at it, let's darken the road, too. Just press-and-hold the **Option (PC: Alt) key** and drag the Curves adjustment layer you just created down above the road layer. Holding the Option key copies (not moves) the adjustment layer to wherever you drag it.

STEP SEVEN:

There is some pretty bright light coming from behind the clouds, but we don't see any of it in the foreground, and we really want to take people's attention off the city. So, we'll use a trick used in Chapter 4. Press **G** to select the Gradient tool from the Toolbox. Click on the down-facing arrow next to the gradient thumbnail in the Options Bar to open the Gradient Picker, and choose the second gradient from the top left, which is Foreground to Transparent (circled here). To the right of the gradient thumbnail are the gradient type icons. Click on the Reflected icon (the second from the right), then set your Foreground color to white by pressing **D**, then **X**.

STEP EIGHT:

Click on the Create a New Layer icon at the bottom of the Layers panel to create a new blank layer. Then, position your cursor in the middle of the buildings and click-and-drag downward to the bottom to add the gradient on this layer. It creates a white gradient in the middle, and the gradient appears to fall off as it gets further away from the middle. This gives the appearance of adding a lot of light to the background. If it's too bright, then reduce the Opacity of the layer to around 70%. It's a bright light wash like this that lets us "sell" the composite more easily and keep the focus on the subject that we'll be adding. When you're done, go to File>**Save** and save this as a PSD file.

THE PORTRAIT SETUP AND EXTRACTION

If you're shooting this type of photo with processing it in Photoshop in mind, one of the best things you can do is give yourself a lot of options. Get multiple poses and multiple angles, so you have more options in Photoshop later. Set up one pose and fire off two photos. Then, have the model move and fire two more off. Then, change your angle and get down lower. Don't overshoot the same pose. Constantly move and constantly have the model move. That way, when you're done, you have lots of photos to work with and lots of options for compositing, depending on the background you choose.

STEP ONE:

Here's a photo of the studio setup for this example. You can see the two strip lights with grids on the sides. This gives us that nice edge light, which is not only great for adding some mood to the photo, but also helps us extract the photo from the background a lot faster. Directly in front of him is a beauty dish with a diffuser on it.

STEP TWO:

Just so you know, I'll typically take at least 100 photos during a shoot like this. Sometimes I know exactly what I'm looking for, and I'll start with a certain pose. Sometimes I don't, so I'll take a bunch of different poses from different angles. In this example, I kinda knew the general pose I wanted. It was a low camera angle with him either bouncing the ball or slamming it on the ground. However, I wasn't sure what background I was using yet, so I made sure to take a few different angles of the same photo. Some were close up at a wide-angle focal length, and some were pulled back a bit for a more normal view. You can see a few of them here in my Lightroom window.

STEP THREE:

Go ahead and open the photo we'll be working with. As you can see here, I opted for the wider-angle close-up photo of the basketball player. The photo will open in the Camera Raw window. Right off the bat, I can tell it's a little warm, but I'm not going to make any adjustments yet. We'll want to make sure we give ourselves a way back and forth to Camera Raw, so press-and-hold the Shift key and click the Open Object button at the bottom right of the window to open the photo as a Smart Object. This way, when we see the photo in the final composite, we can always double-click on its thumbnail to come back to Camera Raw and make adjustments.

STEP FOUR:

Press **W** to get the Quick Selection tool, and start painting a selection on the basketball player. And, because I've said it so many times before, I won't even mention here that you should zoom in and use a smaller brush to make sure you get all the details around him (oops, I said it, didn't I?). Anyway, since he's wearing such dark clothes that contrast with the background, the Quick Selection tool should make a good selection pretty easily here. Once you've got the general outline, zoom in to the feet and get them as close to perfect as possible, because that's a key area to pull off the composite and make it look real. If you over-select an area, then press-and-hold the **Option (PC: Alt) key** to subtract from the selection.

STEP FIVE:

When you're ready, click the Refine Edge button up in the Options Bar and then press the **W key** to change the View setting to white. Since we have hair in this one, turn on the Smart Radius checkbox and set the Radius to 10 pixels to try to pick up the edges. Now, move your cursor over the photo and brush around his hair at the top of his head, as well as along his arms and legs to get all the details. Set the Output To setting to **Layer Mask**, and click OK when you're done. You'll have one layer in the Layers panel with a layer mask attached to it. Don't forget, if any of the edges seem to have dropped out, you can get the Brush tool **(B)**, set the Mode in the Options Bar to **Overlay**, set your Foreground color to white, and paint over those edges on the layer mask to bring them back. Go to File>**Save**, save it as a PSD, and get ready to move on to the composite.

CREATING THE COMPOSITE

This composite was a lot of fun to create. Once the background is done and the athlete is selected, our main goal is to make him fit into the final image. Because you often need to actually put someone onto the background before you can figure out what to change, I used a Smart Object and Camera Raw to help out a lot. After that, the shadows on the ground played a huge part of pulling this one off. And perhaps the most fun part for me was the cracked concrete on the ground. It really helps to add to the intensity of the overall image.

STEP ONE:

Open the background image we created earlier. If you didn't follow along, don't sweat it. The finished background is ready for you to download. If you did follow along, though, then go to Layer>**Flatten Image** to flatten all of your layers into one.

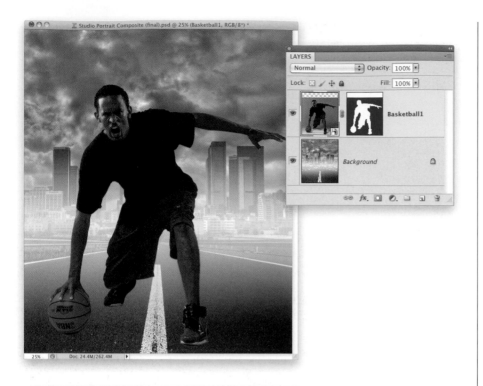

STEP TWO:

Now, open the selected basketball player. Again, if you didn't follow along, just download the image and you'll already have the selection done for you. First, we need to move him, so press **V** to get the Move tool and drag him onto the background image.

STEP THREE:

He's a little too bright to fit into the background right now, so let's fix that first. Double-click on his layer thumbnail to reopen the photo in Camera Raw. Reduce the Exposure to around –0.80, increase the Fill Light to 70 to bring out some details in the shadows, and reduce the Vibrance to –26 to take some of that color away from the photo. Don't click OK yet. We still have one more change to make.

STEP FOUR:

His arms, legs, and shoes are still too bright compared to the rest of the photo. So press **K** to select the Adjustment Brush tool from the toolbar up top. First, set the Exposure to –0.10 and the Brightness to –5, then paint over his arms (including the ball) and his legs. Don't worry about being precise, because we won't see any of the spillover, since he's already selected.

Then, click the New radio button at the top of the Adjustment Brush options, so we can create a new adjustment and darken his feet separately. Set the Exposure to –1.05 and the Brightness to –20, then paint over his feet. When you're done, click OK to go back to Photoshop.

STEP FIVE:

Next, we're going to use a trick we used in a few other tutorials to give a slightly desaturated and edgy look to the athlete. Right-click on the layer and choose **New Smart Object via Copy** to make a copy of the original Smart Object layer. Double-click on the new layer's image thumbnail to reopen it in Camera Raw, go to the HSL/Grayscale panel (the fourth icon from the left, shown circled here), and turn on the Convert to Grayscale checkbox to remove all of the color.

STEP SIX:

Go back to the Basic panel and reduce the Exposure setting to –0.45. Set the Fill Light slider to 100 to really open the shadowy areas, set the Blacks to 10 to darken the blacks a little more, then set Contrast to 0, and Clarity to 35. Finally, press K again to get the Adjustment Brush and then press the Clear All button at the bottom right to remove all of the selective adjustments we created earlier. Click OK when you're done. To complete the edgy effect, change the layer's blend mode to **Hard Light**.

STEP SEVEN:

Let's warm him up a little to add to the fiery mood that the photo is building. Click on the Create New Adjustment Layer icon at the bottom of the Layers panel and select **Photo Filter**. Make sure the Filter pop-up menu is set to **Warming Filter (85)**, then click the Color radio button and increase the Density to 55%. Next, add a Hue/Saturation adjustment layer and set the Saturation to –60 to decrease it just a little more. Command-click (PC: Ctrl-click) on each adjustment layer in the Layers panel to select them both, and go to Layer>**Create Clipping Mask** to force each one to clip to the layer right below them.

TIP: SAVE YOUR FILE REGULARLY

If you haven't already, it's probably a good idea to go to File>**Save** to save the image as a PSD file, in case Photoshop or your computer accidentally crashes. In fact, I press the shortcut for Save (**Command-S [PC: Ctrl-S]**) all the time, just to make sure I'm always covered.

STEP EIGHT:

It's time for some shadows. Click on the Create a New Layer icon at the bottom of the Layers panel and drag the new layer below both of the basketball player layers. Press **B** to select the Brush tool from the Toolbox and choose a small, soft-edged brush. Make sure your Foreground color is set to black, set the Opacity to 75% up in the Options Bar, and paint a dark, hard shadow that comes out from under both of his feet. It doesn't have to spread too far away from the feet, though. Remember, it's just a shadow that his shoes are casting on the ground.

STEP NINE:

Create another new layer on top of the last one. This time, press the **Right Bracket key** to make your brush larger and set the Opacity to 10%. Now, paint some more shadow areas on the ground in front of him. There's a light source coming from behind him, so we want to make sure we're casting some shadow on the ground in front. Since you're painting with a 10% opacity brush, the more you paint, the darker it'll get, and you'll be able to build up the effect. Also, it's a good idea to start double-clicking on the name of each layer and giving them more descriptive names at this point.

STEP 10:

Now, it's time for some really cool stuff. I photographed him in this pose specifically because I had the idea that I wanted to make it look like the ball was being slammed into the ground. In order to do that, we'll need a photo of some damaged concrete. Go ahead and open the damaged concrete photo and use the Move tool to drag it into the composite. Make sure you position it directly above the Background layer, but below all of the other layers. Don't close the concrete image yet, because we'll need it again.

STEP 11:

Of course, it doesn't fit yet, so we'll have to transform it. Press **Command-T (PC: Ctrl-T)** to go into Free Transform mode. Press-and-hold the Command (PC: Ctrl) key, click on the top-left corner handle, and drag in toward the center. Then Command-click on the top-right corner handle and do the same. Drag the top-middle handle down a little to make it seem like the cracks have the same perspective as the road. Also, you'll want to position the cracks in the ground so that the hole appears as if it's under the basketball. When you're done, press **Return (PC: Enter)** to lock in the transformation.

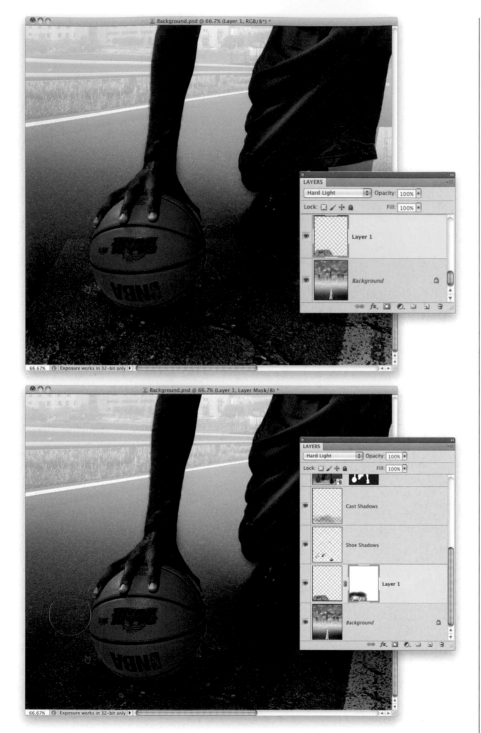

STEP 12:

Change the blend mode of the concrete layer to **Hard Light**. This fades the actual concrete portion of the layer into the original road, and just leaves the cracks. Sometimes, the Multiply blend mode works, too, and sometimes it may be Soft Light or Overlay. Depending on the color, you'll have to experiment with which one works best.

STEP 13:

Click on the Add Layer Mask icon at the bottom of the Layers panel to create a layer mask for this layer. Press **B** to get the Brush tool, make sure your Foreground color is set to black, and paint with a small, soft-edged brush set to a low Opacity to fade away the edges of the cracked concrete image, so it blends better with the road around it.

STEP 14:

Remember how I asked you not to close the concrete image yet? Well, go back to the original cracked concrete photo and go to Image>Image Rotation>**Flip Canvas Horizontal**. This way, the cracks will go out in another direction. Then, drag it into the composite and repeat Steps 11–13. Also, rename these layers, so you know which one is which.

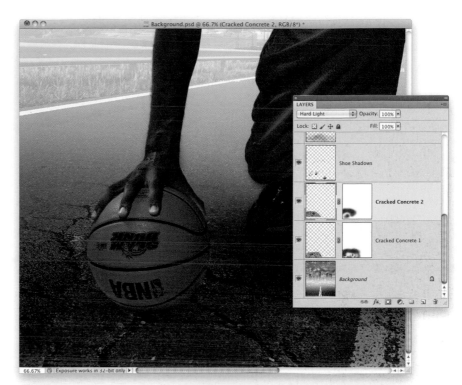

STEP 15:

If we want the ball to look like it's sunk into the ground, then we have to hide part of it. Create a new blank layer at the very top of the layer stack. Press **S** to get the Clone Stamp tool and make sure that the Sample pop-up menu is set to **All Layers** in the Options Bar up top. Option-click (PC: Alt-click) on an area of concrete with cracks on it to sample the texture. Then, start brushing upward with a small, hard-edged brush to cover the bottom of the basketball. You may have to Option-click a few more times as you're painting to continue to pull in the right texture from the ground.

STEP 16:

Press **O** to get the Dodge tool. Up in the Options Bar, set the Range to **Midtones** and the Exposure to 20%, and use a small brush to paint along the very top edge of the concrete you just created to add a highlight. Then press **Shift-O** to get the Burn tool. Use the same settings, and paint to darken the concrete, so it appears the ball is casting a slight shadow on the ground.

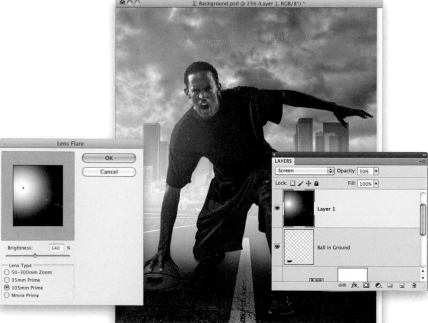

STEP 17:

Next, we'll add some light from behind him. As you can see, the sky is pretty bright on the middle left of the photo, so we'll work with that. Create another new blank layer at the top of the layer stack and go to Edit>**Fill**. Set the Use setting to **Black** and click OK to fill the layer with black. Then go to Filter>Render>**Lens Flare**. Set the Brightness to 140%, the Lens Type to 105mm Prime, then position the lens flare on the middle left, and click OK. Change the layer's blend mode to **Screen** to hide the black and reduce the Opacity setting to around 50%–60% to make the effect more subtle.

STEP 18:

All right, we're almost done. Just a couple of finishing touches left. Press **Command-Option-Shift-E (PC: Ctrl-Alt-Shift-E)** to merge everything together into one new layer on top. I mentioned a way to add an edgy sharpening effect in Photoshop at the end of Chapter 2. But my favorite way to do this is to use the Tonal Contrast filter in Nik Color Efex Pro, so that's what I'll use here at its default settings. If it gets too textured in the cloud or skin areas, just add a layer mask and paint them away with a low-opacity black brush, as I did here.

PHOTOSHOP COMPOSITING SECRETS

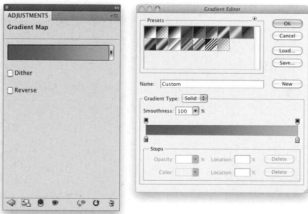

STEP 19:

There's one more finishing touch for this photo, though. I really want a warmer feel to it and color is a great way to add mood. And for composites, it's a wonderful way to tie all of the random parts of the image together. One way to do this in Photoshop is to click on the Create New Adjustment Layer icon at the bottom of the Layers panel and select **Gradient Map**. Then, click on the gradient thumbnail in the Adjustments panel to open the Gradient Editor. To change the color of the gradient, just double-click on the little color stops (the tiny squares) under the gradient ramp in the middle of the dialog. When the Color Picker appears, choose an orange color (I used R: 176, G: 79, B: 6) for the left color stop, and a greenish-yellow (I used R: 186, G: 186, B: 53) for the right color stop. Click OK to close the Gradient Editor, then change the layer blend mode to **Overlay** and the Opacity to 80%. Now, it's got a very fiery, warm color tone to it.

TIP: USING NIK COLOR EFEX PRO INSTEAD

If you have Nik Color Efex Pro Complete, you can also use a filter called Bi-Color Filters. In fact, I used it for this image and, personally, I like it a little better, because it seems to still add some nice color, but it keeps the skin tones fairly removed from the effect. Again, though, either one will work.

STEP 20:

So, here's the final image with Nik's default Bi-Color Filters run on it. Lastly, one of the secrets to compositing people's feet on the ground is to darken the entire area to keep people's attention away from them. We'll use a gradient for this. Create a new blank layer above all of the other layers, and then press **D** to set your Foreground color to black. Press **G** to select the Gradient tool, click on the down-facing arrow next to the gradient thumbnail in the Options Bar to open the Gradient Picker, and choose the second gradient from the left (Foreground to Transparent). Then, drag the gradient from the bottom right of the photo to about a third of the way up, as seen here. This gradually darkens the entire area and you can always reduce the Opacity if it gets too dark.

As you can see on the next page, there's room for some ad copy on the top, or maybe even the athlete's name. Or, you can just as easily select the Crop tool and crop the image to remove some of that space up top.

FINAL IMAGE 1

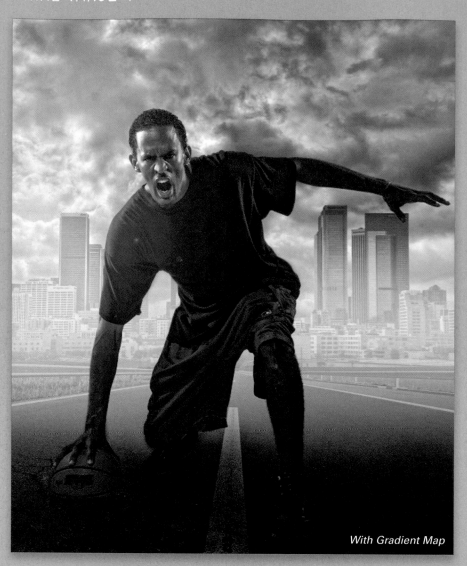

With Gradient Map

FINAL IMAGE 2

With Bi-Color Filters

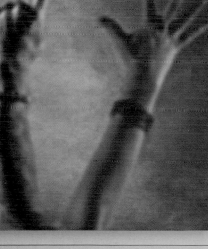

LIVE CONCERT

8

This composite is one I wanted to put in the book for two reasons: First, it was just plain fun to create—from the concept, to the actual shoot, all the way through to the execution of putting everything together in Photoshop. But, I also wanted to include it because it's a great example of how creative we can be with compositing. The idea is to envision a cool-looking scene and then work to make it a reality. Especially, when maybe we can't (or simply don't have the access to) create it in real life without Photoshop.

PREPPING THE BACKGROUND

I knew I needed a background with lights, smoke, etc., to really pull this off. The great part about using separate photos, like this background, to put this entire composite together is that we can change them at will. If I were photographing at a real concert, I'd be stuck with whatever lights the venue had to offer. But, with Photoshop, we can not only control those lights and their brightness, we can also change their color and the entire mood of the image we're looking to create.

©ISTOCKPHOTO/NIKADAI

STEP ONE:
Open the background we're going to use for this photo. The idea is to place a rock star on a stage with all of the concert lights and smoke behind him.

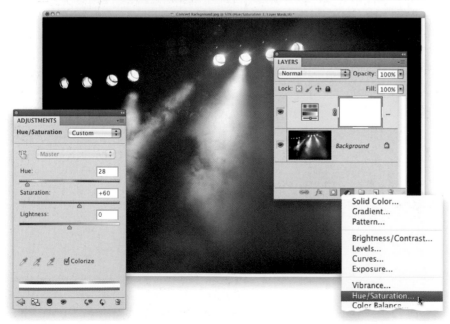

STEP TWO:
I always envision a red/orange hot feel to a rock concert, so let's change the color of the background. Click on the Create New Adjustment Layer icon at the bottom of the Layers panel and choose **Hue/Saturation**. In the Adjustments panel, turn on the Colorize checkbox, set the Hue to 28 for a nice orange color, and then move the Saturation slider to 60 to add some more color saturation to it.

STEP THREE:

The lights in the background look great already, but let's enhance them with a little lens flare. There's actually a Lens Flare filter in Photoshop, but you can't apply it to an adjustment layer. So, click on the Create a New Layer icon at the bottom of the Layers panel to create a new blank layer. Then, go to Edit>**Fill**, set the Use pop-up menu to **Black**, and click OK to fill the new layer with black.

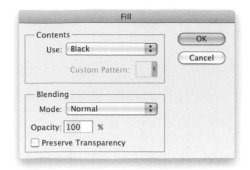

STEP FOUR:

Now, go to Filter>Render>**Lens Flare**, set the Brightness to 100%, and the Lens Type to 50–300mm Zoom. Move your cursor over the preview area in the dialog and drag the flare toward the top right of the photo, placing it in the general area where the lights are. Click OK when you're done to apply the filter.

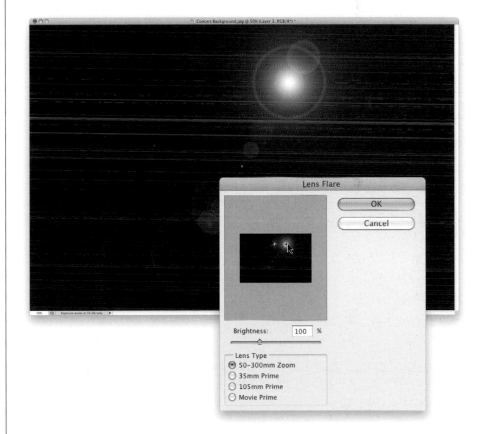

STEP FIVE:

Of course, we can't see the lights in the background image, because we added the lens flare to a black layer. So, change the blend mode of the lens flare layer to **Screen** to hide the black. Then use the Move tool **(V)** to reposition the flare, so it's over one of the real lights on the right (as shown here).

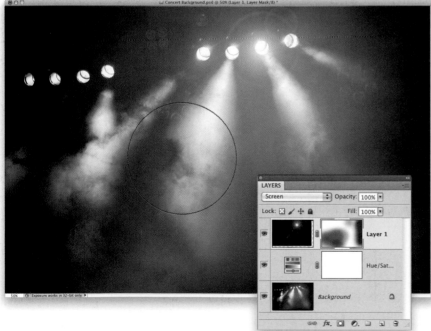

STEP SIX:

Whenever you add a lens flare to a layer, and then move the layer like we just did, chances are you'll end up with a funky edge (you can see it on the right side in Step Five). If that happens, click on the Add Layer Mask icon at the bottom of the Layers panel to add a layer mask to the lens flare layer. With your Foreground color set to black, get the Brush tool **(B)**, and with a large, soft-edged brush, paint on the layer mask to remove the edge from the lens flare layer, so everything blends in nicely. Also, I think the flare gets too distracting toward the middle of the photo, so in the Options Bar, set the brush to 50% Opacity, and paint to hide some of that area, too.

STEP SEVEN:

Repeat Steps Three through Six a few more times for the other lights in the photo—I added one more on the right side and two on the left side. When you're in the Lens Flare filter dialog, change the position of the flare slightly for each one. And since some of the lights aren't pointing right at the camera, make sure you reduce the opacity of some of those layers, so every light isn't equally as bright.

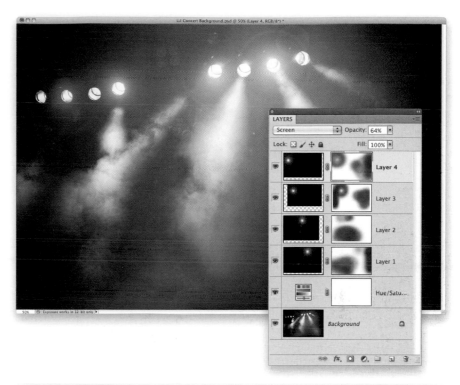

STEP EIGHT:

Also, lens flares change shape and size, depending on how much of the light is pointing at the camera. So, click on one of the outer layers of lens flare and go to Edit>**Free Transform**. Press-and-hold the Shift key and click-and-drag one of the corner handles inward to make it smaller. Press **Return (PC: Enter)** to lock in the transformation and do the same thing for one or two of the other lens flare layers.

STEP NINE:

We're done with the background for now. So, go to File>**Save** and save it as a PSD file, because we're going to need the layers later when we add the rock star in, especially when it comes to the lens flare we added back in Step Four. The flare wouldn't just be behind the rock star, so we'll need to use these layers to bring some of that flare in front of him, too.

SELECTING THE PORTRAIT AND THE ARMS

We have two different selections to make for this composite: the rock star and the arms of people in the audience. I originally thought of using black-silhouetted arms for the foreground in this composite, but then I realized that I already had the lights set up for the singer's photo, and knew they would work perfectly (with a small change that you'll see in a minute) to photograph people's arms in the air, and I could use the real thing.

STEP ONE:

Before we get started, if you're curious, here's a partial setup shot for this photo. It's similar to the setup I used for several other projects in the book. I used two strip lights on each side of the subject for the edge lighting (which you can see here), and one beauty dish directly in front (just a bit to camera right) as the main light.

STEP TWO:

Go ahead and open the photo for the composite. It's a RAW photo, so it's going to open in the Camera Raw window first. When it comes to the RAW adjustments, start by moving the Temperature slider to 4400 to neutralize that warm color it has. Let's also increase the Fill Light slider to 35 to bring out some more of those details in the darker areas. Then, drag the Vibrance slider to –33 to remove some of the redness and color from the photo. When you're done, press-and-hold the Shift key and click the Open Object button at the bottom of the window to open the photo as a Smart Object in Photoshop.

STEP THREE:

We'll use the Quick Selection tool **(W)** to start our selection. This one took a little finessing, though, so make sure you zoom in and get all of the edges with a smaller Quick Selection brush—especially, around the microphone area. The Quick Selection tool is probably going to select too much, so you'll have to zoom in even more, press-and-hold the **Option (PC: Alt) key**, and paint to subtract from the selection, refining it a little more in that background area near his shoulder, microphone hand, and face.

STEP FOUR:

Once the overall selection is looking good, press the Refine Edge button in the Options Bar, and in the Refine Edge dialog, set the Radius to 10. The selection will look a lot better now and, honestly, there's not much more we can do here. The Smart Radius checkbox won't help here, since we don't have many rough edges or wispy hair. And the Refine Radius tool won't help much either, because there are not really any areas that haven't been selected. So, from the Output To pop-up menu, choose **Layer Mask** and click OK.

STEP FIVE:

Now you've got the selection on a layer mask and you're ready to tweak the edges a little. First, Command-click (PC: Ctrl-click) on the Create a New Layer icon at the bottom of the Layers panel to add a new blank layer below the singer. Then, go to Edit>**Fill**, choose **Black** from the Use pop-up menu, and click OK to fill the new layer with black. I think black contrasts strongly with the singer and gives us a good way to see if any of the edges need refining.

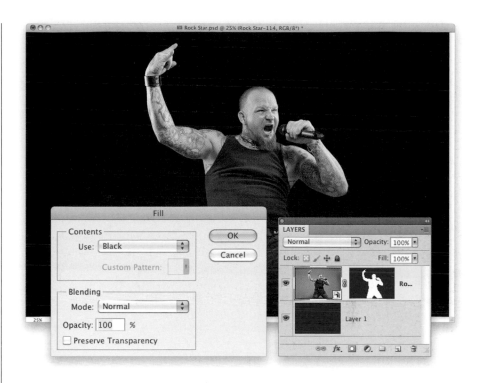

STEP SIX:

Zoom in and check the edges of the singer. I won't lie to you here (well, I guess I wouldn't lie to you in any of the tutorials actually, but especially this one). This image requires a little more manual refining than we've had to do in the past, mainly because Photoshop is getting confused between the tones and colors of his tattoos and the overall background itself. So, when you zoom in on some of the edges, you'll see what I mean. Here's an example of where the edges aren't all selected. At first glance, it looks like they are, but we're definitely missing some detail. Also, keep in mind that your selection is always going to be a little different than mine, so the places I see problems may not be the exact spots that you see them in.

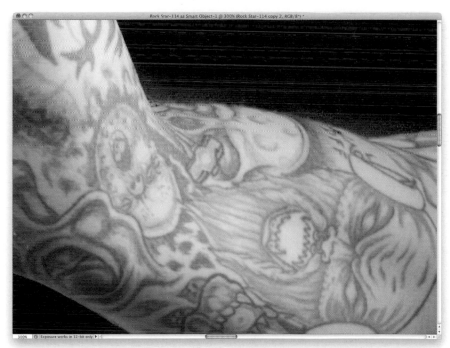

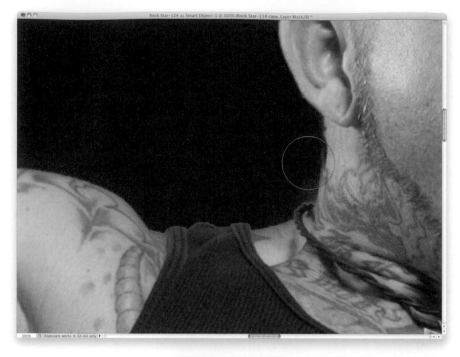

STEP SEVEN:

We'll fix the edges just as we have in the past. Click once on the singer layer's layer mask to target it. Then, select the Brush tool from the Toolbox (or press the **B key**), set the blend Mode in the Options Bar to **Overlay**, and then press **X** to set your Foreground color to white. When you see an edge where the skin seems to be missing some detail, use a small, soft-edged brush to paint it back in. Remember, because we're painting on the layer mask in Overlay mode, you don't have to worry about painting outside of the edge of the skin. Brushing in this mode sees the existing hard edges and keeps them intact. Work your way around the edges of the singer and continue to paint on the mask in Overlay mode. Again, this photo took a little more work than some of the others, so be patient and get all of the missing areas. When you're done, go to File>**Save** and save it as a PSD file, so we can still use the Smart Object and layer mask later.

STEP EIGHT:

Next, open the photos of the arms. The only lighting difference with these photos is that I turned off the main light (the beauty dish), and just used the two strip lights on the sides to give the arms some depth and contours. Oh, and yes, I felt silly asking random people around the office to come in and hold up their hands. I got a few weird looks when I told them what I was doing, but it was just their arms after all, so everyone had fun with it.

STEP NINE:

On the first arm photo, use the Quick Selection tool to paint a selection on the arm and hand. I even included a head in there for a couple of them. You'll have to zoom in on these to make sure you select the fingers well, too. That said, don't worry too much about getting an absolutely perfect edge here. We're going to blur them a little later.

STEP 10:

Once you have the arm and hand selected, click the Refine Edge button. Just use a small Radius setting of around 5, choose **Layer Mask** from the Output To pop-up menu, and click OK.

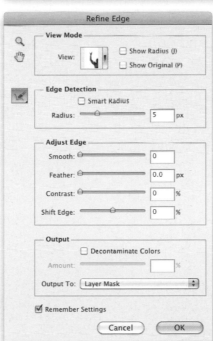

STEP 11:

Do this for all the other arm images, then drag them into one document, and save the image as a PSD file. If you're following along, but don't want to go through all of the selections for all of the arms, I've got a nice PSD file for you with arms in it for the next tutorial. You can just use that one if you want to skip the mind-numbing work of selecting arms from a background.

CREATING THE COMPOSITE

This composite is all about the mood. We'll need to continue with the warm background that we've already created, and keep the same overall feeling with everything else we add. It's also a great introduction to how supporting graphics can really take a composite to that next level. Right now, our subject is just a guy singing with no stage. But, we'll be adding some cheering arms in the air, as well as some smoke, to make this feel like he's really on stage during a concert.

STEP ONE:

Open the background image first and then take a look at the Layers panel for a minute. Notice it has a few layers in there: a Hue/Saturation adjustment layer for colorizing the background, and several lens flare layers added to the lighting. We need to make sure that the photo of the singer goes above the adjustment layer, but below the lens flare layers.

STEP TWO:

Next, open the selected photo of the singer. We started this one in Camera Raw and opened it as a Smart Object into Photoshop. Grab the Move tool **(V)** and then go ahead and click-and-drag the singer into the background image. Then, click-and-drag his layer down in the Layer's panel, so it's above the Hue/Saturation adjustment layer, but below the lens flare layers.

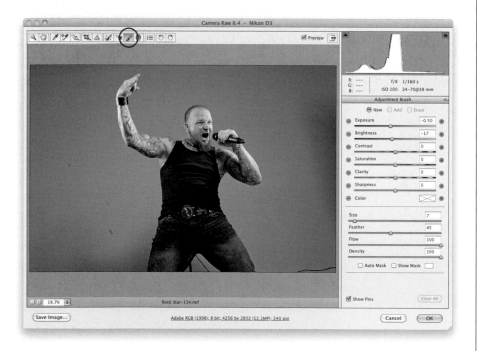

STEP THREE:

He's way too big for the photo, so go to Edit>**Free Transform**. In the Options Bar, enter 62% for the width and height settings, and then press **Return (PC: Enter)**. Then, reposition him in the center of the background image.

TIP: MAINTAIN ASPECT RATIO

If you click on the Maintain Aspect Ratio icon (the little chain link) in the Options Bar between the W and H fields, Photoshop will automatically change the height when you change the width. Also, clicking that icon makes it so you don't need to hold the Shift key if you manually decide to resize the photo using the transform handles.

STEP FOUR:

One of the first things I realized once he was in the photo is that his arms and jeans are too bright. Since he's on a Smart Object layer, we can change that really fast. Just double-click on the singer layer's image thumbnail to reopen the photo in Camera Raw. Grab the Adjustment Brush **(K)** in the top toolbar, then set the Exposure to –0.50 and the Brightness to –17.

STEP FIVE:

Set the Brush size to around 7, and brush along his arms and legs to darken them. Don't worry about brushing on the background, because we've already selected him, so none of that will show up. When you're done, click OK to go back to Photoshop.

STEP SIX:

His skin is also a little too cool for the warm background we've placed him on, so click on the Create New Adjustment Layer icon at the bottom of the Layers panel and choose **Photo Filter**. In the Adjustments panel, increase the Density setting to 60%. Since the Photo Filter adjustment is affecting the entire photo (and we just want it to affect the singer), go to Layer>**Create Clipping Mask**. This forces the adjustment layer to only affect the layer right below it.

STEP SEVEN:

Overall, I think he's still too bright, so click on the Create New Adjustment Layer icon again, but this time, choose **Curves**. In the Adjustments panel, drag the middle of the curve downward, like you see here. Then, go to Layer>**Create Clipping Mask**, again, to force it to only affect the layer below, just like we did with the Photo Filter adjustment layer. Finally, change the blend mode to **Luminosity**.

STEP EIGHT:

If you look at the background, you'll see it already has some smoke in it. But, I think it'll look cooler if we add some more. Images like this are perfect candidates for using stock photos, since we typically don't have photos of smoke just lying around. As you get into compositing more, though, you'll find that you'll start taking photos of anything you see, and smoke is one of those things you should definitely start building a library of. You just never know when you'll use it. Anyway, I went to iStockphoto.com, searched for "smoke," and found this photo on the first page of the results.

STEP NINE:

Go ahead and open the smoke photo (iStockphoto.com was kind enough to allow me to provide it to you in the downloads). Using the Move tool, drag it into the composite image and then, in the Layers panel, make sure it appears directly above the Curves adjustment layer, but below the lens flare layers (as seen here).

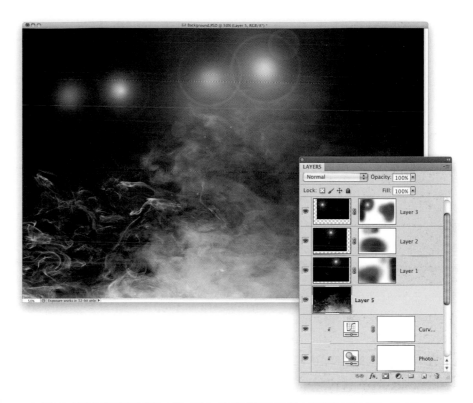

STEP 10:

Change the blend mode of the layer to **Color Dodge** and reduce the Opacity to 85%. This helps the smoke blend into the background more. In fact, whenever you have smoke, mist, fog, or any other texture with black behind it, try the Color Dodge or Screen blend mode. It's a great way to drop the black and only leave whatever texture happens to be on the layer.

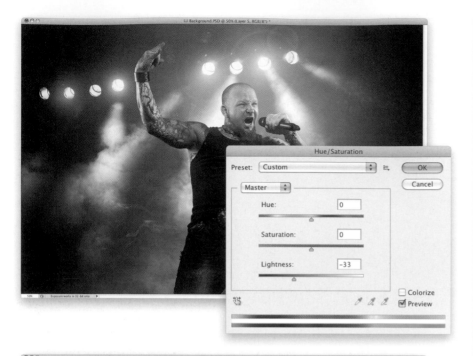

STEP 11:

Let's position the smoke layer toward the bottom of the image a little, so the smoke is rising toward the top, but not in front of his face. Now, the only problem I still see is that it's just a little too bright near the bottom. It almost looks like fire, which can be cool at times, but not for this photo, so let's remove some brightness. Press **Command-U (PC: Ctrl-U)** to open the Hue/Saturation dialog, then drag the Lightness slider to the left to –33, and click OK. We can still see the smoke now, but it just takes the edge off of some of those bright areas.

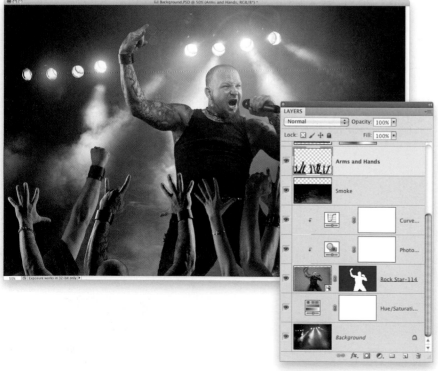

STEP 12:

Every rock star needs their fans, so it's time to add the crowd. Go ahead and open your selected arms photo from the last tutorial and drag it into the composite. Or, if you decided not to make all the arm selections yourself and just downloaded the arms PSD file I created for you, drag the Arms and Hands layer into your composite (that's the one I'm using here). Since the smoke is mainly up on the stage, you'll want the arms to be in front of it, so place the layer above the smoke and position the arms at the bottom of the image.

STEP 13:

Let's use a little depth of field to help pull this off. Since the singer is in focus, we can blur the arms a little. So, go to Filter>Blur>**Gaussian Blur**, set the Radius to 5 pixels, and click OK. Now, the arms have just a little blur to them, which does two things: (1) It helps "sell" the composite—since the focus should be on the singer, the arms would naturally fall out of focus just a bit. And, (2) it helps pull attention away from the arms and onto the singer. We want the arms there, of course, but we don't want them to attract too much attention.

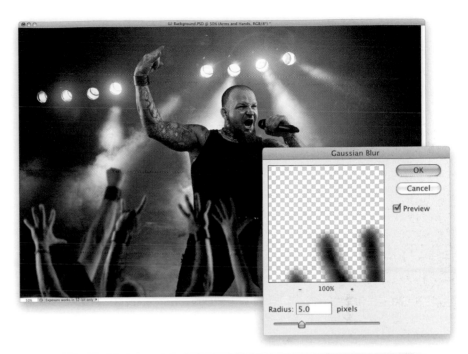

STEP 14:

Whenever I have a lot of lights in the photo, I usually add some extra lighting up front to help give the feeling of a wash of light falling around the subject. So, create a new blank layer at the top of the layer stack. Then, press the **l key** to get the Eyedropper tool, and click on the background to sample a bright orange color. Select the Brush tool (**B**), and with a large, soft-edged brush set to 10% Opacity, paint some light brush strokes over the lights. Just click a few times instead of dragging and actually painting. Remember, this layer is above all the others, so it'll have the appearance that the light is wrapping around the singer from all angles. If it looks too bright, lower the layer Opacity a bit.

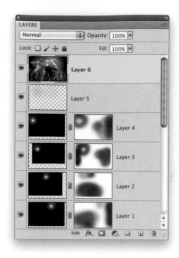

STEP 15:

If you've been following along with any of the other edgy-like composite tutorials in the book, you'll know I like to finish things off with an effect. I've mentioned before that there's a free way built into Photoshop that's good, and a not-free way that I think is better. First, the free way: Press **Command-Option-Shift-E (PC: Ctrl-Alt-Shift-E)** to combine all of the layers into one new merged layer on top of the layer stack.

STEP 16:

Then go to Filter>Other>**High Pass**, use a Radius setting of 9 pixels, and click OK. Now the image looks gray, so change the blend mode of the layer to **Hard Light** to hide the gray. This gives the photo a sharpened/gritty look to it, which works perfectly, considering the subject here.

STEP 17:

The not-free way is with a plug-in from Nik Software called Color Efex Pro 3.0 Complete. If you have it installed, go to Filter>Nik Software> **Color Efex Pro**. I cover this plug-in and the entire plug-in topic in the "10 Things You Need to Know About Compositing" section at the beginning of the book. For now, I wanted to at least show you the way I'd really finish off this photo to get the best effect. When the Color Efex Pro window opens, click on Tonal Contrast on the left, and set the Highlight Contrast, Midtone Contrast, and Shadow Contrast settings (on the right) all to 30. Then, set Saturation to 5 and click OK to apply the filter to the new layer. Now you've got a similar effect to the High Pass filter, but I think it looks better overall.

STEP 18:

Regardless of which method you just used, the effect doesn't look good on the hands or the lens flares. So, click on the Add Layer Mask icon at the bottom of the Layers panel. Then, get the Brush tool, set your Foreground color to black, and use a small, soft-edged brush set to a low Opacity to paint away the effect from the hands up front, as well as around the lens flare.

FINAL IMAGE

What you're about to learn in this chapter is a really popular composite that you'll mainly see used for sports. There's no studio lighting involved. Heck, there's no studio involved. All you need to shoot this one is a subject, a camera, and preferably a tripod. It's a great effect and, although it's been around for a while, your clients, family, friends, or whomever the image is for, will still love it.

TOM BOL

THE SETUP

The setup for this type of shoot is really simple. In fact, if you set it up the right way, you'll make your post-processing in Photoshop really simple, too. I do want to take a quick moment to thank my good friend and very talented adventure photographer, Tom Bol (www.tombolphoto.com). Tom was kind enough to let me use his photos for this chapter. Why? Because I live in Florida and the closest I get to snow is when I open my freezer to get ice. But Tom lives for this stuff. In fact, if it's not below 20 degrees, Tom's out shooting in shorts and a t-shirt, because that's like summer weather to him (he's from Alaska). Thanks Tom!

STEP ONE:

Okay, let's go over what you'll need to make this type of shot happen. For starters, you need a moving subject. It doesn't have to be skiing or snow-boarding, by the way. A lot of sports work—basketball, football, baseball, soccer, motorcross, you name it. Track and field would be awesome, too, by the way. It helps a lot if there's an interesting background or setting, but sometimes the motion of the actual sport can carry the composite by itself. In this example, we'll use a snow-boarder flying through the air.

STEP TWO:

A tripod helps with these multiple-action shots, because it helps steady the overall framing of the photo. So, the scenery behind the subject will stay the same for every shot and only the athlete will be moving, making our Photoshop work really easy. Next, set your camera to Aperture Priority mode and do a quick test shot. Then, remember what aperture you used and make a note of the shutter speed the camera chose. Say you're set to f/8 and the camera chooses 1/500 of a second. Switch to Manual mode and dial in f/8 and 1/500. This way, the camera won't accidentally meter off the wrong area and choose a different exposure as you fire off multiple frames.

STEP THREE:

Now, you need to turn your camera to Continuous or Burst mode. It's going to differ for each camera, but you basically want the camera to take photos as fast as it can. Also, the FPS (frames per second) your camera will shoot will vary. Some entry level DSLRs shoot 4 fps and some of the pro models will shoot 9 or 10 fps. The main difference that FPS makes for this type of photo is the distance between each photo of the subject. The lower the FPS, the more space between each photo. The higher the FPS, the closer they'll be. Sometimes, they'll even overlap if the subject isn't moving really fast. Here's an example of what the spacing may look like using a camera with a lower FPS vs. one that has a higher FPS.

Lower FPS

Higher FPS

ADAM ROHRMANN

STEP FOUR:

Here's a setup shot taken during one of the series of photos while Tom was out shooting. It's of a skier, but the concept was the same for the snowboarder. You can see that Tom has his camera locked down on a tripod as the skier flies through the air.

MULTIPLE-EXPOSURE ACTION COMPOSITE (THE EASY WAY)

If you read the title to this tutorial, you probably noticed I wrote "the Easy Way" at the end. That's because there are two ways to create a composite like this, and I figured I'd show you the easy, automatic way first. Sometimes it works, and sometimes it doesn't, so I'll show you the other way (not really that difficult) in the next tutorial.

STEP ONE:

In Photoshop, we'll need to get all of the images from the series into one document. You could always do it the hard way by opening each photo and dragging them individually into one image, but Photoshop's got a much easier way built in. Just go to File>Scripts>**Load Files into Stack** to open the Load Layers dialog.

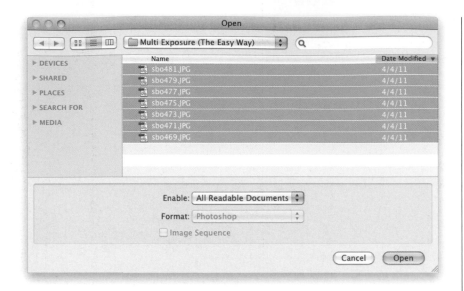

STEP TWO:
Click on the Browse button and navigate to the series of photos that you've captured (or just follow along by downloading the ones I'm using here). When you get to the series in the Open dialog, click on the topmost photo and then Shift-click on the bottom one to select them all.

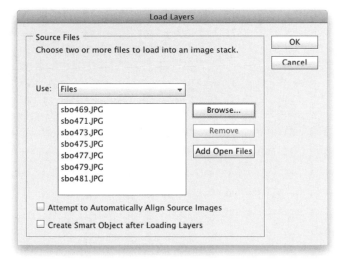

STEP THREE:
When you've got all of the photos selected, click the Open button, and then click the OK button in the Load Layers dialog to start stacking them. It took about 30 seconds for Photoshop to stack the ones I'm using here.

STEP FOUR:

When it's done, you'll have one image window with a bunch of layers in the Layers panel. In the Layers panel, click on the bottom layer, then press-and-hold the Shift key and click on the top layer to select them, along with all the layers in between.

STEP FIVE:

Remember how I said we're going with the easy way first? Watch this. Go to Edit>**Auto-Blend Layers** and then, in the Auto-Blend Layers dialog, in the Blend Method section, click on the Stack Images radio button (if it's not already selected). Then, make sure the Seamless Tones and Colors checkbox at the bottom is turned on, and click OK. This one can take a while depending on how many photos you used—it took almost two minutes on my computer, so be patient with it. It's definitely worth the wait if it works.

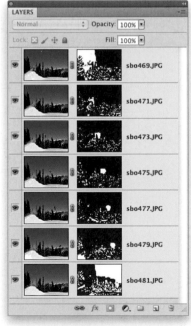

STEP SIX:

When it's done, if you're following along with the photos I used here, you should have something that looks like this. You have to admit, that's pretty sweet, huh? No masking, no brushing, no nuthin'! The Auto-Blend Layers feature seamlessly put all of the photos together. Just take a look at the Layers panel and you'll see some crazy layer masking going on there. It's done an almost flawless job in my example. Everything looks good, except for the second frame from the left, where we have a little ghosting, which can be cleaned up with a little painting on the layer mask.

Before we move on, I feel like I have to tell you that it doesn't always work as well as it did here. One of the reasons Auto-Blend Layers worked so well here is because there was some distance between each copy of the snowboarder. If they overlapped in any way (which they will in the next tutorial), or they interact with the background too much, you'll see it doesn't work as well. Whew, now that I got that off my chest let's move on to the other way of doing this.

MULTIPLE-EXPOSURE ACTION COMPOSITE (THE NOT-QUITE-AS-EASY WAY)

The previous tutorial showed you the easy way to blend multiple copies of the snowboarder together. I mentioned at the end that if the subject doesn't overlap in any of the photos, the Auto-Blend Layers feature works really well. But, I cheated there. I actually only used half of the photos that were taken in the series (every other one). It looks cool enough, but I think it looks like an even better composite when there are more versions of the snowboarder in the photo. In fact, I actually think it looks really cool when they do overlap. Unfortunately, the automatic method doesn't work that way, so we'll need to do it manually.

STEP ONE:

Before we get started, let's just take a look at what would have happened if we used Auto-Blend Layers for this composite using all of the photos—not just every other one, like I did in the last tutorial. As you can see here, some copies of the snowboarder are ghosted. Because of the extreme masking that Photoshop does with Auto-Blend Layers, it's not worth even trying to go back and fix them. It's just easier to do it the manual way, like we'll do here.

STEP TWO:

All right, we'll start this one out the same way we did in the last tutorial. Go to File>Scripts>**Load Files into Stack** to open the Load Layers dialog. Click on the Browse button and find the series of the same photos we used earlier. They're actually the same exact series of photos, just more of them this time.

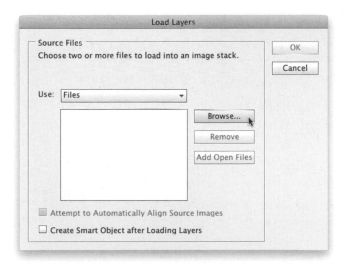

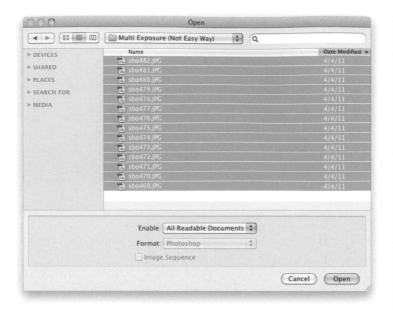

STEP THREE:

When you get to the Open dialog, click on the topmost photo and then Shift-click on the bottom one to select them all. When you've got all of the photos selected, click the Open button, and then click the OK button in the Load Layers dialog to start stacking them.

STEP FOUR:

You'll end up with a new image with a bunch of layers in the Layers panel. Think of the bottom layer as a sort of home base here. That's going to be our main photo and everything else will end up blending in with that one. Right now, we won't even see it, though, since there are so many layers on top of it. So, click on the top layer to target it, then **Option-click (PC: Alt-click)** on the Add Layer Mask icon at the bottom of the Layers panel. This adds a layer mask in hide mode (black), so the entire layer is hidden right now.

STEP FIVE:

Now, we just need to repeat this for every layer except the bottom layer. But, instead of Option-clicking to add a black layer mask to each layer, try this: press-and-hold the **Option key**, then click on the layer mask on the top layer, and drag it down to the layer below it. By holding down the Option key first, you're telling Photoshop you want to copy the mask (not move it). So, it'll copy the same exact black mask to the layer you drag it to.

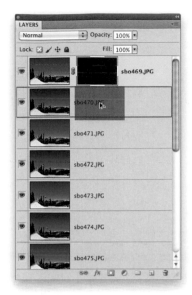 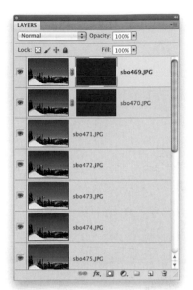

STEP SIX:

Just repeat Step Five for all of the other layers, except the bottom layer. Leave that one without a layer mask. Since we've just hidden all the layers except the bottom one, you should now only see the snowboarder at the very end of his jump.

STEP SEVEN:

Get the Zoom tool **(Z)** and zoom in on the left of the photo where the flags are at the beginning of the jump. We'll start there and reveal each layer and each frame of the snowboarder as he goes through the air. Here's the problem, though: you can't see where the snowboarder is in that photo because we hid that layer with a black layer mask, right? I suppose you could paint with white haphazardly until you see him, but there's a better way. Shift-click on the top layer's layer mask to temporarily disable it. You'll see a big red X appear on the mask to let you know it's disabled and that'll let you see where the snowboarder is.

STEP EIGHT:

Shift-click on the layer mask again to turn it back on and then make sure it's active. Then, select the Brush tool **(B)** from the Toolbox and choose a small, soft-edged brush. Press **D** to set your Foreground color to white (because the mask is black) and start brushing where you remember the snowboarder to be. As you brush with white, he'll start to reappear. Disabling the layer mask, like we did in Step Seven, just gives you a good starting point for where to paint.

STEP NINE:

For the first layer of the image, go ahead and paint with white all the way down the ramp on the far left of the photo. That way, you'll reveal the snow that he kicked up as he was starting his jump.

STEP 10:

One layer down, 12 more layers to go. The process is pretty much the same. Move to the next layer down and Shift-click on the layer mask to disable it (so you see the big X over it). Then, take a good look to see where the snowboarder is in that image.

STEP 11:

Shift-click on the mask to re-enable it, then click on it to make sure it's active, and with a white brush, start painting on the next image of the snowboarder to reveal him. It's okay if you're not perfect when you paint the edges, but try to stay as close to the edges of the snowboarder as possible. Now you've got two snow-boarders revealed.

STEP 12:

We'll continue working down the Layers panel, revealing each image of the snowboarder. But, when we get to the third layer from the top, something interesting happens. Take a look at the image here. I started painting around the snowboarder and, as you can see, I wasn't really careful with the brush size and it extended pretty far away from the snowboarder. See what happened as a result? The sky appears to be a lighter blue on this layer than it is on the other layers. This can happen for a couple of reasons: First, if you had your camera set to Aperture Priority (and not Manual) mode, the exposure could have changed slightly. Also, if you have your camera set to Auto White Balance, the white balance may have changed a little, too. It's easy enough to fix this, though.

STEP 13:

If the background does change in brightness or color, then it just means you need to be more precise when painting the subject back into the photo. I mentioned that I was pretty loose with the brush in this example, and went way outside the boundaries of the snowboarder for this layer when I painted with white. So, just press the **X** key to swap your Foreground color from white to black. Then, zoom in even closer, decrease the size of your brush, and paint the unmatched sky away. But, don't go too far or you'll hide the snowboarder again.

STEP 14:

Continue down the layer stack until you get to the bottom. If you come across any layers where the images of the snowboarder overlap (which can look really cool, by the way), you just have to pick which image you're going to choose to be in front. I usually choose the version that's in the direction they're moving. In this case, he's moving to the right, so I'll choose the version on the right to be the one that's in front and hide any parts of the version on the left behind it. You may have to go to the previous layer's layer mask to adjust it to hide the overlapping parts. It's kind of a creative choice, though, so try it both ways to see what looks best.

PHOTOSHOP COMPOSITING SECRETS

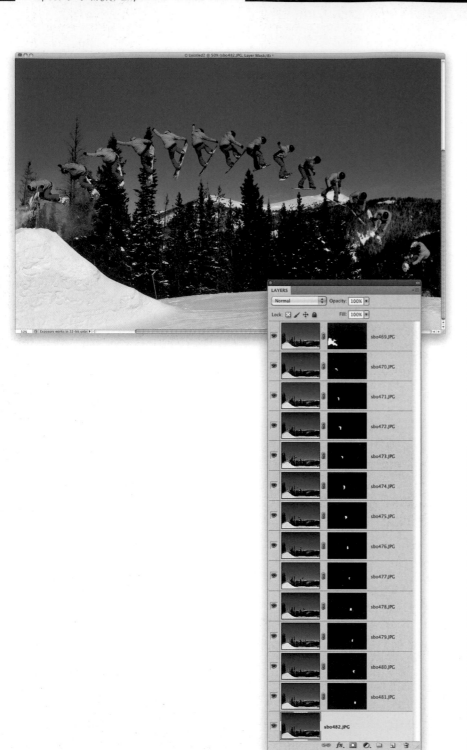

STEP 15:

When you're done, you'll have the snowboarder flying through the air. Make sure you save this one as a PSD file with all of the layers, in case you need to change anything later. You don't want to have to do all of that work all over again.

FINAL IMAGE

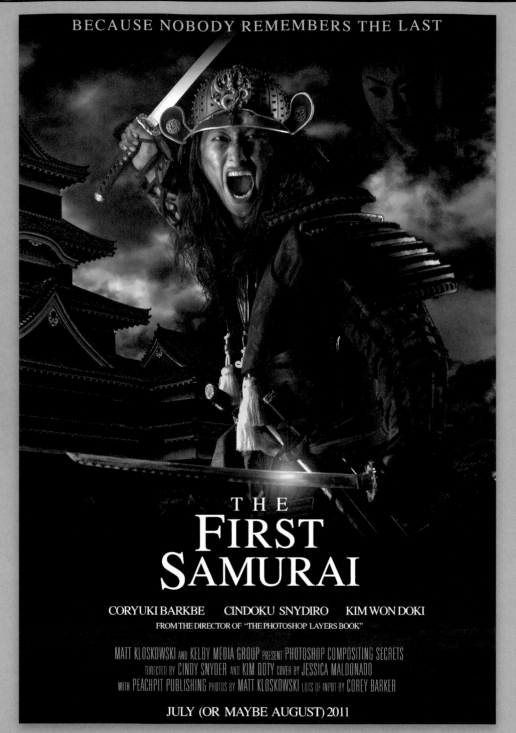

BECAUSE NOBODY REMEMBERS THE LAST

THE
FIRST
SAMURAI

CORYUKI BARKBE   CINDOKU SNYDIRO   KIM WON DOKI

FROM THE DIRECTOR OF "THE PHOTOSHOP LAYERS BOOK"

MATT KLOSKOWSKI AND KELBY MEDIA GROUP PRESENT PHOTOSHOP COMPOSITING SECRETS
DIRECTED BY CINDY SNYDER AND KIM DOTY COVER BY JESSICA MALDONADO
WITH PEACHPIT PUBLISHING PHOTOS BY MATT KLOSKOWSKI LOTS OF INPUT BY COREY BARKER

JULY (OR MAYBE AUGUST) 2011

MOVIE POSTER

10

If there's ever a final product that absolutely screams of compositing, it's a movie poster. Think about it. Movie posters often depict something that's not real. The artist and designers creating the poster have to take all the elements they're given and create this unrealistic scene that actually looks real. Real enough to sell the movie.

THE SETUP

We'll approach this from the aspect of someone creating a movie poster who's been given certain photos and information to work with. The movie's name is *The First Samurai* and we've got a samurai, a Japanese castle, and a few other things to put together.

BACKGROUND:
The background is a Japanese castle. The sky is pretty nice, but we'll want something a little more dramatic. That's where our next photo comes in.

CLOUDS:
Here's a photo of some dramatic clouds. I carry my camera around with me all the time (even on cloudy days), just to take photos to add to my background collection. Clouds and skies play a huge role in some composites, so I've got a big library of them.

SAMURAI:

Here's a photo I took of a samurai. Now, he's not a real samurai. The photo was taken at the Westcott lighting booth on the tradeshow floor at the Photoshop World Conference & Expo.

LOVE INTEREST:

We've got to have a love interest in the movie, so here's another photo we'll use in the background. But, we'll only be using part of the woman here.

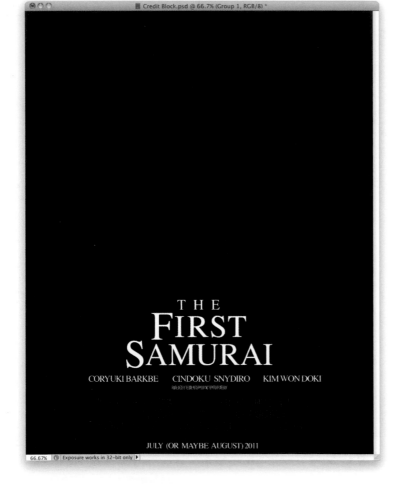

SAMURAIS FIGHTING:
To help add to the "action" feel of the movie poster, we'll use a photo of two samurais fighting. Like the previous photo, it's more of a secondary photo, though. We won't see much of it.

MOVIE TITLE AND CREDIT BLOCK:
And, of course, what movie poster is complete without the movie's title and text at the bottom (also called a credit block)? We'll take a look at how to create the text and what fonts work best.

PREPPING THE BACKGROUND

The background is nowhere near as dramatic as we need yet. Movie posters like this always have something dark and stormy as the background setting. If you haven't realized it yet, I love dramatic clouds, so we'll definitely add some of those. Then we need to darken it (we have a couple of tricks to do this), so everything looks a little more ominous. Let's get started.

STEP ONE:

First, open the two photos we'll need for the background—we'll need the castle and we'll need the clouds to put behind it. By the way, I already resized the castle photo to the dimensions needed for a movie poster. Just in case you're wondering, most posters are generally 27x40". Now that's huge for what we're creating here, so I've sized it down a bit. But, the actual aspect ratio here is still 27x40.

STEP TWO:

Grab the Quick Selection tool from the Toolbox (or just press **W**) and make a very quick selection of the castle image's sky. Then, click on the Refine Edge button in the Options Bar. When the Refine Edge dialog opens, turn on the Smart Radius checkbox and set the Radius to around 40 pixels, so we pick up any little details on the castle. From the Output To pop-up menu, choose **Selection** and click OK.

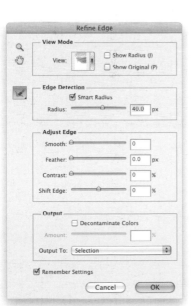

STEP THREE:

Switch over to the cloud photo, go to Select>**All** to select the entire photo, and then go to Edit>**Copy** to copy it. Switch back over to the castle photo (where you already have a selection active) and choose Edit>Paste Special>**Paste Into**. This pastes the clouds into the sky, but automatically creates a layer mask, so the rest of the cloud photo is hidden.

STEP FOUR:

Now, we need to grunge it all up to get a more dramatic look. It's a movie poster, after all, and they usually have a very dramatic feel to them. I'm going to show you a way to do it in Photoshop first, but then I'll show you what I think is a much better way. Photoshop's HDR Toning adjustment is a good way to get an instant grunge look, so go to Image>Adjustments>**HDR Toning**. Photoshop will ask if it's okay to flatten your document, so just click Yes to continue.

STEP FIVE:

When the HDR Toning dialog opens, enter settings similar to what I have here. By really cranking up the Radius, Strength, and Detail settings, you'll get a very detailed and dramatic look. Click OK when you're done.

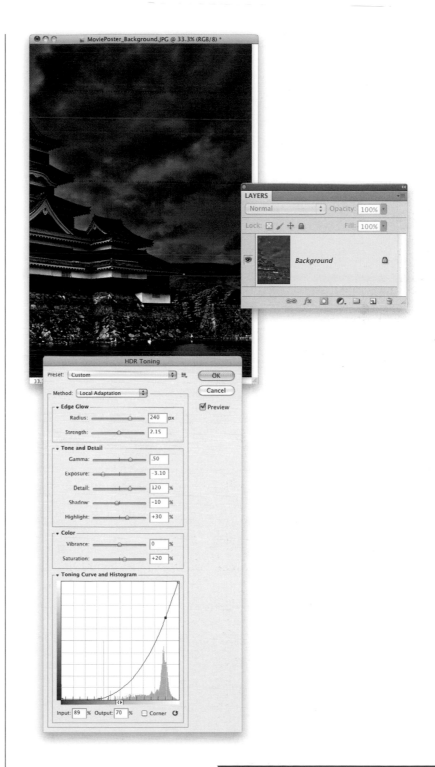

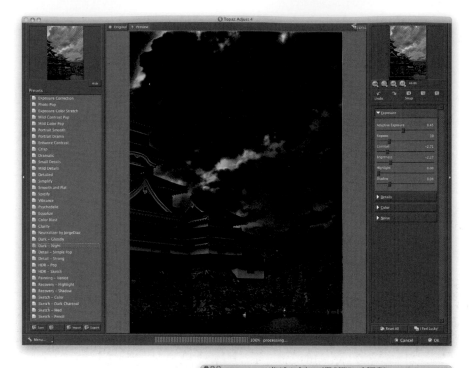

STEP SIX:

The HDR Toning adjustment looks pretty good for creating that dramatic look. But if you want to step it up a notch and want to learn the real secret, it's from a plug-in called Topaz Adjust. First, though, you'll need to undo the HDR toning (press Command-Z [PC: Ctrl-Z]). Then, create a new merged layer to apply the filter to by pressing **Command-Option-Shift-E (PC: Ctrl-Alt-Shift-E)** to create a new merged layer at the top of the layer stack. If you've installed the plug-in (you can find it at www.topazlabs.com/adjust, and they do have a free trial), you'll find it under Filter>Topaz Labs>**Topaz Adjust**. When you open the plug-in window, you'll see a bunch of presets along the left side. I use the Dark – Night preset all the time. It's a great way to take a daytime photo and turn it into night with just one click. And it gives a much better result than anything I've seen in Photoshop. I've also included the completed background image at this point, so even if you don't have the plug-in, you can still follow along with the same photo I'm using.

SELECTING THE SAMURAI

The samurai breaks most of the rules about selections that I've talked about so far. Black is probably one of the hardest colors to work with when you have someone with black hair (especially wispy hair, like we have here) and dark details in their clothing (again, like we have here). But, sometimes, we can't set everything up in the studio like we want, so we have to work with what we're given.

STEP ONE:

Open the samurai photo. It's a RAW photo, so it'll open in the Camera Raw window. First things first, click the Rotate Image 90° Counter Clockwise button in the top toolbar (or just press the **L key**) to rotate the photo.

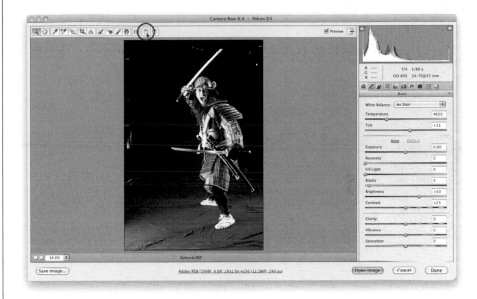

STEP TWO:

From a selection standpoint, we know it's always good to have contrast with the background. Since the background is so dark, move the Fill Light slider up to 30. This'll brighten it a bit and give us a better chance at a fast, clean selection. Then, press-and-hold the Shift key and click the Open Object button in the bottom right to open the photo as a Smart Object in Photoshop.

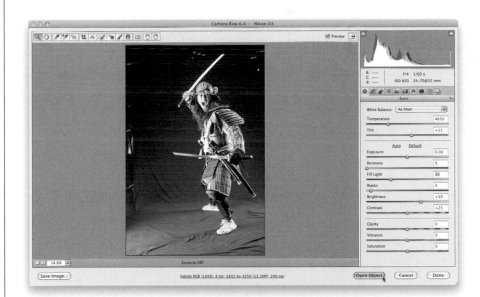

STEP THREE:

Use the Quick Selection tool **(W)** to get a rough outline selection around the samurai. You'll have to use the Left Bracket key **([)** to make the brush really small to grab the sword blade and some of the smaller details. I probably sound like a broken record if you've been reading the other tutorials in the book, but it's definitely worth spending about two minutes now to zoom in and make sure you get all of the smaller details, so you don't have to go back and do it later. Also, don't worry about the feet. We're only going to use the top half of the photo, so you can stop at his knees when selecting.

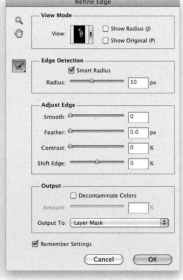

STEP FOUR:

Click the Refine Edge button in the Options Bar and, when the dialog opens, press **B** to set the View setting to black. We're putting him on a dark background, so the darker the preview we have, the better. Set the Radius to 10 and turn on the Smart Radius checkbox, so it helps even the selection around the hair and some of those edges that are harder to see. Use the Refine Radius tool and brush on his hair, just below the hand that's holding the sword up. Choose **Layer Mask** from the Output To pop-up menu, and click OK.

STEP FIVE:

Command-click (PC: Ctrl-click) on the Create a New Layer icon at the bottom of the Layers panel to create a new blank layer under our existing Smart Object layer. Go to Edit>**Fill** and set the Use pop-up menu to **Black**, so that we have a similar background to fix our selection If we need to. Then, go back and work on the layer mask with the Brush tool (**B**) set to black or white to add or remove any areas that were missed by Refine Edge. I actually got a really clean selection the first time (especially on the hair) with this image, so there's not much work to do.

STEP SIX:

Lastly, double-click on the Smart Object layer's image thumbnail to go back to Camera Raw. Bring the Fill Light setting back down to 0 and click OK. You're done with this photo now. I know there's another photo with the woman, however, that one's just going to be a faded background element in the photo, so we don't need to select anything like we did in this photo. We'll just fade it when we get to that point in the composite, and you'll never see its background.

CREATING THE COMPOSITE

Most of the composites we're creating in this book have a background and a subject, and our main goal is to put them together so they look like they were photographed together. With movie poster composites, we usually add more photos into the mix. But, as you'll see here, we use many of the same techniques we've already covered to get those photos to fit into the overall image.

STEP ONE:

First, open the castle background photo. Remember, this is already sized to our final image, so we'll make this our home base, so to speak. All of the other images we add will get moved into this one. We don't need all of the layers anymore, so choose Layer>**Flatten Image**. Then, open the selected samurai photo and, using the Move tool **(V)**, drag him onto the background, so both images are in the same document.

STEP TWO:

Go to Edit>**Free Transform** to resize the samurai, so he fits in the background. You probably won't be able to see the transform handles, so press **Command-0** (zero; **PC: Ctrl-0**) to automatically zoom out so you can. Then, press-and-hold the Shift key and click-and-drag one of the corner transform handles inward. Keep an eye on the width and height in the top Options Bar, until you reduce the size to around 80%. Press **Return (PC: Enter)** when you're done. I know it looks like I've placed him fairly high in the layout, but remember, we've got the title and credits that need to go at the bottom, so I'm just leaving some space for them.

STEP THREE:

The samurai looks too bright and too cool (he has a bluish tint) for the background we've placed him on, but since it's a Smart Object layer, it's easy to fix. Just double-click on the layer's image thumbnail to reopen the samurai in Camera Raw. Set the Exposure setting to –2.00, the Recovery to 25 to tone down some of those bright high-lights, and the Temperature setting to 5400 to warm it up a little.

STEP FOUR:

Even though we've reduced the Exposure to darken him, I still think his clothes are too bright, so click on the Adjustment Brush tool (**K**) in the top toolbar, and then set the Exposure to –0.50 and the Brightness to 10. Now, use a medium-sized brush and paint over his torso, arms, and hand at the top. Don't worry about being precise. We've already made a selection of him, so none of the spillover will affect our final image. Click OK when you're done to go back to Photoshop.

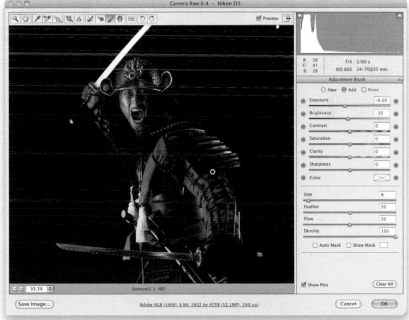

STEP FIVE:

Things are looking good, but there's one more key ingredient to making the samurai look like he was there. Sometimes, images need a common color theme to bring them all together and I think that's the case here. So, I want to show you a neat trick to let the people in the photo pick up some of the overall background and environment color. First, press **Command-Option-Shift E (PC: Ctrl-Alt-Shift-E)** to merge all of the layers together into one new layer at the top of the layer stack.

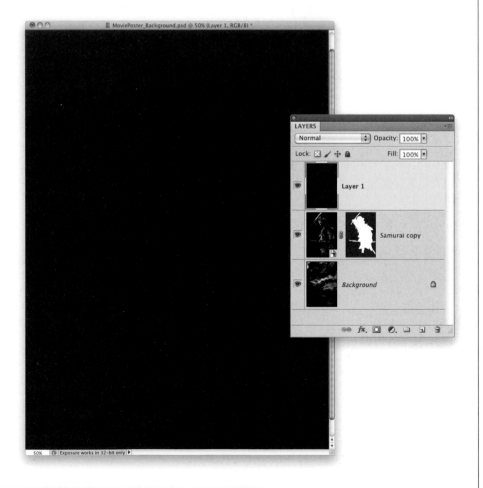

STEP SIX:

Go to Filter>Blur>**Average**. This filter doesn't have any settings, so you won't see a dialog—it'll just run automatically when you choose it. It simply picks the average color of the photo and blurs the entire photo so much that it turns into just one color (the average). So, now we can see what the overall color of our environment here is.

STEP SEVEN:

Go to Layer>**Create Clipping Mask**, which forces the blurred layer we just created to only affect the layer right below it (the samurai). Change the layer's blend mode to **Color**, to only affect the underlying color of the samurai, and set the Opacity to 20% to soften the effect. It's always hard to pinpoint what this trick does, but I'm tellin' ya, it's a great way to tie everything together if you have trouble making your subjects fit into the composite, because the color looks just a little off.

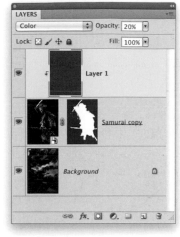

STEP EIGHT:

Next, open the photo of the two guys fighting, and using the Move tool, drag it near the bottom in the composite. Then, choose Layer>**Release Clipping Mask**.

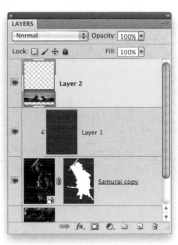

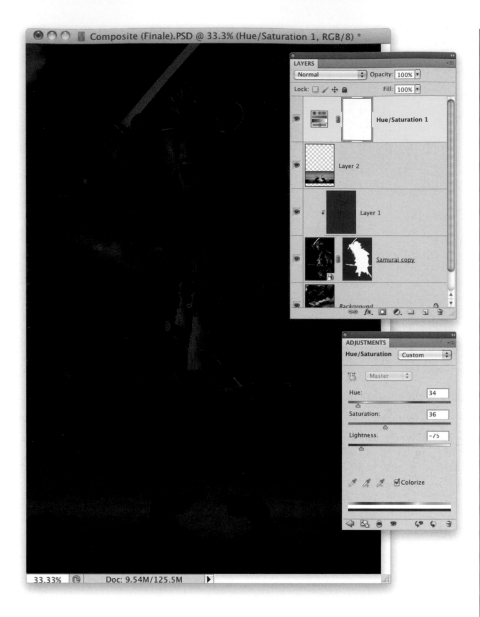

STEP NINE:

For starters, the colorful sunset in the photo doesn't fit too well with the muted warm image we're working on here. So, that's our first task. Click on the Create New Adjustment Layer icon at the bottom of the Layers panel and select **Hue/Saturation**. Then, in the Adjustments panel, turn on the Colorize checkbox, set the Hue setting to 34, the Saturation to 36, and Lightness to –75 to make it really dark. This gives the photo the same desaturated, yet warm, feeling the rest of the image has.

STEP 10:

Since the Hue/Saturation adjustment layer we just added is affecting the entire photo, go to Layer>Create Clipping Mask to force it to just affect the layer below it (the layer of the two guys fighting).

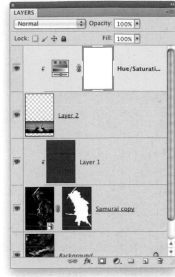

STEP 11:

You'll probably notice the photo we just added doesn't fit in too well because of the straight lines at the top and bottom of it. To fix that, we'll add a black gradient to make the transition smoother. Select the Gradient tool from the Toolbox (or just press the **G key**). Then, in the Options Bar, click on the Reflected Gradient icon (the second one from the right), then click on the down-facing arrow to the right of the gradient thumbnail, and from the Gradient Picker, choose the Foreground to Transparent gradient (the second one from the left in the top row). Finally, press **D** to set your Foreground color to black.

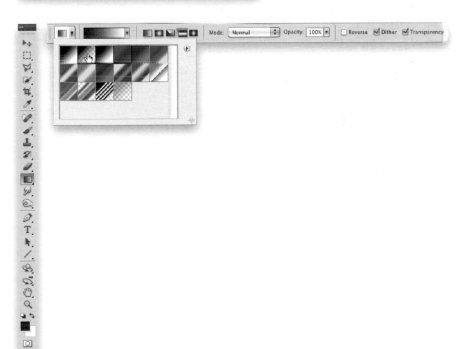

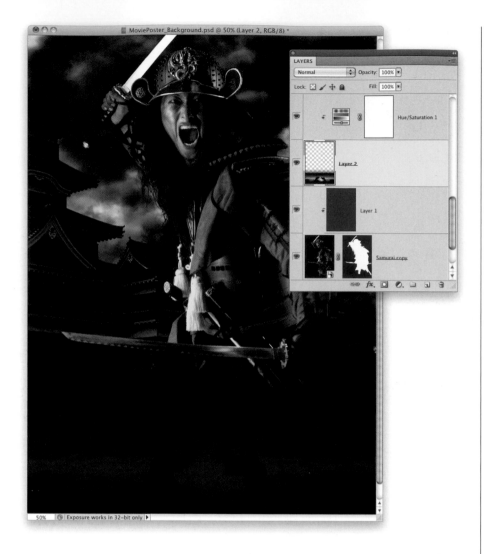

STEP 12:

Click on the layer with the two samurais fighting to target it. Then, position your cursor just above the photo and click-and-drag downward about a third of the way into the photo to create the gradient. You'll see that Photoshop starts the gradient with black, at the top where you started dragging, but then the gradient fades to transparency as it gets to where you stopped dragging. This gives us a nice way to fade the harsh edges of the photo and help it blend in with the background better. Do the same thing for the bottom of the photo to get rid of that edge, as well.

STEP 13:

Now, open the photo of the Japanese woman with the samurai. Every movie needs a love interest, right? So, using the Move tool, drag this image into the composite. Then, move the layer to the top of the layer stack, choose Layer>Release Clipping Mask, and reduce the Opacity to about 20%. Now, move her, so her face appears near the top right.

STEP 14:

Click on the Add Layer Mask icon at the bottom of the Layers panel to add a layer mask. With your Foreground color set to black, select the Brush tool **(B)**, and use a fairly large, soft-edged brush to paint on the mask to hide most of the photo. We just want her head and part of her hands to show.

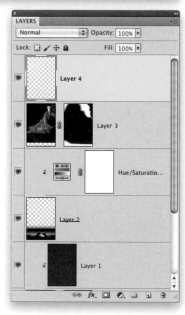

STEP 15:

It's time to add a light source. We can see that there's a light source coming from the top left area, so let's enhance it. Click on the Create a New Layer icon to create a new blank layer at the top of the Layers panel. Then, with the Brush tool still active, in the Options Bar, set the Opacity to 20%, and then press **X** to set your Foreground color to white.

STEP 16:

Use a large, soft-edged brush and just click a couple of times in the top left part of the image to add a bright wash of light. It just helps the samurai blend into the background a little and makes it actually seem like that light from the background is partly causing the light on the left side of his face. Remember, the white is on its own layer, so you can always reduce the layer's opacity if you think it's too bright.

STEP 17:

I think we can add some flare to the sword in front of him. So, create another new blank layer, then go to Edit>**Fill**, and choose **Black** from the Use pop-up menu to fill it with black. Then go to Filter>Render>**Lens Flare**. Select the 105mm Prime option, set the Brightness to 80, and click OK to apply the flare.

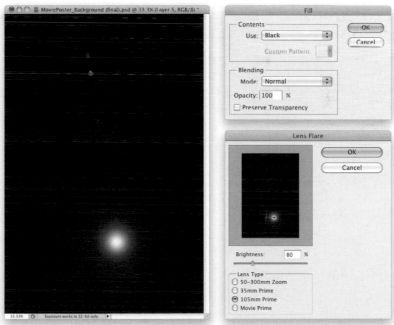

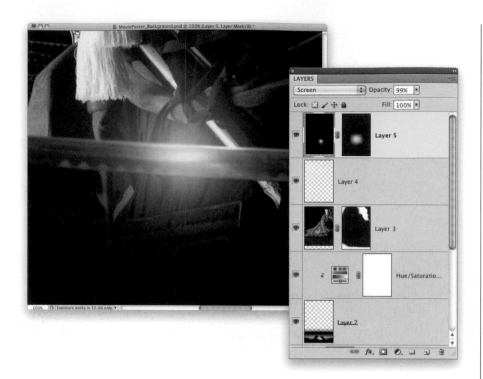

STEP 18:

Change the blend mode of the layer to **Screen** to hide the black and use the Move tool to position the lens flare right onto the sword. If the flare is too bright, **Option-click (PC: Alt-click)** on the Add Layer Mask icon to create a black layer mask, which hides the lens flare. Then, press **X** to set your Foreground color to white, and with a large, soft-edged brush set to a low opacity, paint to bring the lens flare back into the image. This will help remove some of the excess flare and brightness. You can also reduce the Opacity of the layer to tone it down a bit.

STEP 19:

Finally, we need some movie poster text. I've included the text I'm using here on its own layer on the download website for you to follow along with. Keep in mind, it's rasterized text, meaning it's not the actual non-destructive Type layers. I can't give you the Type layers, because they won't work if you don't have the fonts I used. And I can't give you the fonts, because it's illegal to distribute fonts without paying for them. So, you can use the layer in the download file, but I'll also go over what fonts I used to create them in the next steps.

STEP 20:

For the main title, I selected the Horizontal Type tool **(T)** and in the Character panel (choose Window> **Character**), I set the Font pop-up menu to **Times New Roman**. You can see that all the letters in the word "THE" are the same point size. But, for the words "FIRST SAMURAI," I typed the word first and then selected the first letter and made it a little larger than the rest of the word. I used the same font for the actors' (well, fake actors) names below the title, as well as the movie's tagline at the top of the image (and I lowered the Opacity of the tagline's layer before I merged and rasterized the text layers).

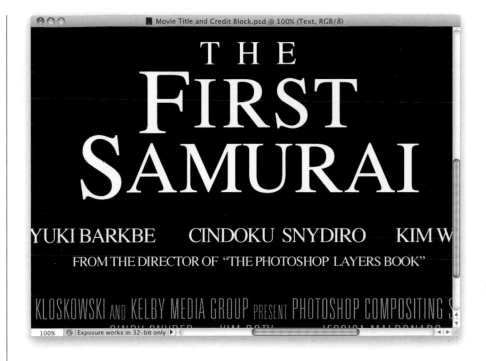

STEP 21:

For the credit block text, I used a font called Univers 39 Thin Ultra Condensed (it's available for purchase on several websites). While movie titles use hundreds of different fonts, I've found the credit blocks tend to only use a few, and Univers is one of the most popular ones. The only trick here is that the actual names of any people or companies are slightly larger than the words and titles ("AND," "DIRECTED BY," etc.) that go between them.

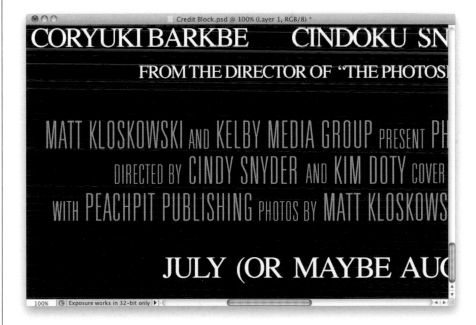

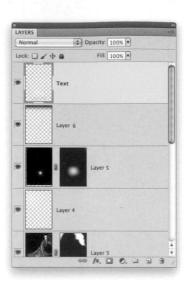

STEP 22:

Just drag the layer with the text on it into the composite image and place it at the top of the layer stack. If you press-and-hold the Shift key while dragging the layer into the document, Photoshop will automatically place it in the exact middle of the image, so it should fit right in. I also added a blank layer right below the text and used the gradient trick from Step 12 to darken the top of the image, behind the text.

STEP 23:

And, of course, we need to finish the image off with a little sharpening and extra contrast. So, press **Command-Option-Shift E (PC: Ctrl-Alt-Shift-E)** to merge all the layers into one new one at the top of the layer stack. I covered the High Pass sharpening/contrasty look you can achieve with just Photoshop at the end of Chapter 8, but my favorite way is with the Tonal Contrast filter in Color Efex Pro. I leave the settings at their defaults and usually add a layer mask afterward to paint that edgy look away from the clouds and wherever it looks too strong.

FINAL IMAGE

ULTRA-GRUNGY/EDGY HDR BACKGROUND

11

Whew! What a chapter name, huh? This one shows one of the most popular portrait compositing styles today. The style was pioneered by photographer, lighting pro, and Photoshop artist, Joel Grimes. He's a true pro when it comes to this stuff. His vision behind the camera and in the studio, along with what he can do in Photoshop, really makes him one of the best compositors out there today. Make sure you head over to his website at www.joelgrimes.com for some inspiration and training. Now, one of the common themes in Joel's composites is that many of the backgrounds he uses are HDR photos. This really takes the feeling of the image to a different level. When you combine that with the dramatic lighting and some edgy Photoshop portrait techniques, you've got the makings of a very cool-looking image.

CREATING THE BACKGROUND

The background for this style of compositing is usually really dark and grungy. There are lots of things we can do to make a photo look this way, but one of the best ways is to use the HDR feature that's right within Photoshop.

STEP ONE:

Let's take a quick look at the original parking garage photos in Bridge. HDR photos start from taking several photos of the same thing, but using different exposures. For example, you'll typically set your camera on a tripod and choose an aperture for the photo. Then, by varying shutter speeds, you're able to get over- and underexposed versions of the image. Most DSLRs have a feature called Auto Exposure Bracketing that does it automatically for us, so make sure to look up AEB in your camera's manual to see how to turn it on. When you put the images together, you get an image with a lot of detail in the shadow and highlight areas.

STEP TWO:

Let's go to Photoshop and go to File>Automate>**Merge to HDR Pro**. In the Merge to HDR Pro dialog, click the Browse button and go to the folder with the original RAW files in it. In the Open dialog, click on the top one and then Shift-click on the bottom one to select all of them, then click Open.

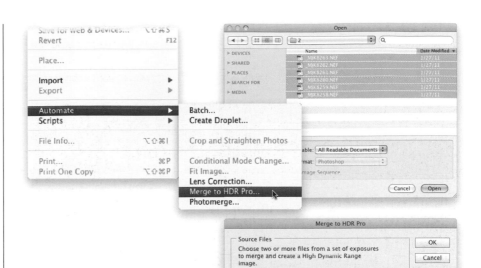

STEP THREE:

When you're back in the Merge to HDR Pro dialog, click OK to start creating the HDR image. It takes a minute or two, but when it's done, you'll see the Merge to HDR Pro settings dialog. The first thing I always do when going for the grungy look is crank the Detail setting way up to get some of that gritty effect. Then, set the Radius to 145 and the Strength to 2.05. Bring the Highlight slider all the way to the left to darken the highlights and bring the Shadow slider all the way to the right to brighten the shadow areas. Set Gamma to 0.21 and leave Exposure alone. Click OK when you're done.

STEP FOUR:
Photoshop then starts merging all of the detail from all of the various exposures to create an HDR image. When it's done, you'll see the photo open in Photoshop. At this point, it's just like any other image and you can start working on it like usual. So, first, let's fix the perspective problems we have here by going to Filter> **Lens Correction**. When the Lens Correction dialog opens, go under the Auto Correction tab on the right and turn on the Geometric Distortion checkbox. Photoshop reads the camera and lens information and automatically fixes some of the distortion problems we have.

STEP FIVE:
Then, click the Custom tab and set the Vertical Perspective setting to +7 and the Angle to 0.10. While you're at it, drag the Vignette slider to –45 and the Midpoint slider to 20 to darken the edges a little, so we don't have to do it later. Click OK when you're done.

STEP SIX:

Get the Crop tool **(C)** and crop out some of the edges, so the whole background has a more centered and symmetrical feel to it.

STEP SEVEN:

Now, we've got a pretty grungy looking background. I do think it's looking a little flat, though. So, let's add some interest and mood to the background area with a dusty smoke-like effect. Click on the Create a New Layer icon at the bottom of the Layers panel, and then press **D** to set your Foreground and Background colors to the default black and white. Then, go to Filter>Render> **Clouds**. There are no settings for this one. You'll just immediately see a black-and-white cloud-like image appear on the new layer.

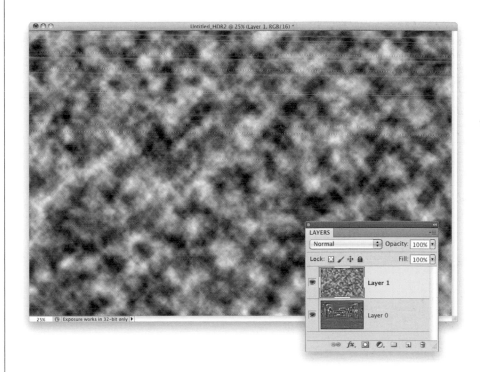

STEP EIGHT:

Change the blend mode of the layer to **Screen** to hide the black and reduce the Opacity to 70%. The effect is still a little harsh looking, though, so go to Filter> Blur>**Gaussian Blur**, set the Radius to 78 pixels, and click OK. That does a good job of softening it a bit. Now, click on the Add Layer Mask icon at the bottom of the Layers panel to add a mask to the layer. Press **B** to get the Brush tool from the Toolbox, press **X** to set your Foreground color to black, and then paint along the top and bottom of the layer mask with a large, soft-edged brush to hide the smoke effect, so it just appears in the middle.

STEP NINE:

Let's just darken the entire image before moving on. Click on the Create New Adjustment Layer icon at the bottom of the Layers panel and choose **Levels**. Drag the top black slider toward the right, until it hits the edge of the histogram where it starts climbing. Finally, go to File>**Save** and save the image as a PSD file.

SELECTING AND PREPARING THE PORTRAIT

Along with a dark and grungy background, you need someone that looks like they fit into this style of composite. So, photographing a little girl with her mom probably won't cut it. Remember, we need edgy to make this work. You'll notice our model here, Willie, is not looking happy. I deliberately used a really mean expression for this one, since we were working with a grungy-style composite. Funny thing, though, because Willie is about as nice a guy as they come, so don't hold the mean look against him. He is, however, a world champion athlete, so you don't want to mess with him.

STEP ONE:
Open the photo of the subject for this composite. Press **W** to get the Quick Selection tool and paint over him to make a selection. The only area that was hard to select here was near his upper arm and shoulder on the right side. The highlights from the flash are mixing with the bright background, so I had to zoom in and use a really small brush to get the selection right. To remove any areas from the selection, just press-and-hold the **Option (PC: Alt) key** and paint over them.

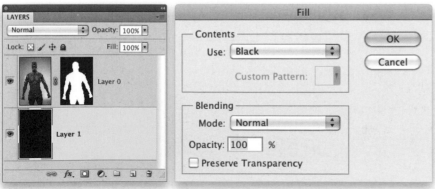

STEP TWO:
Once you've got the subject selected, click the Refine Edge button up in the Options Bar. There's not much work to do here, since we don't have any details. So, just set the Radius to 10, the Output To setting to **Layer Mask**, click OK, and it will create a layer mask for your subject.

STEP THREE:
Command-click (PC: Ctrl-click) on the Create a New Layer icon at the bottom of the Layers panel to add a new blank layer below the layer with your subject. Then, go to Edit>**Fill** and, from the Use pop-up menu, choose **Black**. Click OK to fill the bottom layer with black to give us a black background to work with.

STEP FOUR:

Right off the bat, I can see we've got a thin, bright fringe around him. So, we'll use the Defringe trick we've seen a few times throughout the book. Command-click (PC: Ctrl-click) on the layer mask to load its selection, and then click on the layer's thumbnail to target it. Press **Command-J (PC: Ctrl-J)** to copy the selected area up onto its own layer and then click on the Eye icon to the left of the layer with the mask on it to hide it for now.

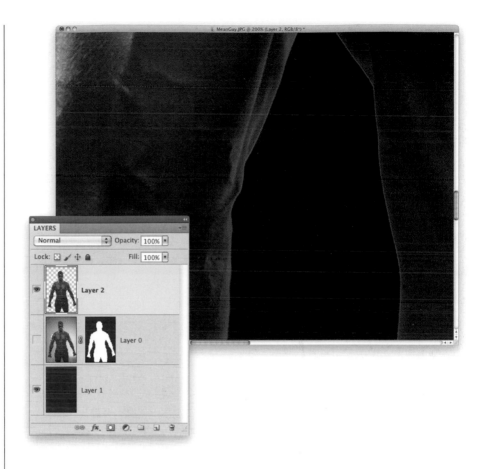

STEP FIVE:

With the top layer active, go to Layer>Matting>**Defringe**. Set the Width to 1 pixel and click OK to get rid of the bright fringe around him.

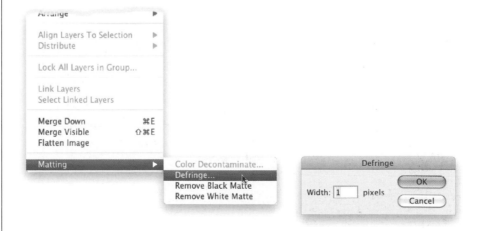

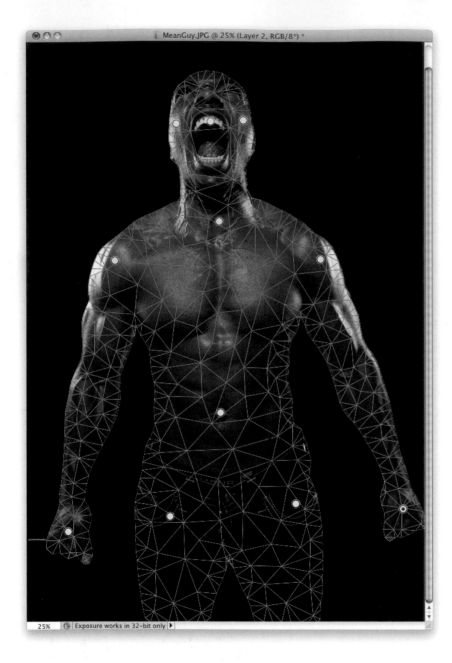

25% | Exposure works in 32–bit only ▶

STEP SIX:

Lastly, his arms look like they're just a little off balance. I wanted them to be as symmetrical as possible and they're not. No sweat, though, because we've got a tool in Photoshop CS5 called Puppet Warp that can work great for compositing. Go to Edit>**Puppet Warp** and you'll see a grid-like outline appear over the subject. First, we need to add points that will eventually serve as hinges for using Puppet Warp. I usually just click on the major joint areas or body parts, as you can see here. Each time you click, you add a point that you can eventually move.

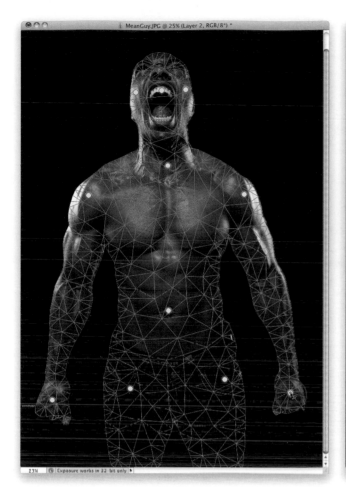

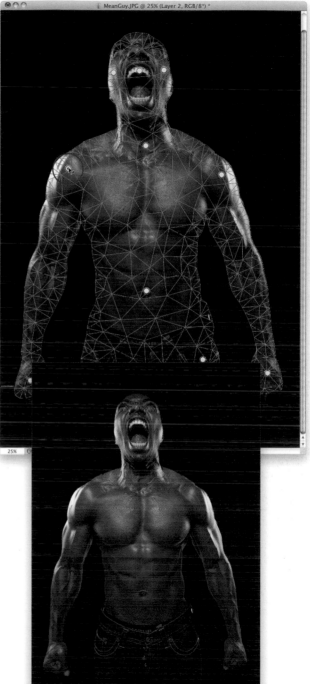

STEP SEVEN:

Once you've got all the points created, click on the point on his hand on the right to select it (circled here). Then drag it inward, so his arm appears similar to the other one. Then, click-and-drag the point on his shoulder on the left up just a little bit. When you're done, press **Return (PC: Enter)** to lock in the transformation. Pretty sweet, huh? Go to File>**Save** and save the image as a PSD before we move on.

CREATING THE COMPOSITE

Like most of the other composites, once the background and selections are done, just putting them together is easy. It's the process of "selling" the composite and making the subject look like they belong there that takes the most time. With a few adjustment layers and blend modes, though, you'll be amazed at how quickly we can pull this composite off.

STEP ONE:

Open the background image for the composite. If you didn't start with the first tutorial in this chapter, I've got the background already created for you, so you can follow along here (you can download it from the book's download site). We don't need all the layers that are there, so go to Layer>**Flatten Image** to flatten all of the layers into one. Next, open the selected photo of Willie from the last tutorial (like with the background image, I've already got him selected and available on the download site, so feel free to download that image, if you haven't already selected him). Press **V** to select the Move tool and drag him into the middle of the parking garage background.

STEP TWO:

The first thing I noticed is that he's got a very warm look to him and the background has a colder feel to it. We could go either way on this one—warm the background or cool him down a little—but I think I'd rather make the background match him. So, click on the Create New Adjustment Layer icon at the bottom of the Layers panel and choose **Photo Filter**. Use the default **Warming Filter (85)** preset and set the Density slider to 30%. Then, click-and-drag this adjustment layer between the portrait and background layers, like I have here.

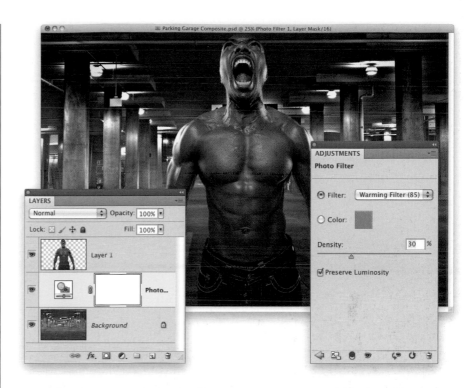

STEP THREE:

Next, we're really going to take the edginess up a notch. Click once on the portrait layer to target it, and then press **Command-J (PC: Ctrl-J)** to create a copy, so now there are two portrait layers in the Layers panel. First, we'll need to desaturate the duplicate by going to Image> Adjustments>**Desaturate**. Then, change the blend mode of the duplicate layer to **Hard Light** and reduce the Opacity to 50%.

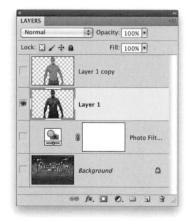

STEP FOUR:

Okay, that's a good start. His skin definitely has an edgier look to it now, but we need more. So, go to Image>Adjustments>**Shadows/ Highlights** and crank the Shadows Amount setting up to the maximum of 100. Now, you should start seeing every single vein on his body stand out. Then, start increasing the Midtone Contrast setting (under Adjustments; if you don't see all of the settings shown here, just turn on the Show More Options checkbox at the bottom of the dialog) and watch how the grit really seems to show up on his skin. Don't go too high here— increasing it to around 25 works pretty well. Click OK when you're done to apply the adjustment.

STEP FIVE:

We're getting that edgy look, but he's still too bright and saturated for the background. So, let's tackle the brightness first. There's a really cool Channels-related selection trick that'll help us target both the highlight areas and the shadow areas separately when darkening our subject. When you're compositing, it helps to be able to control both. Sometimes, the overall brightness is okay, but the highlights may be too dark. First, hide all of the layers, except for the one with the color version of the portrait on it, by **Option-clicking (PC: Alt-clicking)** on the Eye icon to the left of the color portrait layer.

STEP SIX:

Now, go to the Channels panel (Window>**Channels**) and Command-click (PC: Ctrl-click) on the RGB channel (the top one) to load its selection. Photoshop will load the luminosity, or overall brightness, of the image as a selection.

STEP SEVEN:

Go back to the Layers panel, click on the Create New Adjustment Layer icon, and choose **Curves**. In the Adjustments panel, click-and-drag the curve downward and you'll notice that the bright areas (especially the highlights on his arms and face) of the portrait become darker. But everything else stays pretty much the same. This is a great way to control those highlights once you change a person's background.

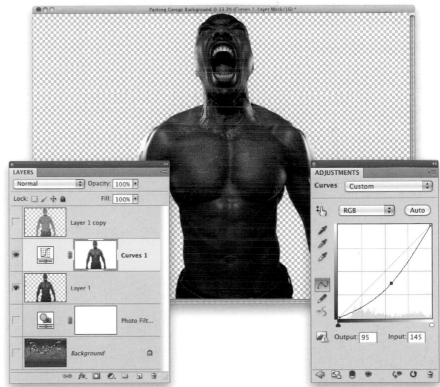

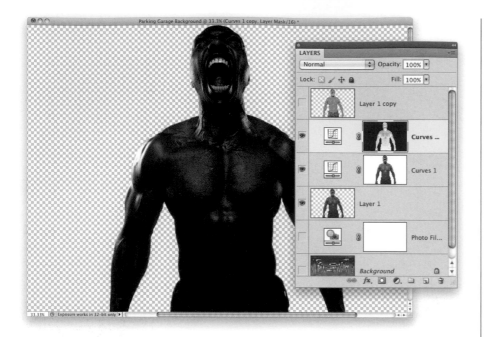

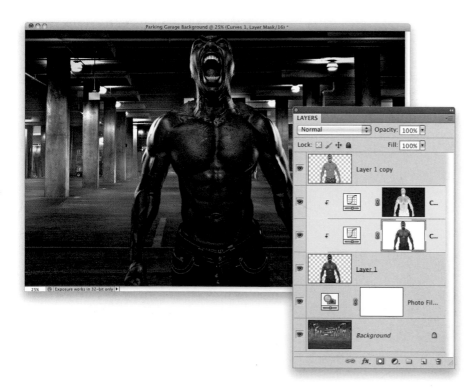

STEP EIGHT:

Press Command-J to duplicate the Curves adjustment layer, then press **Command-I (PC: Ctrl-I)** to Invert the layer mask. Whatever was being targeted by the adjustment is now reversed, and you've just given yourself a way to work specifically on the darker parts of the portrait.

Note: A question I get a lot when showing this technique is whether one simple Curves adjustment (with no mask) would have worked. It would have, but here's the deal: When you're compositing, you constantly try to get your subject to fit into the background. Having total control over their shadows and highlights, like we just did, gives you an easy way to make small (and targeted) adjustments as you work on the composite.

STEP NINE:

Go ahead and click where the Eye icons were for the hidden layers to show them again, and you'll notice that those two Curves adjustment layers we just added apply to everything below them (not just the portrait). So, with one of them targeted, Command-click (PC: Ctrl-click) on the other, and then go to Layer>**Create Clipping Mask** to force them to only apply to the portrait and not the background.

STEP 10:

Now, I still think he's a little too saturated for the photo, but that's an easy fix. Click once on the top Curves adjustment layer to target it, then click on the Create New Adjustment Layer icon and choose **Hue/Saturation**. In the Adjustments panel, reduce the Saturation to –45, then go to Layer>Create Clipping Mask, again, to force it to only affect the portrait layer below.

STEP 11:

One of the last things we need to do is add some lights to the background. You'll see there are two lights hanging from the ceiling pretty close to him, and he's got some fairly hard light on his shoulders and arms. So, let's work with that and enhance it a little. Click on the Create a New Layer icon at the bottom of the Layers panel to create a new blank layer, and then drag it to the very top of the layer stack. Press **B** to get the Brush tool from the Toolbox, and press **D**, then **X** to set your Foreground color to white. Using a medium-sized, soft-edged brush, click once on the light at the top right of the image, then press-and-hold the Shift key, and click again toward the bottom middle of the image to draw a straight (but soft) line. (*Note:* I used a Wacom pen here to create my lines, so if you're using a mouse, your lines may be wider.)

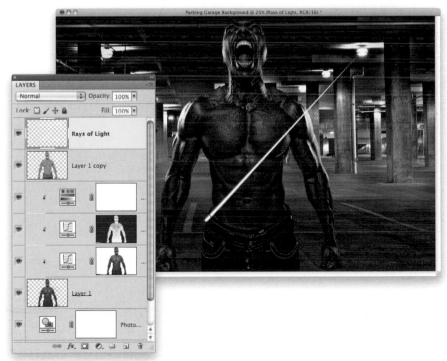

STEP 12:

Repeat this process of clicking on the light, and then Shift-clicking somewhere else near the bottom of the photo to create some fake light beams. It's okay if they're different sizes, because we want them to be a little random. And, you don't need many. Just seven or eight beams should do, as seen here.

STEP 13:

Next, go to Filter>Blur>**Gaussian Blur** and set the Radius to about 70 pixels to blur the lights. Click on the Add Layer Mask icon at the bottom of the Layers panel to add a layer mask to the layer and then, using a large, black, soft-edged brush, paint away the lights from his body and the opposite side of the image. If the light beams look too bright, just lower the Opacity of the layer.

STEP 14:

Press Command-J to duplicate the layer, then go to Edit>Transform> **Flip Horizontal** to flip the layer. Using the Move tool, move the duplicate layer over to the other side of the image, on top of the light on the left (as shown here).

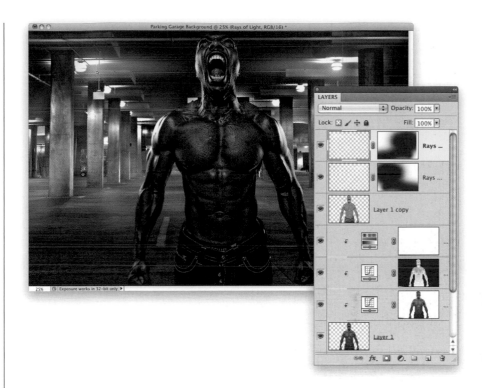

TIP: ADD SOME EXTRA GRIT

We've already got a lot of grunge here, but if you want some extra grit in the image, try using either the High Pass technique or Nik Software's Tonal Contrast filter, both of which we used at the end of Chapter 8. In the final image here, I used the Tonal Contrast filter to add some extra grit to the background.

FINAL IMAGE

FALL 2011 SPORTS

FOOTBALL

2/3	VS.	NEW YORK	7:30PM
2/10	VS.	PITTSBURGH	3:30PM
2/17	VS.	ATLANTA	7:30PM
2/24	VS.	MIAMI	3:30PM
3/1	VS.	ORLANDO	3:30PM
3/8	VS.	ALABAMA	1:30PM
3/15	VS.	PENN STATE	7:30PM
3/22	VS.	WEST MERCER	1:30PM

SOCCER

2/5	VS.	CAROLINA	7:30PM
2/12	VS.	JACKSONVILLE	3:30PM
3/17	VS.	ALABAMA	7:30PM
3/19	VS.	AKRON	3:30PM
3/26	VS.	STONY BROOK	3:30PM
4/10	VS.	SYRACUSE	1:30PM
4/14	VS.	VILLANOVA	7:30PM
5/21	VS.	RUTGERS	1:30PM

SPORTS TEMPLATE

Creating sports templates and collages is another one of those instances that compositing seems perfect for. First off, people love sports. Whether it's a young child, a high school or college student, or a professional, people love to see their favorite athletes in action. By mixing some text, team logos, and a cool texture, you've got all the makings of a season calendar, promo poster, or just about anything where you want to showcase multiple photos for a sports team or school.

12

CREATING THE BACKGROUND

We'll be creating a school's sports calendar here, and you'll see that most of the work for a composite like this is on the background. When we add the athletes in the next tutorial, you'll see that it's mostly just a quick selection and you're done. But, the background has to look cool to pull it off. You not only need to leave room for the people, but also for the logos, graphics, and any text that needs to be added. So that's where we'll start.

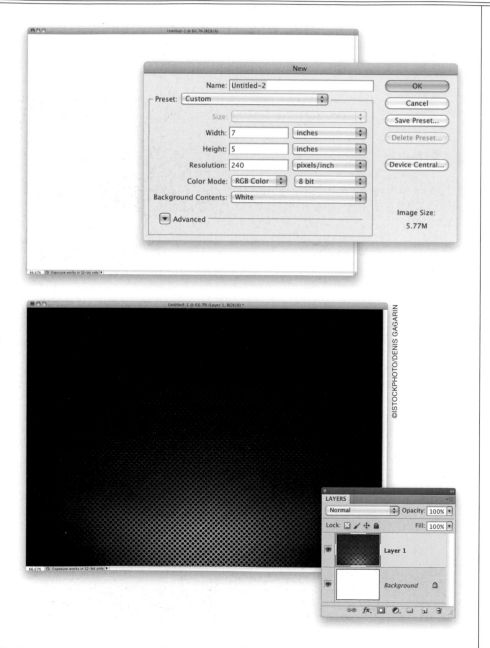

©ISTOCKPHOTO/DENIS GAGARIN

STEP ONE:
Start out by going to File>**New** and creating a new image based on the size you want your final composite to be. In this example, let's go with a 5x7 aspect ratio. Set the Width to 7 inches, the Height to 5 inches, and the Resolution to 240 ppi.

STEP TWO:
Next, open the background texture. This one is from iStockphoto (www .istockphoto.com). Just do a search for "background textures" and you'll find plenty. Once you have your background open, get the Move tool **(V)**, and click-and-drag it into the new image you just created, on top of the Background layer. Since it's larger than the image we created, press **Command-T (PC: Ctrl-T)** to go into Free Transform, and press **Command-0** (zero; **PC: Ctrl-0**) to be able to see the Free Transform handles. Click-and-drag the side or corner handles until the image is the same size as your document and then press **Return (PC: Enter)** to lock in the change. Also, we want the bright spot to be at the bottom, so go to Image> Image Rotation>**180°**.

STEP THREE:

Select the Ellipse tool from the Tool-box (it's nested with the Shape tools, but you can also press **Shift-U** until you get to it). Then, click on the Shape Layers icon up in the Options Bar (the first icon on the left). Press **D** to set your Foreground color to black and draw an ellipse at the top of the image, like you see here.

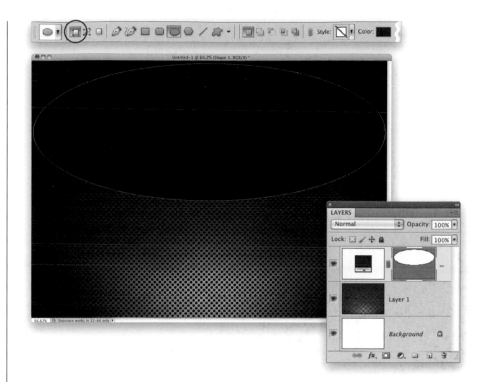

STEP FOUR:

Go back into Free Transform. Press-and-hold Option-Shift (PC: Alt-Shift) to constrain the proportions and expand from the center, click on one of the corner handles, and drag outward. You can even go past the boundaries of the document and Photoshop will still transform the shape larger, even though you can't see the handle anymore. Click-and-drag inside the Free Trans-form boundaries to move most of it out of the document, so you only see the lower part of the ellipse. When you're done, press Return to lock in the change.

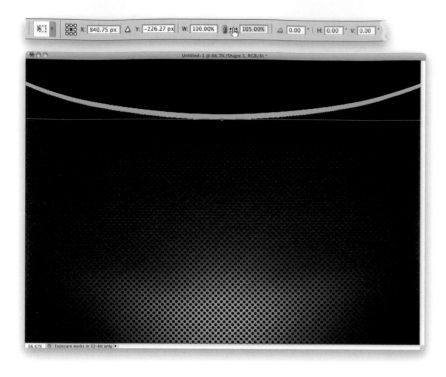

STEP FIVE:

Press **Command-J (PC: Ctrl-J)** twice to create two more copies of the ellipse layer. Double-click on the layer thumbnail on the bottom copy and, in the Color Picker, set the color to R: 201, G: 181, B: 126, and click OK. Even though you changed the color, you won't see it yet, since it's behind another Shape layer. Still working on the bottom copy, go into Free Transform again, put your cursor over the H (height) setting in the Options Bar, and use the scrubby hand icon (as seen here) to drag to the right to increase it, so just part of the shape shows through.

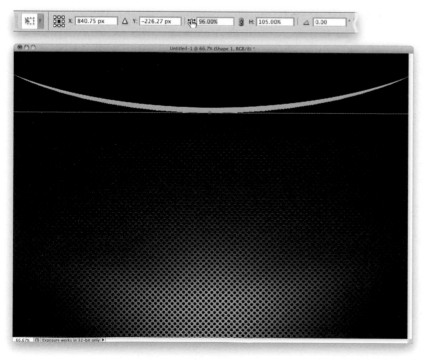

STEP SIX:

Then move over to the W (width) setting and decrease it a little, so the amount of the tan shape that shows through changes as it gets toward the center. Press Return when you're done. This created a tan outline, but the outline also changes in shape and has a much cooler look to it, since it's not perfectly symmetrical with the top shape.

STEP SEVEN:

Do the same thing with the middle layer, but this time change the color to white instead. Again, this just adds a little more depth to the overall design. I went back and re-adjusted the bottom Shape layer a little after I adjusted the middle layer, too. Those outlines really stand out when you see the final image.

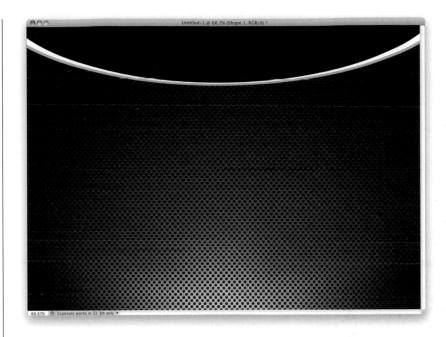

STEP EIGHT:

Click on the top copy of the ellipse to target the layer. Let's start getting the school colors on the image. Click on the Add a Layer Style icon at the bottom of the Layers panel and choose **Gradient Overlay**. Click on the Gradient thumbnail in the dialog to open the Gradient Editor. To change the color of the gradient, just double-click on the little color stops (the tiny squares) under the gradient ramp in the middle of the dialog. When the Color Picker appears, choose a semi-dark green for the left color stop, and an even darker green for the right color stop. Click OK to close the Gradient Editor.

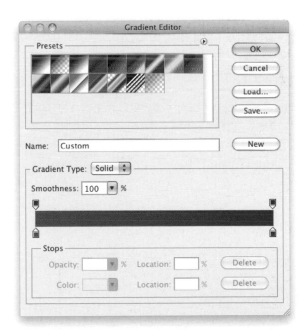

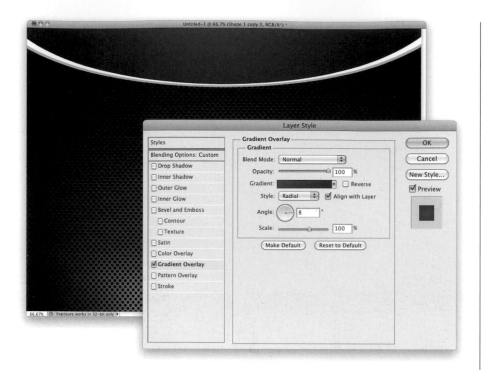

STEP NINE:

Back in the Layer Style dialog, set the Style to **Radial**, the Angle to 8°, and click OK. Now your top layer has a green gradient on it. Gradients really help add that extra dimension to your designs, which is why we rarely use just a flat color in images like this. It doesn't have to be (and it probably shouldn't be) a severe color difference in the gradient, but something subtle (like the two greens we used here) really helps add to the overall look of the image.

STEP 10:

Okay, the top is done. Click on the top shape layer in the Layers panel and Shift-click on the bottom one to select all three. Then go to Layer> **Group Layers** (or press **Command-G [PC: Ctrl-G]**) to put these into a group. Groups (which look like folders in the Layers panel) help us keep the various layers organized when the Layers panel starts to grow. Double-click on the group name and rename it something more descriptive, like I did here.

STEP 11:

Right-click on the group and choose **Duplicate Group** to make a copy, and in the Duplicate Group dialog, re-name it to something more descriptive. Then, select the Move tool and click on the duplicate group layer in the Layers panel to target it. Because we've selected the group, and not an individual layer, most things we do will affect all the layers inside. So, drag the group downward toward the bottom of the photo, like I have here. Feel free to go inside and trans-form any layers like we did in Steps Five through Seven. Now, the bottom of the image is done.

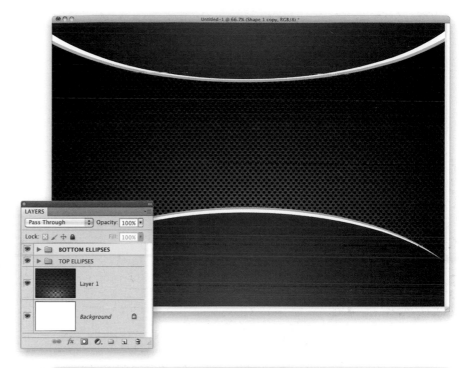

STEP 12:

Let's add some text at the top. Select the Horizontal Type tool **(T)**, press **D**, then **X** to set your Foreground color to white, and click to start typing. The font I used here is Varsity Regular (I got it for free from www .dafont.com/varsity-regular .font) set at 30 points. If you need to move the text after you type, move your cursor away from the text until you see the arrow cursor, then click-and-drag it. Press **Command-Return (PC: Ctrl-Enter)** to lock your text when you're done, then click on the Add a Layer Style icon at the bottom of the Layers panel and choose Gradient Overlay. This time, add a gradient that goes from the tan we used in Step Five on the right to a slightly darker tan on the left, then turn on the Reverse checkbox, and set the Style to **Reflected**.

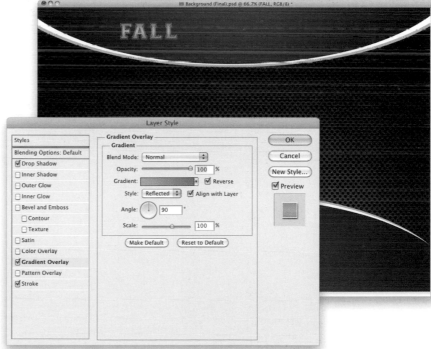

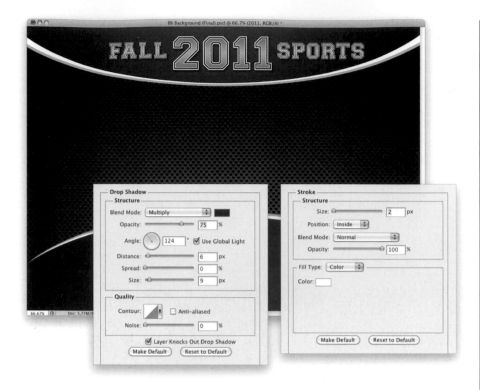

©ISTOCKPHOTO/ID-WORK

STEP 13:

While you're still in the Layer Style dialog, add a Drop Shadow layer style and a Stroke layer style to help lift the text off the background a little (you can see my settings here). Keep the stroke small, though, and make sure you set the Position to **Inside**, so it keeps the edges crisp. Click OK when you're done to close the dialog. Here, I created two more Type layers for the year and the other text. Notice I made the year a little larger (about 62 points), too. Now, **Option-click (PC: Alt-click)** on the Layer Style (*fx*) icon in the Layers panel, and drag it onto each of the other two Type layers to copy the styles to them. I also added all three Type layers to a group to keep things neat.

STEP 14:

Open the logo image and drag it into the composite in the bottom third of the image. Make sure the logo is on a layer above the group with the ellipses at the bottom. Use Free Transform to resize it, if necessary. Then, add the same Stroke layer style as you did to the text, and add a Drop Shadow layer style with the settings you see here.

STEP 15:

Finally, add some text for the dates at the bottom. The font for this text is Myriad Pro, and I used Bold for the two headers at the top (Football and Soccer) and Regular for the dates and opponents. To help keep things tidy in the Layers panel, group these Type layers together, too.

ADDING THE ATHLETES TO THE COMPOSITE

I mentioned this earlier, but adding the athletes into the composite is probably the easiest part of all this. Once your background is looking good, it's just a matter of a few selections and you're done. Now, none of these athletes were photographed in a studio. These were all taken during live games, so our backgrounds aren't nice to work with. But you'll see that the Refine Edge dialog still totally rocks here.

STEP ONE:

Open the first athlete photo. Use the Quick Selection tool **(W)** to select as much detail as you can. I say this over and over again in this book, but I think it's most important here. Make sure you spend the extra time to zoom in and get that selection as good as possible. You'll probably have to make your brush really small to get all of the edges of the uniform, the hands, helmet, etc., but because we don't have a nice clean background, we need this edge to be as close to perfect as possible. That way, when we go to Refine Edge, all we have to do there is smooth it out a little. Don't worry too much about the feet, though, because they'll be hidden.

STEP TWO:

Click the Refine Edge button up in the Options Bar, or just press **Command-Option-R (PC: Ctrl-Alt-R)**. Turn on the Smart Radius checkbox and set the Radius to 6 px. There are no stray or wispy hairs or edge details to worry about, so we don't need the Refine Radius tool for this one. However, if you were photographing female athletes or men with longer hair, then you definitely would want to make sure you use the brush to select the hair. Okay, back to our story. Set the Output To setting to **Layer Mask** and click OK when you're done.

STEP THREE:

Now, you've got the player selected from the background with a layer mask. Open the background image we created in the previous tutorial (you can download the final image if you didn't follow along) and use the Move tool **(V)** to drag the football player in and place him on the left side (I'll rename each layer as I drag it in to keep them straight). Here's the catch: we want to make sure to position this layer above the top ellipses (so his hands and head will appear above them), but below the bottom ellipses (so his feet will be hidden). Take a look at the Layers panel here to see what I mean.

STEP FOUR:

The photo is probably too large for the background, so press **Command-T (PC: Ctrl-T)** to bring up Free Transform. Because it's so much larger than the image area, you won't be able to see the Free Transform handles. So, press **Command-0** (zero; **PC: Ctrl-0**) to automatically resize the window, so you can reach all four handles (as seen here). Then just click on a corner handle, and drag it in to resize the photo. Don't forget to press-and-hold the Shift key to keep it proportional.

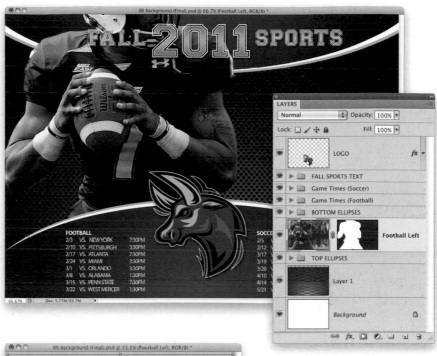

STEP FIVE:

All right, that's one photo. Do the same for the other four photos. Select the players and drag them into the final composite. Arrange them so all the players are facing toward the center of the image. I didn't have much of a fringe problem on these, but if you do, make sure you refer back to Chapter 1 to see how to get rid of it. You'll tend to have fringed edges if you have a dark uniform with a bright sky or grass behind it. One more thing: try to mix it up a little. Notice how some of the hands and heads appear over the top ellipses. That helps give some depth and an almost 3D quality to the image. Also, the photo in the middle is above everything else (I had to move the text at the top below his layer in the Layers panel, so he would appear over the text). The photos on the far right and far left come next, and all the football players are in front of the two soccer players. This helps the soccer players look like they could be the same size as the football players, but they're just farther away from them. It's important to think about those little details, because they help make the final composite look more dynamic. You can just drag the layers up and down in the layer stack once they are all in the image to see what looks best.

TIP: DOWNLOAD FILES HAVE SELECTIONS

Oh yeah, all of the download images have a hidden layer with the layer mask on it already. So they're selected for you, if you want to save time and follow along. See, I care.

STEP SIX:

Now, if you look at the soccer player on the left, his face is in shadow. We need to fix that, so click on his layer, then click on the Create New Adjustment Layer icon at the bottom of the Layers panel and choose **Levels**. In the Adjustments panel, drag the shadows (left) slider under the histogram to the right a little to 12, drag the midtones (center) slider to the left to 1.19, and drag the highlights (right) slider to the left to 209. You'll see that this also lightens everything below him, so Right-click on the layer and choose **Create Clipping Mask** to clip this adjustment to just the soccer player.

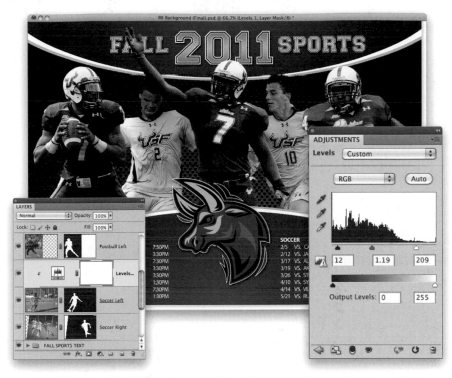

STEP SEVEN:

The only problem now is that the left side of him is too bright. So, click on the layer mask to make it active, then press **Command-I (PC: Ctrl-I)** to Invert it and hide the adjustment. Press **B** to get the Brush tool, make sure your Foreground color is set to white, and with a medium-sized, soft-edged brush, paint across the right side to bring the lightening back, until both sides match.

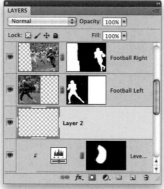

STEP EIGHT:

Okay, since the three football players are in front of the soccer players, they should be throwing a shadow on the soccer players. The way the football players are lit, you can see that the light was coming from the left side of the image, so we are going to create a shadow on the right side of the player on the left and the player in the center. Start with the player on the left by clicking on his layer, then Command-clicking (PC: Ctrl-clicking) on the Create a New Layer icon at the bottom of the Layers panel to create a new blank layer beneath him. Now, we're going to need the selection of the football player, so Command-click on the layer mask we used as his selection to bring up the selection. Because we moved the layer to the left, your selection will also include the blank right side of the layer, so grab the Rectangular Marquee tool **(M)** and, while pressing-and-holding the **Option (PC: Alt) key**, click-and-drag around that area to remove it from the selection.

STEP NINE:

With your selection in place, go to Edit>**Fill**, then choose **Black** from the Use pop-up menu, and click OK. We'll need to blur it a little, so go to Filter>Blur>**Gaussian Blur**, set the Radius to 8, and click OK. Now, since it's a shadow, we'll need to lower the layer's Opacity to fade it a bit. Here, I lowered mine to around 45%. Then, because the light (from the sun) is coming from the top left, we want to make the shadow cast down and to the right. So, go into Free Transform again, move the shadow to the right, and change its angle. Now, we don't want the shadow falling on the background, so grab the Eraser tool (E) and erase that area away. Do the same thing with the football player in the center, and make sure you rename your layers to keep them organized. The shadow next to the center player's head was a bit too dark, so I set the Eraser tool's Opacity to 10% and erased some of it away.

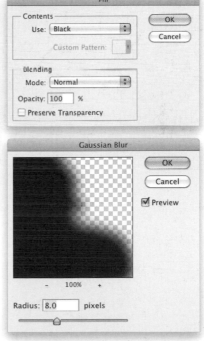

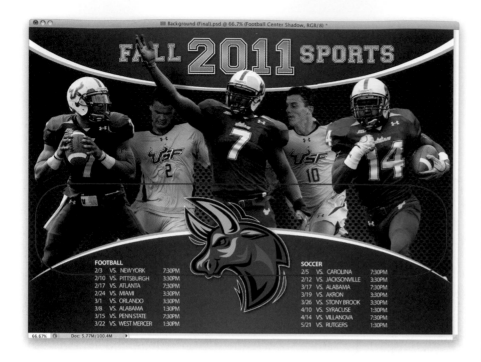

STEP 10:

There's one last little finishing effect. Notice how bright the athletes look, from top to bottom. These were all taken outdoors in the middle of the day. Well, one thing about this composite is that we don't show their feet. In fact, we want to draw people's attention away from their feet and legs as much as possible. Remember, that's one of the keys to compositing when someone's legs or feet are in the photo—take the attention away from them. Now, when someone looks at this, we don't expect they'll even think it's real, right? But anything we can do to take their focus away from the lower half of the athletes' bodies (circled here) will help.

STEP 11:

Click on whichever layer is the top athlete in the image to target it (here, it is the football player in the center). Then, click on the Create a New Layer icon at the bottom of the Layers panel to create a new layer above the athletes, but below the ellipses at the bottom, as seen here.

STEP 12:

Press **D** to set your Foreground color to black. Press **G** to get the Gradient tool, then in the Options Bar, click on the down-facing arrow to the right of the gradient thumbnail to bring up the Gradient Picker. Click on the second gradient from the left in the top row (Foreground to Transparent), and then make sure you have the Linear Gradient icon selected (the first icon on the left). Now, click-and-drag from the bottom of the image upward to about halfway from the top to create a gradient that's black, but fades to transparent. You'll see it darkens the lower part of the bodies. If it doesn't look right, press **Command-Z (PC: Ctrl-Z)** to Undo, and try again. Remember, you just want to darken the lower part of their bodies, but the gradient shouldn't go much higher than their waists. And, because the gradient layer is below the bottom ellipse layers, they look the same—we're only darkening the athletes.

STEP 13:

Now, this made the football player on the left really dark. In fact, he's too dark. So, let's add a layer mask and mask him out. Bring back his selection again, and remove the right side of the layer from the selection like we did in Step Eight. Then, **Option-click (PC: Alt-click)** on the Add Layer Mask icon at the bottom of the Layers panel to mask just that selection. The edges of his pants are a little bright, so just grab the Brush tool, and with your Foreground color set to white, brush over those edges.

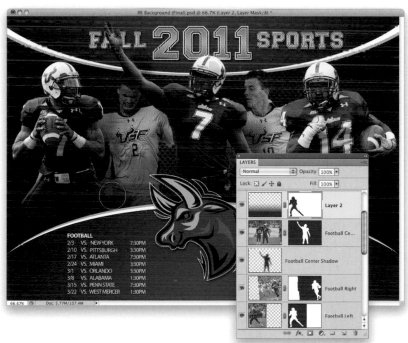

FINAL IMAGE

The single-photo composite is a great idea when you only have one photo to work with, but you want it to look like there's more going on in the image. You'll see this used a lot with sports photos, but I've also seen it used with regular portraits and even product ads. The idea is to make a copy of your original photo, make it way bigger, and fade it into the background. Because it's faded, most people don't really pay attention to the fact that it's the same photo. Let's take a look.

SINGLE-PHOTO COMPOSITE

The beauty of this tutorial is its simplicity. Once you have a nice background to use, all you need is one photo. That's it. With some creative use of multiple layers, blend modes, layer styles, and some text, you'll have a catchy sports collage in no time flat.

STEP ONE:
Open the background photo. I'm using a texture downloaded from iStockphoto (www.istockphoto.com), here. I found it by searching for "background texture." If you're into compositing, though, definitely keep your camera (it can even be a point-and-shoot camera) with you whenever you can. As you come across a cool-looking texture on a wall or floor, just grab a quick photo of it and start building your own background image library.

STEP TWO:
Click on the Create New Adjustment Layer icon at the bottom of the Layers panel and select **Hue/Saturation**. In the Adjustments panel, turn on the Colorize checkbox and then set the Hue to 49 and the Saturation to 8 to remove most of the color. By the way, this step is totally adjustable, depending on your background photo—sometimes it may work to leave more color in the photo and sometimes you'll want to add color saturation. It really depends on the image, but in this example, I was trying to match the background with the pale gold color in the uniform of the faded version of the football player we'll be placing here.

STEP THREE:

Open the photo of the football player now. Press **W** to get the Quick Selection tool and make a selection of the football player. The busier the background, the more important it is to get a good selection here. So, zoom in on his helmet and his hand carrying the ball, and make sure you have everything selected. Press-and-hold the **Option (PC: Alt) key** and paint to remove anything you don't want included in the selection.

STEP FOUR:

Press the Refine Edge button up in the Options Bar. If you spent the time to create a good selection in the previous step, then there's not much to do here. We don't have any hair or many tiny details, so the Refine Radius tool won't help much. Just set the Radius to 5 pixels and everything should be looking pretty good, then choose **Layer Mask** from the Output To pop-up menu, and click OK.

STEP FIVE:

Press **V** to get the Move tool and then click-and-drag the football player onto the background image. You'll see the entire layer, with the layer mask, show up in the background image now. The photo is too large for the background, though, so go to Edit> **Free Transform**. But, because it's so much larger than the image area, you won't see the Free Transform handles, so press **Command-0** (zero; **PC: Ctrl-0**) to automatically resize the window, so you can reach the handles. Then, press-and-hold the Shift key, and just click on a corner handle and drag inward to resize the photo. I dragged until the width and height settings in the Options Bar were about 80%. Press **Return (PC: Enter)** when you're done to lock in the transformation, and then position the player in the center of the background.

STEP SIX:

Press **Command-J (PC: Ctrl-J)** to duplicate the football player layer. We want to make the bottom copy really large and fade it into the background, so click on it in the Layers panel to target it, and then go to Edit>Free Transform, again. It's going to be hard to use the transform handles to enlarge this as much as we want. So, instead, click on the Maintain Aspect Ratio icon in the Options Bar (the little chain link icon in between the width and height fields), then enter 200% for the width and the height will automatically change, too. Move the photo over to the left a little and press Return when you're done.

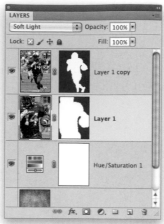

STEP SEVEN:

The larger photo in the background is supposed to play less of a role in this image, so we need to fade it. Try changing the blend mode of the layer to **Soft Light**, and now the photo fades into the background and even picks up some of the background texture. That said, Soft Light worked in this example, but it's not always going to be the one. Sometimes Overlay will work. Give Multiply, Screen, and Hard Light a try, too. It really depends on the brightness and color of the original background.

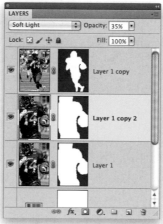

STEP EIGHT:

I think the football player is faded a little too much into the background, so we're losing too much detail. Just press Command-J to duplicate the layer and you'll instantly see the photo better. But, now it's too colorful. Remember, it's not supposed to draw a lot of attention. So, first, go to Image>Adjustments>**Desaturate** to remove the color. That gives it more of a muted look. Then reduce the Opacity of the layer (30%–40% works well here).

STEP NINE:

Click on the Create New Adjustment Layer icon at the bottom of the Layers panel again, and add another Hue/Saturation adjustment layer. In the Adjustments panel, set the Saturation to –30 and the Lightness to 40, then go to Layer>**Create Clipping Mask** to force the adjustment to only affect the layer right below it. This tones down the background image just a little more, but more importantly, it gives us a lot of options. The way your photo looks may be way different than mine, depending on the background and athlete you used. This adjustment lets us really refine the way the background copy appears, because you can add more or less color and brighten or darken it with just a couple of sliders.

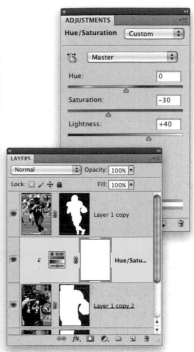

STEP 10:

Now for a couple of finishing touches: First, we need some text, so click on the top layer in the layer stack, then press **T** to get the Horizontal Type tool from the Toolbox. Press **D**, then **X** to set your Foreground color to white. Type the player's name and number in the lower-left corner. I used Futura Bold here, at around 118 points, but any bold font (maybe even Arial Black) will work. Also, as you can see, because of the way the player is running, the text fits better in the bottom-left corner. You may need to reposition it if your subject looks different.

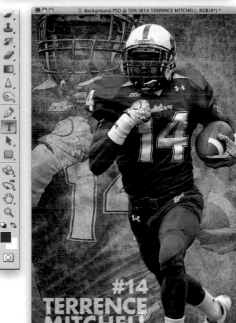

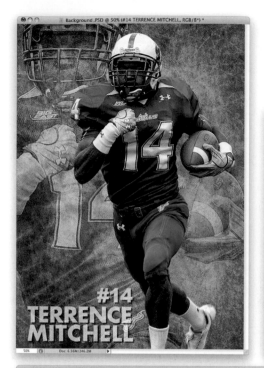

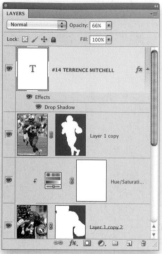

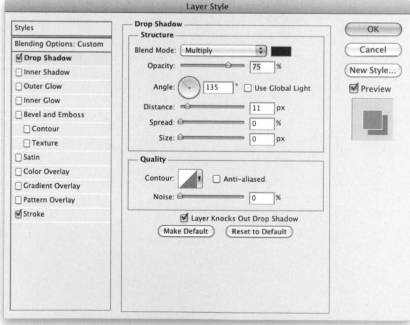

STEP 11:

Next, click on the Add a Layer Style icon at the bottom of the Layers panel, select **Drop Shadow**, and add a very slight drop shadow to help lift the text from the background. I set the Angle to 135°, the Distance to 11, and the Size to 0 (to make the edge more crisp). Click OK when you're done, and then lower the Opacity of the Type layer a bit.

STEP 12:

Finally, let's darken the edges of the composite a little. Press **Command-Option-Shift-E (PC: Ctrl-Alt-Shift-E)** to merge all of the layers together into one new layer at the top of the Layers panel. Get the Burn tool from the Toolbox (or just press **Shift-O** until you have it) and, in the Options Bar, set the Range to **Midtones** and the Exposure to 15%. Then, using a large, soft-edged brush, paint around the edges of the image to burn them in. Edge vignetting is always a nice finishing effect and really helps draw attention into the middle of the image. By using a brush, you can control exactly what you paint over to darken. For example, you don't want to paint over the football player's head at the top center.

Okay, so that wraps up the sports composite, but check out the next two tutorials for some optional ideas to change it up a little.

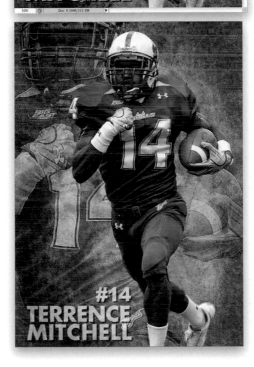

PHOTOSHOP COMPOSITING SECRETS

SINGLE-PHOTO COMPOSITE OPTIONAL TRICK #1

The first option is to put a glow around the smaller version of the football player. This is an old compositing trick to help hide any stray edges or fringes around the subject. I think our selection went really well, so we don't have that problem, but it's still a great way to add some depth to the image.

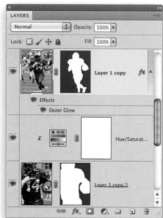

STEP ONE:

Click on the smaller version of the player layer to target it and then click on the Add a Layer Style icon at the bottom of the Layers panel and choose **Outer Glow**. You can go two ways with this: First, you can leave the default color set to yellow and just increase the Size setting to around 25 and reduce the Opacity to 50%–60%.

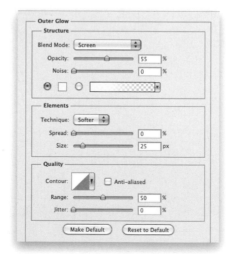

STEP TWO:

Or, you can click on the color swatch and change the color from yellow to black, change the Blend Mode to **Multiply**, increase the Size, and decrease the Opacity. This puts a dark shadowy outline behind him. I kinda like the dark one better here, but both will work, depending on the background. For a darker background, I'd go with the brighter glow. For a brighter background like this one, I'd stick with something darker.

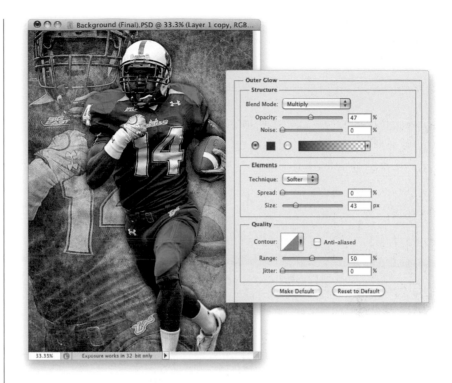

STEP THREE:

If you zoom in, though, you'll see there is a bright fringe around the football player that we didn't see earlier, because he's on a brighter colored background. But when you put the dark outer glow around him, it stands out a little more. I showed you how to get rid of this in Chapter 1. First, we need to copy him from the layer with the layer mask, so Command-click (PC: Ctrl-click) on the layer mask to put a selection around him. Then, click on the layer's image thumbnail to target it and press **Command-J (PC: Ctrl-J)** to copy the selected area (the football player) onto his own layer.

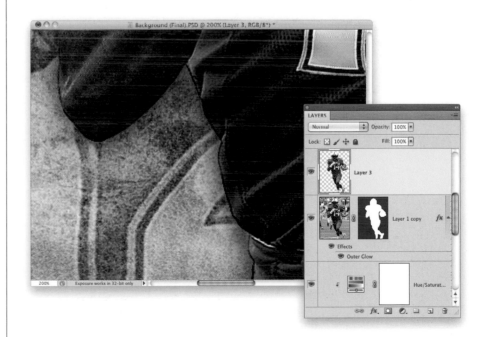

STEP FOUR:

Click on the little Eye icon to the left of the original layer with the layer mask to hide it. Then go to Layer>Matting>**Defringe**, enter 1 pixel, and click OK to remove the bright fringe. Then **Option-click (PC: Alt-click)** on the Outer Glow layer style icon on the hidden layer below and drag it onto the newly defringed layer of the football player.

SINGLE-PHOTO COMPOSITE OPTIONAL TRICK #2

One more optional trick for this type of composite is to add another texture or pattern over the background. Especially when you selectively include it in just parts of the photo, it's a really nice way to finish things off.

STEP ONE:

Open the hexagon pattern image. You'll see the pattern is on its own layer, so using the Move tool **(V)**, drag it into the composite and position it in between the top copy of the football player and the Hue/Saturation adjustment layer that's on top of the larger versions of him for the background.

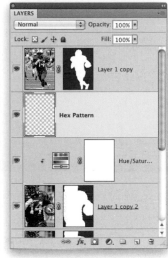

STEP TWO:

The pattern is black right now, so let's flip it to white, which will work better here. Press **Command-I (PC: Ctrl-I)** to Invert the layer from black to white. Then, change the layer's blend mode to **Overlay** to fade the texture into the background some more.

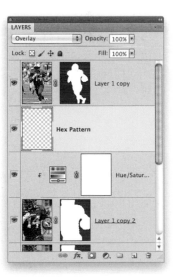

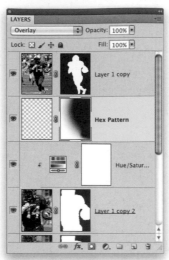

STEP THREE:

It also helps to randomize where the hexagon texture appears, so it's not over the entire background. Click on the Add Layer Mask icon at the bottom of the Layers panel, press **B** to select the Brush tool from the Toolbox, and then make sure your Foreground color is set to black. Use a pretty large, soft-edged brush to paint the hexagon texture away from the upper- and lower-right parts of the photo, so it only appears over the larger version of the football player in the background.

FINAL IMAGE

#14
TERRENCE
MITCHELL

I was in my office one day, working on this book, and my good friend RC Concepcion had a photo shoot going on in the studio right down the hall. As fate would have it, I was in the process of working on some ideas for this very chapter, when I decided to stop in on his shoot (and procrastinate). RC was shooting a very talented dancer, Ricky Jaime, and as soon as I walked in, he showed me some photos on his computer. Wow! This guy was incredible. He seemed to float in the air. As I saw more photos, I realized they would work perfectly for this chapter, so I asked (okay, begged) RC to let me use the photos here. Thankfully, he **was** cool with it. The idea here is that you're taking photos of just one person, but you're compositing them together in different poses. The final image has a strong impact, and is a perfect way to show off those times when you have several great photos of someone and you just can't decide which one to use.

RAFAEL CONCEPCION

THE SETUP

I'm all for using Photoshop to help create my composites. So much so, you're reading an entire book on it, right? But there are times where thinking ahead and shooting something the right way (while thinking about using Photoshop later) is just as good a compositing tool as Photoshop itself. This is a perfect example. The setup for this composite makes the Photoshop work nearly non-existent.

STEP ONE:

First off, you need a great subject doing something cool, different, fun, cute, whatever. But they just can't be standing there doing nothing. These dancer photos are perfect. There's lots of movement and they have a very dynamic look to them. But, it could just as easily be a martial artist, a football player, or even a child.

STEP TWO:

In fact, here are a few photos taken of some children on the same background. You can see the direction this is going, with the letters they're holding. We'll talk more about this one later in the chapter at the end of the compositing tutorial. I'll show you a couple of different ways we can go with this type of composite.

STEP THREE:

The lighting setup is similar to some of the other setups in the book: a beauty dish in front as the main light, and two strip bank softboxes with grids on the sides. Here's the absolute key, though: there's a light pointed at the background here to turn it white. This way, we don't need a new background for them later in Photoshop. They're already on the background we want. This makes the time you spend on compositing a fraction of what you'd spend if you had to place them on a different background.

STEP FOUR:

Just a quick side note: You don't have to shoot everything on white. The composite could just as easily have a black background, and it would work exactly the same.

RAFAEL CONCEPCION

STEP FIVE:

Finally, you'll want to have the subject stand in the same general location and you'll want to stay put, too. I tend to use a piece of tape on the ground (circled here). If either of you move closer or farther away, you'll lose the correct height perspective. One photo will be larger than the other depending on which way you moved. It's not the end of the world, though. We always have Free Transform in Photoshop to re-size a photo, but again, I'm trying to save you some time later and this step is key to doing that.

CREATING THE COMPOSITE

Once you've got the photos, creating the multiple-pose composite is simple. In fact, this will probably be one of the easiest we create in the book, mainly because we really don't have to worry about selections, backgrounds, or lighting. All that stuff is already done.

STEP ONE:

In Photoshop, we'll need to get all of the images of the dancer into one document. There's always the hard way, which is opening each photo and dragging them individually into one image. But Photoshop's got a much easier way built in. Go to File> Scripts>**Load Files into Stack**. This opens the Load Layers dialog. Click on the Browse button and navigate to the photo series that you've captured, or just follow along by downloading the ones I'm using here. When you get to the Open dialog, click on the topmost photo and then Shift-click on the bottom one to select them all.

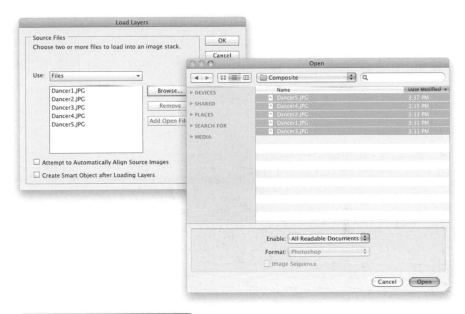

STEP TWO:

When you've got all of the photos selected, click the Open (PC: OK) button to go back to the Load Layers dialog. Then, click OK to start stacking them. When it's done, you'll have a new image open with several layers in the Layers panel.

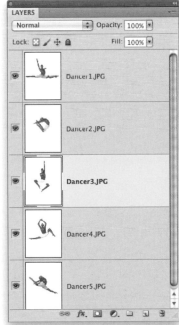

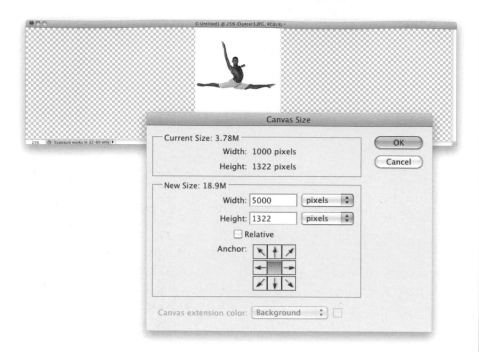

STEP THREE:

Before we go any further, we need to make room for all of the photos. Go to Image>**Canvas Size** and change the unit of measurement to **Pixels**. Since we have five photos, we need to make the width of the image five times as wide. So, in this example, the Current Size Width reads 1000 pixels. Multiply that by 5 and you've got 5000 pixels (I always did well in math). So, type 5000 pixels in the New Size Width field, click OK, and Photoshop automatically adds some extra background area.

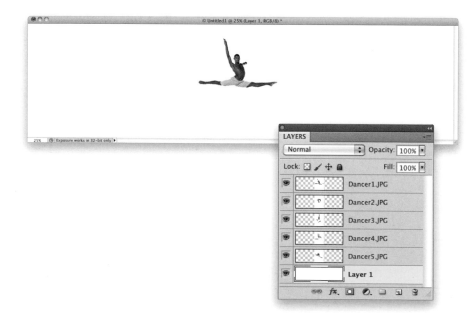

STEP FOUR:

You'll notice that part of the background is transparent now. We need it to be white. Click on the Create a New Layer icon at the bottom of the Layers panel to create a new blank layer. Then, drag the layer so it appears at the very bottom of the layer stack. Go to Edit>**Fill** and change the Use setting to **White**. Click OK, and now you'll have a white background for the entire image.

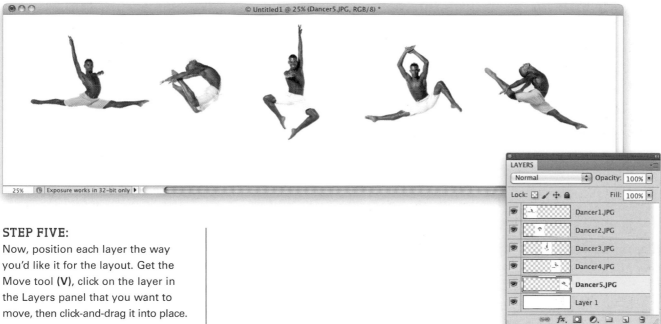

STEP FIVE:

Now, position each layer the way you'd like it for the layout. Get the Move tool **(V)**, click on the layer in the Layers panel that you want to move, then click-and-drag it into place. (*Note:* Press-and-hold the Shift key while dragging to move them along the same horizontal line.) I already have them in numeric order if you're following along, so start with Dancer1, then Dancer2 next, then Dancer3, and so on. As long as you don't put them too close together or overlap any photos, you shouldn't have to do any masking right now (we'll talk more about that in a minute). This is actually one of the most important parts, because there is some strategy to it. First, I always take a look at the photos and see which one would be a good focal point. That photo should go in the middle. The rest of the positioning kinda becomes an art form. I played with several different layouts before I found this combination and I think it works well, since some of the angles in the body of one pose complement the angles of the body in the pose next to it.

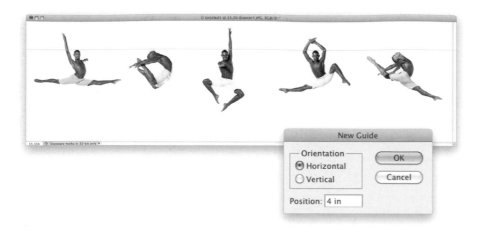

STEP SIX:

The other thing you'll want to be careful of is to make sure the heads are all on the same level. So, we'll use Photoshop's guide feature. Go to View>**New Guide**. Click on the Horizontal radio button, enter 4 inches as a starting position, and click OK to create the guide. You'll see a cyan-colored horizontal guide appear across your image. Chances are it's not in the right place, though. With the Move tool still active, position your cursor over the guide. Then, just click-and-drag it so it's directly over the head in the middle. Then, reposition each layer, so all of the heads appear right below the guide.

TIP: CLEARING THE GUIDES

Once you're done with the guide, you can go to the View menu and choose **Clear Guides** to get rid of it.

STEP SEVEN:

Okay, you could be done here. Notice I said "could," right? All that's really left is to crop the extra space out of the image. So, just grab the Crop tool **(C)** and drag the cropping border out over the image to crop it, as shown here. So, why'd I say "could" earlier? Well, I think the layout looks cool, but it's a little too plain for me. Each pose is separate and in its own space, so to speak. None of them intersect, or even come close to intersecting, with each other. When you're creating a composite like this, I think it significantly improves the final image to bring them all closer together, and even have them appear as if they were in the same frame.

STEP EIGHT:

Let's start at the left side. Click on the Dancer1 layer, where he's doing a split in the air (wow!), to target it. Then, using the Move tool, while pressing-and-holding the Shift key, move it to the right, closer to the next photo. Eventually you're going to see the white background from the Dancer1 layer (which is on top) overlap on the layer below it (the Dancer2 layer). That's the problem we run into when we start moving the photos closer to each other.

STEP NINE:

The fix is simple. With the Dancer1 layer still targeted, click on the Add Layer Mask icon at the bottom of the Layers panel to add a layer mask. Press **D**, then **X** to set your Foreground color to black, get the Brush tool **(B)**, and paint with a small, soft-edged brush on the mask to hide the white background, so we can see his feet from the Dancer2 photo. Since the actual body parts don't overlap each other, the masking should be pretty painless. You'll be able to get away with some simple and quick brushing to hide the background, and you shouldn't have to get really detailed just yet.

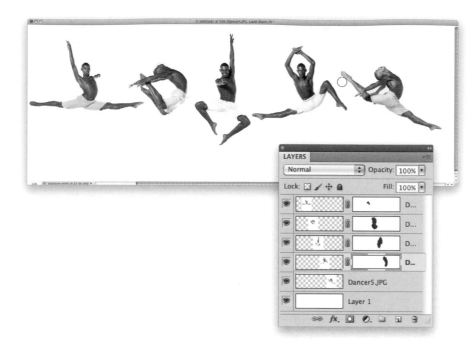

STEP 10:
Go ahead and work through the other layers to bring them closer to each other and add layer masks to paint away the background. To me, this final image looks *way* better than the original one. Instead of five individual photos, it now looks like we have five poses that flow together.

STEP 11:
One more idea for this example is that you could move them so close to each other that they actually overlap. Personally, I don't think it works very well here. To me, each dance move deserves its own space and intersecting with another photo makes it look cluttered. But, it does have its place, so I at least want to show you how to do it. Try moving the Dancer1 layer over toward the right even more, so that his foot actually intersects with the second pose. Because the Dancer1 layer is above the Dancer2 layer, the white background from the topmost layer will start to show up again.

STEP 12:

With the Dancer1 layer still targeted, use the Quick Selection tool **(W)** to make a selection of the dancer. Click the Refine Edge button to open the Refine Edge dialog. Since he contrasts so well with the background, this one is simple. Set the Radius to 5 pixels to pick up any tiny details on the edges. Set the Output Io setting to **Layer Mask** and click OK. Now, you should be able to see that his leg in the pose on the far left goes in front of the pose that's second from the left. For some images, it may work, but for something as artistic as dance, I think it takes something away from the photo and makes it appear too cluttered.

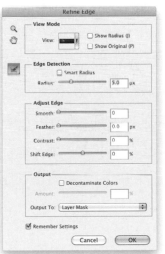

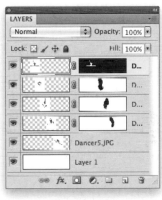

ALTERNATE IDEA #1:

Here's an alternate idea using something different than dance. I totally understand that not everyone is shooting dancers jumping in the air. These photos were taken in the studio, using the same setup as the dancer photos. The subject is just a little different, though. So, even if you're not photographing dancers, but doing family portraits instead, you can still create a similar composite that parents (and kids) will love.

ALTERNATE IDEA #2:

With some pre-planning and a couple of props bought at a local crafts store, you've got another alternative. It's the same studio setup as before and I created the MOM and DAD versions for Mother's Day and Father's Day. But, you could just as easily use the child's name, or maybe a favorite sports team.

FINAL IMAGE

I first thought of the idea for this composite from watching a Mountain Dew commercial. It was, of course, a video of a skateboarder jumping various obstacles, but what I really thought was cool was that there were these illustrative streaks and shapes following him. That's when I first got the idea of mixing a real photo with fake shapes. Shapes we know couldn't possibly be there in real life, but still look cool anyway.

EXTENDING THE BACKGROUND

My idea for this composite had more of a wide-angle view. I wanted it to look like the skateboarder had moved a good distance into the photo with the illustrative graphics following him. In order to do that, we have to widen the background a little first.

STEP ONE:

Open the background photo. In this example, the background image plays a larger part in our final image, since it has the skateboarder in it.

STEP TWO:

Select the Rectangular Marquee tool from the Toolbox (or just press **M**), and then, starting in the upper-left corner of the image, click-and-drag down and to the right to create a rectangular selection similar to the one you see here. Then, press **Command-J (PC: Ctrl-J)** to copy the selected area onto its own layer.

STEP THREE:

Grab the Move tool (**V**), then press-and-hold the Shift key and drag the new layer over toward the left side of the image (holding the Shift key keeps the layer aligned, so you don't accidentally drag it up or down). Keep dragging it until you can just barely see the edge of it (as shown here).

STEP FOUR:

Since you dragged most of the copied area outside the edge of the image window, you can't see it anymore. So, go to Image>**Reveal All** and Photoshop will automatically extend the canvas to show the copied selection.

STEP FIVE:

At this point, we're not concerned with the background behind the skater—we're going to replace that in the next tutorial. What we do need to fix here is the sidewalk, so the perspective looks right. So, go to Edit>Transform>**Skew**. Then click-and-drag the top-middle transform handle to the right, until the sidewalk matches the perspective of the left edge of the original sidewalk. Press **Return (PC: Enter)** when you're done to lock in the change.

STEP SIX:

Click on the Add Layer Mask icon at the bottom of the Layers panel to create a layer mask. Then, press **B** to get the Brush tool from the Toolbox and, with your Foreground color set to black, use a medium-sized, soft-edged brush to paint away the duplicate background over the skater's arm near the top of the image. Also, paint on the layer mask with black to hide the seam at the bottom on the sidewalk (I lowered my brush's Opacity setting in the Options Bar a bit and gradually painted this area away).

STEP SEVEN:

We need to extend the sidewalk just a little more, so press Command-J to duplicate the layer we've been working on. Then, switch back to the Move tool and move that copy over toward the left as far as you can, while still making sure the sidewalk looks okay and no seams are showing. Again, don't worry about the wall; we're going to cover that up later.

STEP EIGHT:

Let's merge everything together now by pressing **Command-Option-Shift-E (PC: Ctrl-Alt-Shift-E)** to create a new merged layer at the top of the layer stack, while keeping all of the layers below still there. Then, press **J** to select the Spot Healing Brush from the Toolbox, make sure the Content-Aware radio button is turned on up in the Options Bar, and use a small brush to paint away the two duplicate cast shadows on the sidewalk (as shown here). Zoom in and try to just paint over the actual shadow without spilling over on the rest of the sidewalk or rocks. Also, don't kill yourself to make this perfect. We're going to darken this area in the next tutorial, so you'll never really see much of the sidewalk when it's all done. Finally, go to File>**Save** and save the image as a PSD file.

CREATING THE COMPOSITE

The main idea for this composite is that we'll have these cool swirl shapes following the skateboarder. Since the background image is also our main photo for the composite, our work mostly involves making a good selection of the skateboarder and replacing the texture behind him. Once we have that done, we're free to add all the shapes and graphics we need (you'll see that I recorded a video about using the Pen tool to add these shapes when you get to that part).

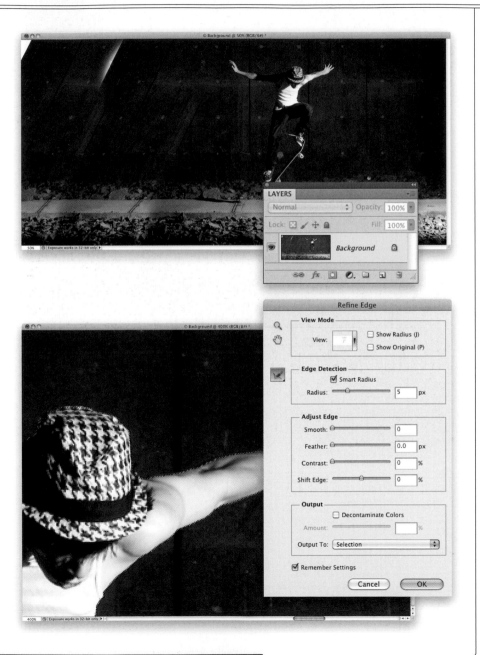

STEP ONE:
Open the extended background we created in the last tutorial (in case you didn't follow along with the last tutorial, you can download the finished background from the book's companion website and pick up right at this point). For starters, we don't need all of the layers anymore, so go to Layer>**Flatten Image**, so you're left with just the Background layer.

STEP TWO:
Using the Quick Selection tool **(W)**, paint a selection on the skateboarder and his skateboard. He's got a lot of tiny little details, so you'll need to zoom in pretty tight here and use a small brush to paint in the details. Press-and-hold the **Option (PC: Alt) key** while painting to remove any areas that you don't want selected. When you've got the skater selected, click on the Refine Edge button in the Options Bar, then in the Refine Edge dialog, set the Radius to 5 pixels, and turn on the Smart Radius checkbox to help pick up some of those stray edges. When you're done, choose **Selection** from the Output To pop-up menu at the bottom of the dialog, so this will be output to a selection (rather than a layer mask, which is what we've been doing in most of the book).

STEP THREE:

Now that we've got our selection in place, we're ready to add the textured background. We're going to paste this background in, but first go to Select>**Inverse** to invert the selection. We don't want to paste the background into the skateboarder; we want to paste it into everything but him.

STEP FOUR:

Open the textured background image. (*Note:* I've mentioned iStockphoto [www.iStockphoto.com] before as a great resource for design graphics and textures for your composites. But, if you're really getting into compositing, it's good to start taking photos of random textures. Seriously, this opens a whole new world of photography to you, because you'll find backgrounds, textures, skies, and whatever else you can think of just about anywhere.) Once you have the textured image open, go to Select>**All**. Then go to Edit> **Copy** to copy it.

STEP FIVE:

Now, go back to the skateboarder image. The inverted selection you created in Step Three should still be in place. Go to Edit>Paste Special>**Paste Into**. This pastes the texture you just copied into the selection, on its own layer with a layer mask. You'll need to make this new background bigger, so press **Command-T (PC: Ctrl-T)** to enter Free Transform, then press-and-hold the Shift key, grab a corner transform handle, and drag the image out to fit the background. Press **Return (PC: Enter)** to lock in your transformation.

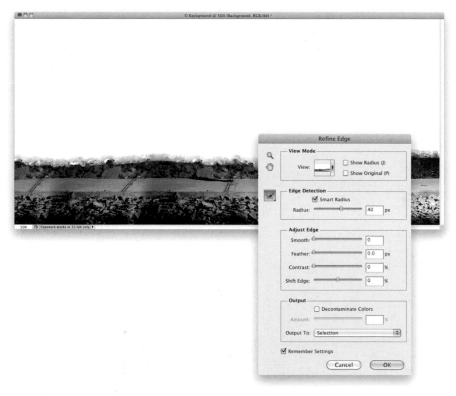

STEP SIX:

The only problem now is that the new textured background covers part of the sidewalk and rocks, too. So, click on the little Eye icon to the left of the textured background layer to hide it for a minute, then click on the Background layer to target it. Once again, use the Quick Selection tool to make a selection of the sidewalk, the rocks in the foreground, and the rocks that lead up to the wall. Click the Refine Edge button in the Options Bar, and then turn on the Smart Radius checkbox and crank the Radius setting up to 40 pixels this time (also, my View pop-up menu is set to **On White** here). We want a wider radius, so the edge isn't perfect. Make sure the Output To pop-up menu is set to **Selection** and click OK.

STEP SEVEN:

Now, we've got a selection of the sidewalk and rocks, but we need to modify the layer mask on the textured background layer, so it doesn't hide them anymore. Click where the Eye icon used to be next to the textured layer to turn it on again, then click on the layer mask on that layer to target it. Go to Edit>Fill, choose **Black** from the Use pop-up menu, and click OK to fill the selection (on the layer mask) with black. This will hide the textured layer covering the rocks and sidewalk and show the layer below. Press **Command-D (PC: Ctrl-D)** to Deselect.

STEP EIGHT:

It's time to add some graphics to the background. So, first open the splatter image (it's a layered PSD file). Get the Move tool **(V)**, click-and-drag the top layer (the splatter) onto the skateboard photo, and move it directly over the skateboarder. At the top of the Layers panel, change the layer's blend mode to **Overlay**, so that the splatter blends into the background. Press Command-T to use Free Transform if you need to resize the splatter.

STEP NINE:

Of course, the splatter is covering the skateboarder, since it's on the layer above him, right? So, press-and-hold the **Option (PC: Alt) key** and click-and-drag the layer mask from the textured layer to the splatter layer. Holding the Option key copies the mask from the layer you're dragging it from and makes an exact duplicate on whatever layer you put it on.

STEP 10:

Let's draw some illustrative lines next. Select the Pen tool from the Toolbox (or just press **P**), and press **D**, then **X** to set your Foreground color to white. On the left side of the Options Bar, click on the Shape Layers icon (the first one on the left, circled here) to set the Pen tool to draw a Shape layer.

STEP 11:

Click once on the left side of the image with the Pen tool to start the shape. Then, click-and-hold slightly above and to the right of where you clicked before to add another point. Continuing to hold your mouse button down, drag to the right to extend the path to make it curve upward. Next, click on the skateboarder's leg and, again, with your mouse button held down, drag to the right to extend another anchor point, so it looks like you've created a wavy line.

If you're like most people using the Pen tool for the first time, you'll probably throw your arms up in despair at this point. It's one of the harder tools to get used to, and it's definitely easier to watch someone use it than to read about how to use it. So, I've recorded a video about using the Pen tool and how to make these shapes (you can find it on the book's download site). Plus, the Pen tool is a great selection tool, so I'll cover that, as well.

STEP 12:

Option-click (PC: Alt-click) on the last anchor point (on his leg), then click right below it to make the path go downward. Click-and-drag a few times back the other way until you're back where you started (again, if you're having trouble, go watch the video I recorded on this). Finish it off by clicking on the original point (you'll see a tiny circle appear to the right of your cursor when you hover over it) to close the path.

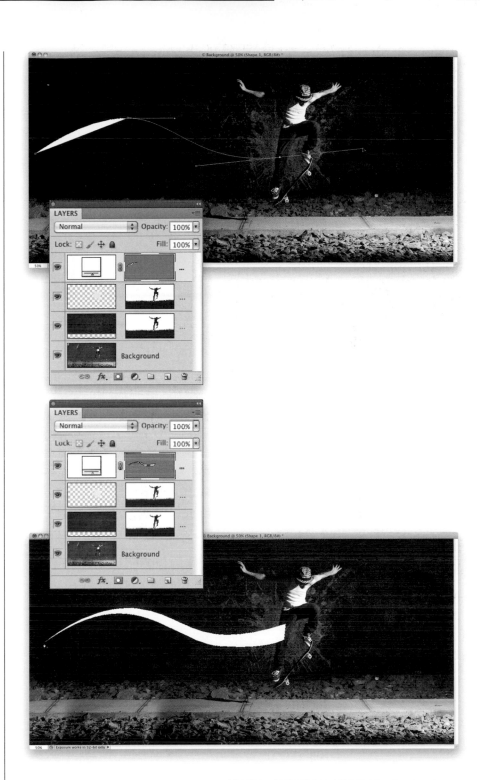

STEP 13:

The Shape layer automatically picks up whatever color your Foreground color was set to. We had set it to white, so that we could see the shape as we created it, but we're going to change it now. Click on the Add a Layer Style icon at the bottom of the Layers panel and choose **Gradient Overlay**. In the Gradient Overlay options in the Layer Style dialog, click on the down-facing arrow on the right side of the Gradient, and choose the Orange, Yellow, Orange gradient from the Gradient Picker (the second one from the left in the second row). Then, set the Angle to 0 and click OK.

STEP 14:

Now, if you look at the image in the next few steps, you'll see I drew some more shapes. If you already know how to use the Pen tool, then you'll look at these and think, "No sweat, I got it." But, if you don't know how to use the Pen tool, then no amount of text I write here will help. Trust me. It's just one of those tools that is really difficult to read/write about. But, when you actually get to watch it being used, it all starts to make sense. So, I've done two things: First, like I mentioned earlier, I recorded a video that goes over how I created the shapes you see in the image here. Next, I've created an image with all of the shapes already in it that you can download from the book's download site. This way, if you want to follow along and finish the tutorial, you can without having to go online and watch the video first. Sound good? (Yes, I know you really can't answer me back. That's why I love books.)

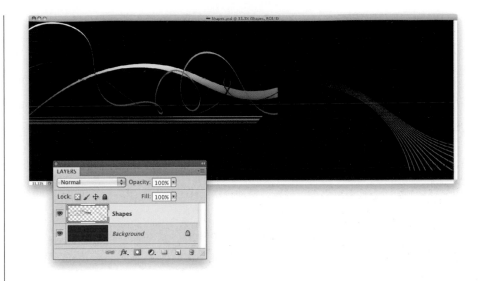

STEP 15:

Once you have the shapes image open, using the Move tool, drag the Shapes layer into the composite and position it like I have here. We'll need a layer mask for the next part, so click on the Add Layer Mask icon at the bottom of the Layers panel to add a mask to the Shapes layer.

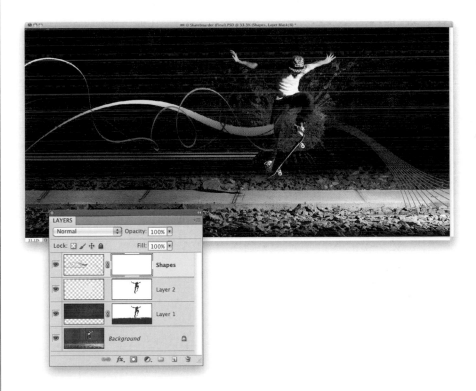

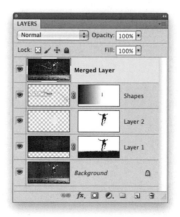

STEP 16:

Press **G** to select the Gradient tool from the Toolbox. Then, in the Options Bar, click on the down-facing arrow on the right of the gradient thumbnail to open the Gradient Picker, choose the third gradient from the left in the top row (the Black, White gradient), and click-and-drag from left to right on the layer mask. This fades the shapes on the far-left side of the image into the background and makes them appear brighter as they get closer to the skater—almost like they're following him. Then, press **B** to get the Brush tool, press **X** to set your Foreground color to black, and use a small brush to paint away the area where the shapes overlap the skateboarder.

STEP 17:

After all the shapes are done, click on the topmost layer in the Layers panel and press **Command-Option-Shift-E (PC: Ctrl-Alt-Shift-E)** to merge everything into one new layer at the top of the layer stack. Now, we can apply some finishing touches on the entire image.

STEP 18:

You'll probably remember from the background tutorial that the sidewalk was copied-and-pasted a few times to extend it. Since the lighting is a little off (and bright in certain parts), we'll do some burning to darken the whole bottom of the image. Get the Burn tool from the Toolbox (or press **Shift-O** until you have it), and then in the Options Bar, set the Range to **Midtones** and the Exposure to 10% (Exposure is similar to Opacity—the more you paint, the more you build up the burning effect).

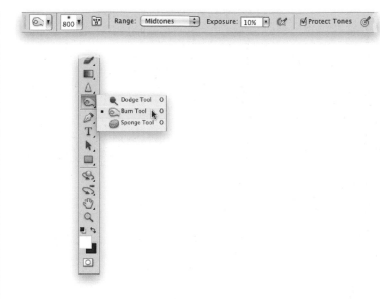

STEP 19:

Use the Right (]) and Left ([) Bracket keys on your keyboard to make the brush roughly the size of the sidewalk and start painting over the bottom of the image to darken the entire area. The more brush strokes you add, the darker it'll get. It's okay to keep the area under the skateboarder brighter, but make sure you darken the left and right sides, as well as the rocks all around.

STEP 20:

Lastly, you know I always like to finish things off with an edgy sharpening effect. There's a free way that I described in Chapter 8 (the concert composite) that uses the High Pass filter, but as I also mentioned there, I really prefer the effect I get from Nik Software's Tonal Contrast filter, which is included with the Color Efex Pro 3 Complete plug-in. So, if you have it installed, choose Filter>Nik Software>**Color Efex Pro** and, in the Color Efex Pro window, choose **Tonal Contrast** from the filters on the left (as shown here). At the top right of the window, set the Highlight Contrast, Midtone Contrast, and Shadow Contrast settings all to 30, set the Saturation to 20, and then click OK to apply the filter.

STEP 21:

It not only has the effect of sharpening the entire image, but it adds a certain grit and contrasty effect that makes everything pop out at you. And, of course, feel free to reduce the layer's opacity or add a layer mask to hide areas where it's too intense. Here, I reduced the layer's Opacity and painted with black, with a low brush opacity, on the layer mask on parts of the wall that became a little too gritty as a result of the Tonal Contrast filter.

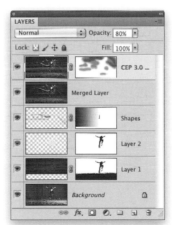

FINAL IMAGE

I added "Advanced" to the title of this chapter, because it takes a little bit of everything we've done so far in the book and puts it all together. While you don't have to read the book in order, I do suggest that you work through a few of the other composites before trying this one. At this point in the book, you may or may not have noticed that most of the compositing we've done has been portrait-related. This means that the face, expression, or likeness of the person (or people) is the main part of the photo. Well, there's another area of compositing that has a more commercial, or advertising, side to it. Sure, there are still people in the image, but the main point of the image isn't to show off the people. It's usually to sell something or make some type of statement. Now, I mentioned in the introduction that this book is more about portrait compositing. However, I wanted to leave you with one last composite that will, at least, whet your appetite for something that has more of a commercial nature to it.

BRAINSTORMING FOR A COMMERCIAL COMPOSITE

Believe it or not, this is probably one of the hardest parts of this type of compositing. When the sky is the limit, it's hard to focus in on just one idea. And when you finally come up with that idea, executing it is just as difficult. That's why I thought it'd be cool to start off by showing the beginnings of the idea we're working with here.

PETE COLLINS

THE INITIAL IDEA:

With commercial composites, the initial idea usually comes from a client. Sometimes they'll have a hand-drawn sketch, and sometimes all they do is verbally communicate what they want. In this example, the initial idea was to create an ad for a new (and fictitious) TV show called *Extreme Green*. It's about a family that gave everything up to live green...well, almost everything. Sure, it's a little quirky, but many commercial or advertising composites have a certain quirk-factor to them. That's what makes them catchy. Even if you don't draw, it's a good idea to try to sketch something out. It gives you something to work from. Once you have a sketch, you can start thinking about how to make it a reality. And, once you have a sketch, you can show it around and brainstorm with other people. Commercial composites are in no way a one-person job.

THE ROUGH COMP:

I highly suggest you create a rough Photoshop comp after the sketch phase. You'd do this for two reasons: (1) It gives you something to show your client to see if you're on the right track. And, (2) it lets you work with "stunt" images to create the composite, while not investing the full amount of time, money, and resources to the photography and work it will eventually take. Let me explain: Once I had the idea, I built the background. Then, I took random photos from my surroundings or used free "comp" images from a stock photography website to start laying it out. Sure, the lighting was all off, the shadows were horrible, and the people weren't really in the poses that I wanted. But, from seeing all of the things that I didn't want, I was able to more accurately (and quickly) photograph the things I did want. Plus, the rough comp helps get people thinking and talking. Once they see it come to life, all-new ideas come out, and that's exactly what happened here. Poses changed, placement changed, colors changed, and it was all because we had something rough to look at.

©FOTOLIA AND ISTOCKPHOTO

CREATING THE BACKGROUND

One of the first trends you'll notice in commercial compositing is that the background is rarely ever just one photo. In fact, it's rarely ever even two photos. When you get to this style of compositing, the background that you need typically doesn't exist anywhere. So, you'll have to build it. In fact, in this example, I tried to photograph the background in one photo for this. I struggled with it for about a week, driving everywhere looking for the perfect place. Once I gave in and decided to build it myself, from several photos, the project became infinitely easier and began to take shape right away.

©FOTOLIA

©FOTOLIA/NEXUSSEVEN

STEP ONE:

Open the photo of the sky. The foreground isn't what we want here, but I like the trees in the back and the blue, partly cloudy sky. It shows a sunny day, but more of a late-afternoon sunny day, so nothing should be overly bright or contrasty.

STEP TWO:

Next, open the grass photo. Using the Move tool **(V)**, drag it into the cloud photo we just opened in Step One. Then, go to Edit>**Free Transform** and click-and-drag the top-middle transform handle down until the grass looks like it's vanishing into the tree line. Press **Return (PC: Enter)** when you're done to lock in the transformation.

TIP: RENAME YOUR LAYERS

You're going to have a lot of layers when you're done with this composite, so start descriptively renaming your layers (double-click on the layer name) right from the start. Trust me, you'll be really happy you did for this image.

STEP THREE:

Now, open the first tree photo. This one is a stock photo, too, so it's got a nice white background. If it didn't have the white background, I'd use the Quick Selection tool/Refine Edge combo and treat the edges of the tree just like I would hair. But, since it does have the white background, let's go to Select>**Color Range**. Click once with the Eyedropper on the white background to select it, then move the Fuzziness slider to the right. I stopped around 135. You'll want to drag until you start to see parts of the tree fading away—that means you've gone too far. Click OK when you're done.

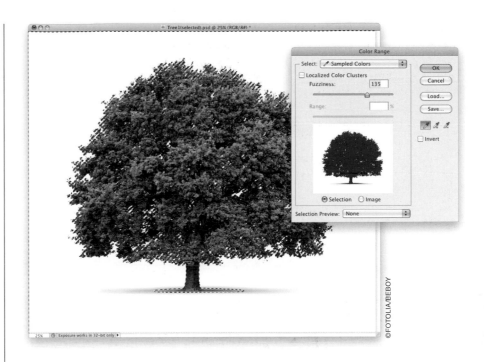

STEP FOUR:

Since we've selected the white background, we need to invert the selection so the tree is selected instead. Go to Select>**Inverse** to invert the selection, and then copy the selected tree. Now, switch over to the background image and paste it in. Go into Free Transform, press-and-hold the Shift key, and click-and-drag a corner handle inward to make it smaller. Press Return when you're done, and then move the tree to the top left. Then, press the **E key** to get the Eraser tool and, using a small, soft-edged brush, erase away the shadow around the tree, because we're going to add our own.

STEP FIVE:

Add a new layer under the tree layer for a shadow, and then press **Shift-M** until you get the Elliptical Marquee tool. Drag a small, wide oval selection beneath the tree and fill it with black. Deselect, then go to Filter>Blur>**Gaussian Blur**, set the Radius to 15 pixels, and click OK when you're done.

STEP SIX:

Reduce the layer's Opacity to 30%, then press **Command-J (PC: Ctrl-J)** to duplicate it. Go into Free Transform and drag the middle handles inward to make it a little smaller (tree shadows are always darker the closer they are to the middle). Set the Opacity of the top copy of the shadow layer to around 20%.

STEP SEVEN:

Since objects that are closer to us tend to be more saturated in color than things that are off in the distance, we'll need to enhance the tree a little. So, click on the tree layer to target it, then click on the Create New Adjustment Layer icon, choose **Vibrance**, and in the Adjustments panel, crank the Vibrance up to 100. Then add a Hue/Saturation adjustment layer, and set the Saturation to 10 and the Lightness to 7. Now, to force each adjustment to only affect the tree layer below them, Command-click (PC: Ctrl-click) on each adjustment layer and go to Layer>**Create Clipping Mask**.

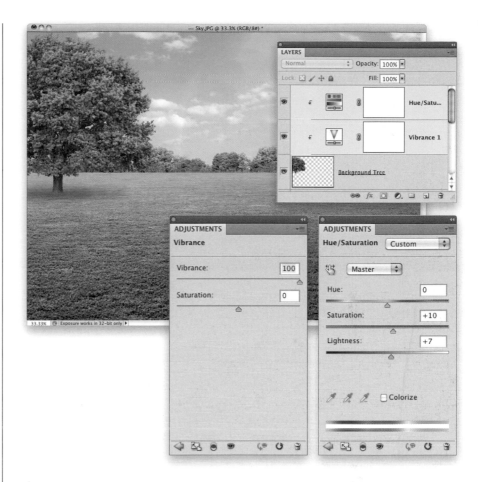

STEP EIGHT:

To make it easier to keep these layers together, click on the topmost layer (Hue/Saturation) and then Shift-click on the bottom shadow layer to select them all. Go to Layer>**Group Layers** to put the tree layers into a folder and rename it, so it's easier to keep track of. It's a good idea to memorize the keyboard shortcut for grouping, which is **Command-G (PC: Ctrl-G)**, because we'll be using groups a lot in this chapter.

PHOTOSHOP COMPOSITING SECRETS

STEP NINE:

Lastly, open the other tree photo and use Color Range, like we did back in Step Three, to select it from the white background, and then copy-and-paste it into the main image. Use Free Transform to make it larger (don't forget to press-and-hold the Shift key to constrain proportions) and position it in the top right (I increased the size of mine to around 200% of the original). Then, add a layer mask to the layer, and use a small, soft-edged brush to paint away the grass at the bottom of the tree, so it blends better with the grass on our new background.

CREATING THE COMPOSITE

As for creating the composite, I think you'll find that once you have a rough comp created and then start creating the actual composite, things start to come together pretty quickly.

STEP ONE:

Before we get started, you may have noticed that in most of the other chapters in the book, I showed you how to select the subject from the background. However, I mentioned earlier that this chapter was more advanced than the others, so I'm assuming you've got a good grasp on selections by now. Plus, these are pretty easy selections here, so they shouldn't give you much trouble. Okay, let's start with the main image. I took quite a few poses of the couple on the couch, so I had a lot of choices. I knew there was going to be a child hanging from the tree, and thought it'd be cute to have the mom with this "What the…?!" look on her face and the dad, well, just bored with a re-mote in his hand (yes, I know they're outside. Remember, they went green and "almost" gave up everything). So, go ahead and open the image of the couple, use the Quick Selection tool/Refine Edge dialog to select them from their background, and move them into our composite.

Note: Don't forget that all of the images (with selections already made) for this chapter (as well as all of the other chapters) are available on the book's download site. So, if you're the lazy type (you know who you are!), you can follow along without having to do all of the selection work (and I wouldn't blame you one bit).

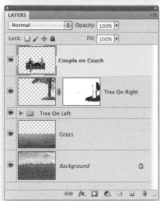

STEP TWO:

Create a new blank layer beneath the couch layer for a shadow. Then, with the Rectangular Marquee tool **(M)**, make a rectangular selection at the bottom of the couch. Fill it with black and then deselect. Now, go to Filter>Blur>**Gaussian Blur**, and apply a 25-pixel radius to it to soften the edges, then reduce the Opacity of the shadow layer to 80%.

STEP THREE:

Next, create a new blank layer above the couch layer. Right now, the legs of the couch look like they're hovering above the grass. So, to fix this, press the **S key** to get the Clone Stamp tool, make sure that **All Layers** is selected in the Sample pop-up menu in the Options Bar, and then Option-click (PC: Alt-click) to sample an area of grass near the couch. Then, with a small brush, paint on the bottom of the legs of the couch, so it looks like there's grass around it.

STEP FOUR:

Repeat Step Three and add some grass around the man's foot, near the bottom-left side of the couch. You'll notice that I'm naming layers here as I go along, because by not doing so, it could start getting really confusing. Also, it's a good idea to group all of these layers into a Couch group, so they're easier to find later.

STEP FIVE:

Create another new blank layer above the cloned grass layers we just created in Steps Three and Four. Then, get the Brush tool **(B)**, set your Foreground color to black, your brush Opacity to 25%, and using a small, soft-edged brush, paint some hard shadows right under the legs of the couch and the man's foot.

STEP SIX:

Now, open the photo we'll use for the boy in the tree. You can see we had some fun shooting this one. I wanted it to be authentic, so we held him upside down. I knew he was going to be hanging in a tree and that his knees and lower legs could be covered, so we didn't worry about covering up his legs. Select him from the background and place him into the composite. Don't worry about the hands on his legs either—just select up to the knee. Use Free Transform to resize and position him up in the tree. Oh yeah, just so you know, I almost always use a layer mask when I create my selections in the Refine Edge dialog. However, in nearly every selection in this chapter, I had to pull the image off of the layer with the mask and use the Defringe feature to get rid of that tiny fringe that we always see. Check out Chapter 1 if you need a refresher on how to do this.

STEP SEVEN:

Create a new blank layer above the boy and use the same trick with the Clone Stamp tool we used in Step Three to put some tree leaves and branches over his legs, so only a small part of them is showing. Option-click to sample the tree near his legs, then paint over part of the legs (leaving just a small area showing), so you can't see that we were really holding him up in the air. You can see in the last step, I created another layer group to hold the layers for this part of the image.

STEP EIGHT:

Next, open the photo of the boy with the water gun. Again, I knew before the photo shoot that he was going to be behind the tree. So, I photographed him behind a large board that we had in the studio, so I could make it as authentic as possible by showing him peeking around something. It also worked out, because the board cast a nice shadow on his leg that the tree would normally be casting if he were really behind it. Select him from the background, move him into the composite, and use Free Transform to make him smaller.

STEP NINE:

Repeat Steps Three and Five and use the Clone Stamp and Brush tool techniques we used there to add some grass and shadows around the boy's feet. Then, select these layers in the Layers panel and press Command-G to group them together.

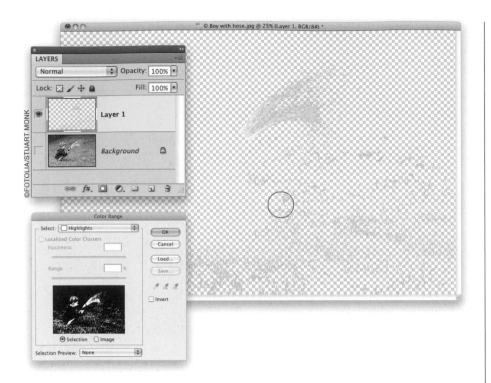

STEP 10:

What's a water gun without water, right? So, open the photo of the boy with the hose. Go to Select> **Color Range** and choose **Highlights** from the Select pop-up menu to just select the bright parts (mostly the water) of the photo, and then click OK. Press **Command-J (PC: Ctrl-J)** to put the selected area onto its own layer. Then, hide the Background layer and use the Eraser tool **(E)** to erase away any excess area that was selected, so you only have the water splash left.

STEP 11:

Switch to the Move tool, and drag the photo of the water into the composite. Then, use Free Transform to reduce the size, Right-click inside the transform bounding box, and choose **Flip Horizontal**, then fit it into place. Press **Return (PC: Enter)** to lock in the changes. Now, it's still got a little green in it from the original background. But, since most of the water goes over a blue sky, all we need to do is change the color. So, press **Command-U (PC: Ctrl-U)** to open the Hue/Saturation dialog and change the Saturation, Hue, and Lightness settings to help the water fit better with the background.

STEP 12:

Next, open the photo of the picture frame with the couple in it (remember... quirky). Drag it into the composite and place it on a layer directly above the tree (so it's below the boy with the water gun), then use Free Transform to reduce the size. Also, move your cursor outside the transform bounding box, and click-and-drag upward to rotate it slightly, and press Return.

STEP 13:

Hide the group with the boy with the water gun for a minute and create a new blank layer under the picture frame. Get the Brush tool and, with your Foreground color set to black and your brush Opacity set to 40%, use a small, soft-edged black brush to paint some shadows on the tree under the frame. Don't forget that, since the tree is curved, the shadows will curve slightly downward to follow the shape of the tree. Lower the layer opacity a bit.

©FOTOLIA/DOGIST

STEP 14:

Every family needs a dog, right? Open the dog photo next and select him from the background. Move him into the composite and use Free Transform to scale his size down quite a bit. He's going to be way off in the background, so he shouldn't be that big. Select the Blur tool from the Toolbox and, in the Options Bar, set the Strength to 25%, then just paint around the edges of the dog, so they're not quite as crisp. Add a new layer under the dog layer and use the same brush from the previous step to paint a shadow under the dog, then create a group for your dog layers, and unhide the group with the boy and water gun.

STEP 15:

Repeat Step 14 (except for the Blur tool) for the pet chipmunk, and place him on the couch near the woman. Be sure to place this new layer group above the Couch group in the layer stack. Again, I know it's quirky, but we're going for that quirk factor here to mix the concept of a living room, a family, and the outdoors.

©FOTOLIA/JAREN WICKLUND

STEP 16:

Now, open the photo of the butterflies, select them from the white background, and add a few around the image. My personal favorite is the one on the man's shoulder. It just seems to fit perfectly with the bored/exasperated look on his face. A quick trick to add some visual interest and take away the cookie-cutter feel extra images like this have is to change their color. Press Command-U to open the Hue/Saturation dialog and move the Hue slider to get a different color for one or two of the butterflies.

STEP 17:

Let's start finishing this one up with some dodging, burning, and overall shadowing. First, click on the topmost layer and press **Command-Option-Shift-E (PC: Ctrl-Alt-Shift-E)** to merge everything together into one new layer. Now, as with most composites, you might have to walk away and come back to it. Then, take a look around and look at details that just don't seem to fit. For example, look at the lighting pattern on all of the people. The two boys have a fairly hard light source coming from the right. You can see it on their clothes and hair.

STEP 18:

The woman isn't facing toward the light source, but we can see she's got some bright areas on her right, which fit in well with the photo. However, the lighting on the man's face on the right isn't as bright as the others. So, select the Dodge tool **(O)** from the Toolbox, and in the Options Bar, set the Range to **Highlights**, since that's primarily what we want to enhance, set the Exposure to 10%, and turn off the Protect Tones checkbox, since it tends to make the skin a peachy color and oversaturated. Now, paint on the right side of the man's face and hair with a small, soft-edged brush. Do the same on the right side of the woman on her hair, shoulder, and back of her arm.

TIP: PROTECTING THE BACKGROUND

You can Command-click (PC: Ctrl-click) on the Couple on Couch layer's thumbnail in the Layers panel to put a selection around them. That way, when you do your dodging and burning on the top-most layer, it won't bleed onto the background.

STEP 19:

Switch to the Burn tool (**Shift-O**), set the Range to **Midtones**, and the Exposure to 10%. Then use a soft-edged brush to darken any areas that should have more shadows. I painted on the ground around the tree a little, and also on the front of the couch. Don't forget, shadows and highlights are one of the hardest parts about putting together a composite like this. Even though it's fake, it has to look like a real fake image, and shadows are a dead giveaway that things are out of place. So, spend some time here searching around your image for things that look out of place. Think about where the light is coming from. Look at real objects around you to see what happens to the shadows (like the couch here) and use low Exposure (or brush Opacity) settings to paint them. It's on a separate layer, so you can always go back and change it if you need to.

STEP 20:

We've got to tie everything together here, so it all has a unified color and tone. Let's use the blurred layer trick we used back in Chapter 10. Press Command-Option-Shift-E again to merge everything together into a new layer. Then, go to Filter> Blur>**Average**. This blurs the entire image into one color that is the average color of everything in the composite. Change the blend mode of the layer to **Color**, and reduce the Opacity to 20%. This unifies everything in the photo and gives every object and person we added a common color tint.

STEP 21:

Finally, press Command-Option-Shift-E to merge everything together one last time. You can use the High Pass filter trick for some extra sharpening and contrast (we covered it at the end of Chapter 8), but I'm going to use my personal favorite, here: the Tonal Contrast filter from Nik Software's Color Efex Pro Complete. I used the default settings, here, and I also added a layer mask and painted the effect away from the couple's faces and arms, and the clouds, since it made them a little too contrasty.

Here's our final image (on the next page) with the fictitious TV show name added to it.

FINAL IMAGE

extreme green
THEY GAVE UP EVERYTHING... WELL, SORT OF

SUNDAYS ON HPO

WHERE TO GO NEXT

If you're reading this, then I figure you're probably looking for more information and inspiration on compositing.
So, I thought I'd take a quick minute to point you to some of my favorite resources for inspiration.

KELBY TRAINING
(www.kelbytraining.com):

We've recently released some online classes from German retoucher and photographer, Calvin Hollywood (who you can find at www.calvinhollywood-blog.com). He does some awesome work with compositing, as well. Plus, we've got work from Corey Barker and Jim DiVitale, and we have videos coming soon (Fall 2011) from Douglas Sonders and Justin Paguia.

JOEL GRIMES
(www.joelgrimes.com):

I've mentioned Joel Grimes several times here in the book. He's been a pioneer in portrait-related compositing. Joel will also be doing some classes over at Kelby Training, so keep an eye out (most likely Fall 2011). He's also teaching at the Photoshop World Conference & Expo (www.photoshopworld.com), and you'll definitely want to check out his website and video tutorials.

DAVE HILL
(www.davehillphoto.com):

Dave Hill caused a big stir a few years ago with his signature post-processing look. He really does have a great finishing style, but Dave's work is so much more than that. He's got some of the absolute best commercial compositing work that I've seen out there, and his website is definitely worth a look.

TIM TADDER
(www.timtadder.com):

Tim Tadder is another commercial and advertising photographer with some awesome compositing work. He's got everything from one-person portraits to group composites.

ERIC DOGGETT
(www.doggettstudios.com):

Eric is a commercial photographer based in Austin, TX. He's got some really clever and incredibly creative composites. In fact, he's got a band composite that I thought would have made a great tutorial for the book. But fortunately, he had already done a tutorial on it on his blog site, so I figured I'd point you there so you can read it and see his work. Here's the tutorial link: www.doggettstudios.com/blog/creating-a-composite-image-for-meagan-tubb-shady-people.

JAMES QUANTZ, JR.
(www.quantzphoto.com):
I first noticed James Quantz's work in the NAPP members' Image of the Week contest. What I like most about his website and blog (aside from his killer photography) is that he often posts animations and information about how he created the composites.

GARY LAND
(www.garylandphotography.com):
Gary Land is a commercial photographer who has shot ad campaigns for Nike, Reebok, Adidas, and Coca Cola. He has a great style to his work and, like many of my favorites here, his website even has some behind-the-scenes photos, so you can see how some of his photos were done.

DOUGLAS SONDERS
(www.sondersphotography.com):
Douglas is a commercial photographer, specializing in on-location photography. Even though much of his work is on-location, there are still a lot of compositing elements to it. Definitely worth a look.

JUSTIN PAGUIA
(www.justinpaguia.com):
Justin is a retoucher who often works with Douglas Sonders (mentioned above), in addition to other photographers. I always love to stop by his website, because his portfolio has the final images, as well as many of the originals, so you can see what he started with.

CHRIS BORGMAN
(www.chrisborgman.com):
I found Chris Borgman's website about a week before this book went to press. Like James Quantz, Jr., he has a great portfolio. But one of the things I like most about Chris's website is that he posts many before and after shots, as well as some videos that show the progression of his composites.

SEVENTHSTREET
(www.seventhstreetstudio.com):
Their portfolio includes a beautiful mixture of photo composites, 3D renders, and all other types of photography elements. They've got a large body of commercial work, and you've probably seen their work featured in just about every Photoshop and design-related magazine out there. Plus, you'll see the before images listed for many of their composites, so it's a great way to learn.

MOTOR IMAGE WORKS
(www.motorimageworks.com):
If you're into cars, then this one is a must see. They've got a full portfolio of CGI and composited car images. Very cool stuff!